storytelling with data

let's PRACTICE!

Cover image: Catherine Madden
Cover design: Flight Design Co.

Published by John Wiley & Sons, Inc., Hoboken, New Jersey.
Published simultaneously in Canada.

For general information on our other products and services or for technical support, please contact our Customer Care Department within the United States at (800) 762-2974, outside the United States at (317) 572-3993, or fax (317) 572-4002.

Wiley publishes in a variety of print and electronic formats and by print-on-demand. Some material included with standard print versions of this book may not be included in e-books or in print-on-demand. If this book refers to media such as a CD or DVD that is not included in the version you purchased, you may download this material at http://booksupport.wiley.com. For more information about Wiley products, visit www.wiley.com.

ISBN 978-1-119-62149-2 (paper)
ISBN 978-1-119-62150-8 (ePub)
ISBN 978-1-1196-2158-4 (ePDF)

Printed in the United States of America.

S10013655_090519

storytelling with data *let's* PRACTICE!

cole nussbaumer knaflic

illustrated by catherine madden

WILEY

contents

acknowledgments   vii

about the author   ix

introduction   xi

chapter 1   understand the context   1

chapter 2   choose an effective visual   51

chapter 3   identify & eliminate clutter   107

chapter 4   focus attention   147

chapter 5   think like a designer   191

chapter 6   tell a story   235

chapter 7   practice more with Cole   285

chapter 8   practice more on your own   355

chapter 9   practice more at work   375

chapter 10   closing words   403

index   407

acknowledgments

Thanks to everyone who helped this book come to be...

Simon Beaumont, Lisa Carlson, Amy Cesal, Robert Crocker, Steven Franconeri, Megan Holstine, and Steve Wexler for your draft manuscript review and thoughtful feedback.

Kim Schefler and Jasmine Kaufman for your sage guidance.

Catherine Madden and Matt Meikle for your creativity and thought partnership. We've made a beautiful book!

Marika Rohn, my dear friend and editor extraordinaire: you've helped the words in my head make sense on paper!

Jody Riendeau for creating order, taking things off my plate, and bringing an awesome sense of levity to all that we do.

Elizabeth Ricks for your dedication and fantastic work sharing SWD lessons with the world. Congrats also on baby Henry!

Avery, Dorian, and Eloise Knaflic, my three beautiful children: you inspire me. You can be anything you want in life.

Randy Knaflic: you are my support, my voice of reason, my confidant, my everything. You hold my heart.

Thanks also to Bill Falloon, Mike Henton, Carly Hounsome, Steven Kyritz, Kimberly Monroe-Hill, Purvi Patel, Jean-Karl Martin, Amy Laundicano, Steve Csipke, RJ Andrews, Mike Cisneros, Alex Velez, Beatriz Tapia, Brenda Chi-Moran, and the team at Quad Graphics. Gratitude goes to all of our clients and everyone reading these words now (that's you!). Thanks for being on this amazing journey with me. Happy practicing!

about the author

Cole Nussbaumer Knaflic tells stories with data. She is the founder and CEO of *storytelling with data* (SWD) and author of the best-selling book, *storytelling with data: a data visualization guide for business professionals* (Wiley, 2015), which has been translated into a dozen languages, is used as a textbook by more than 100 universities, and serves as the course book for tens of thousands of SWD workshop participants. For nearly a decade, Cole and her team have delivered knockout interactive learning sessions highly sought after by data-minded individuals, companies, and philanthropic organizations all over the world. They also help people create graphs that make sense and weave them into compelling stories through the popular SWD blog, podcast, and monthly challenge.

Prior to SWD, Cole's unique talent was honed through analytical roles in banking, private equity, and as a manager on the Google People Analytics team. At Google, she used a data-driven approach to inform innovative people programs and management practices and traveled to Google offices throughout the US and Europe to teach the course she developed on data visualization. Cole has acted as an adjunct faculty member at the Maryland Institute College of Art (MICA), where she taught Introduction to Information Visualization, and regularly guest lectures at prominent universities in the US and beyond.

Cole has a BS in Applied Math and an MBA from the University of Washington. When she isn't ridding the world of ineffective graphs, Cole is undertaking the adventures of parenting three young children with her husband at home in the Midwest and on travels abroad.

introduction

I often receive emails from people who have read my first book, *storytelling with data*, or attended one of our workshops by the same name. There are notes of encouragement, support for the work we're doing, and plenty of questions and requests. I especially love hearing the success stories: reports of having influenced a key business decision, spurred an overdue budget conversation, or prompted an action that positively impacted an organization's bottom line. The most inspiring accounts are those of personal growth and recognition. One grateful reader applied *storytelling with data* principles during an interview, helping him land a new job. All of this success is the result of people from different industries, functions, and roles committing time to improve their ability to communicate with data.

I also hear regularly from people who want *more*. They've read the book and understand the potential impact of telling stories with data, but struggle with the practical application to their own work. They have additional questions or feel they are facing nuanced situations that are keeping them from having the desired impact. It's clear that people crave more guidance and practice to help fully develop their data storytelling skills.

Others reach out who are—or would like to be—teaching the lessons outlined in *storytelling with data*. In many cases, they are university instructors (it's amazing to think that *storytelling with data* is used as a textbook at more than 100 universities around the world!) or they are a part of a learning and development function within an organization, interested in building an in-house course or training program. There are also leaders, managers, and individual contributors who want to upskill their teams or provide good coaching and feedback to others.

This book addresses all of these needs for individuals, teachers, and leaders. By sharing invaluable insight through many practical examples, guided practice, and open-ended exercises, I will help build your confidence and credibility when it comes to applying and teaching others to apply the *storytelling with data* lessons.

How this book is organized & what to expect

Each chapter starts with a brief recap of the key lessons that are covered in *storytelling with data*. This is followed by:

practice with Cole: exercises based on real-world examples posed for you to consider and solve, accompanied by detailed step-by-step illustration and explanation

practice on your own: more exercises and thought-provoking questions for you to work through individually without prescribed solutions

practice at work: thoughtful guidance and hands-on exercises for applying the lessons learned on the job, including practical instruction on when and how to solicit useful feedback and iterate to refine your work from good to great

Much of the content you'll encounter here is inspired by our *storytelling with data* workshops. Because these sessions span many industries, so do the examples upon which I'll draw. We'll navigate between different topics—from digital marketing to pet adoption to sales training—giving you a rich and varied set of situations to learn from as you hone your data storytelling skills.

Warning: this is not a traditional book that you sit and read. To get the most out of it, you'll want to make it a fully interactive experience. I encourage you to highlight, add bookmarks, and take notes in the margins. Expect to be flipping between pages and examples. Draw, discuss with others, and practice in your tools. This book should be beat up by the time you're done with it: that will be one indication that you've utilized it to the fullest extent!

How to use this book in conjunction with the original

SWD: let's practice! works as a great companion guide to *storytelling with data: a data visualization guide for business professionals* (Wiley, 2015; henceforth referred to as *SWD*). It will not replace the in-depth lessons taught there, but rather augment them with additional dialogue, many more examples, and a focus on hands-on practice.

This book generally follows the same chapter structure as *SWD* with a couple of differences, as shown in Figure 0.1. Chapters 7, 8, and 9 are comprehensive exercises that offer additional guidance and practice applying the lessons covered throughout *SWD* and here.

SWD: original book   SWD: **let's practice!**

the importance of context | 1 ●———●	1 | understand the context
choosing an effective visual | 2 ●———●	2 | choose an effective visual
clutter is your enemy! | 3 ●———●	3 | identify & eliminate clutter
focus your audience's attention | 4 ●———●	4 | focus attention
think like a designer | 5 ●———●	5 | think like a designer
dissecting model visuals | 6 ●	6 | tell a story
lessons in storytelling | 7 ●	7 | practice more with Cole
pulling it all together | 8 ●	8 | practice more on your own
case studies | 9 ●	9 | practice more at work
final thoughts | 10 ●———●	10 | closing words

FIGURE 0.1 How *SWD* chapters correspond to this book

If you've picked up both *SWD* and *SWD: let's practice!*, you can use them in a couple of ways. You can read *SWD* once from start to finish to understand the big picture before digging into specifics. From there, you can determine which lessons you'd like to practice and can dive into the relevant sections within this book. Alternatively, you can peruse *SWD* one chapter at a time, then turn here to practice what you've read through hands-on exercises.

If you've already read *SWD*, feel free to jump right in as you will be familiar with these topics.

And if you've only bought this book, there is enough context within to give you the basics. You can always pick up a copy of *SWD* or check out the many resources at storytellingwithdata.com for supplemental guidance.

Do you want to learn or teach?

SWD: let's practice! was written with two different audiences in mind, united by a common goal—to communicate more effectively with data. Broadly, these two distinct groups are:

1. Those wanting to learn how to communicate more effectively with data, and

2. Those wanting to provide feedback, coach, or teach others how to communicate more effectively with data.

While the content is relevant for both groups, there will be subtle differences when it comes to getting the most out of it. Depending on your goal, the following strategies will maximize efficiency.

I want to learn to communicate more effectively with data

Because some later content builds upon or refers back to earlier content or exercises, begin with Chapter 1 and work through in numerical order. After that, you'll likely find yourself revisiting sections of interest and focusing your practice based on your specific needs and goals.

Start by reviewing the lesson recap for a given chapter. If you encounter anything that isn't familiar and you have access to *SWD*, turn back to the corresponding chapter for additional context.

After that, move straight into the ***practice with Cole*** exercises. First, work through each on your own—don't just jump to the solution (you're only cheating yourself!). If you're using this book with others, many of these activities lend themselves well to group discussion. The exercises in this section don't necessarily need to be worked through in order, though they do occasionally build upon prior exercises.

Once you've spent time on the given exercise (not just in your head: I strongly encourage you to write, draw, and use your tools), read through the provided solution. Observe where there are similarities and differences between that and your response. Be aware that there are very few situations where there is a single "right" answer. Some approaches are better than others, but there are usually numerous ways to solve a given problem. My solutions illustrate just one method that applies the lessons covered in *SWD*. Do read through all of the solutions, as many points of advice, tips, and nuances will arise that you will find helpful and insightful.

After completing the *practice with Cole* exercises, turn to the ***practice on your own*** section for more. These problems are similar to those in the first section, except that they don't include any predetermined solutions. If you are working in a group, have individuals first tackle a given exercise separately, then come together to present and discuss. Invariably, different people approach exercises in distinct ways, so you can learn a good deal through this sharing process. Conferring with others is also great practice for talking through your design choices and decisions, which can further clarify thinking and help improve future application. Whether completing on your own or as part of a group, get feedback on your recommended approach. This will help you understand if what you propose is working, as well as where you can iterate to further improve effectiveness.

If, at any time, you find yourself with a current project that would benefit from applying the lessons outlined in a specific chapter, flip straight to the ***practice at work*** exercise section within that chapter. These contain guided practice that can be applied directly to real-world work situations. The more you practice implementing the various lessons in a work setting, the more they will become second nature.

Each chapter ends with discussion questions related to the lessons. Talk through these with a partner or perhaps even use as the basis of a larger book club conversation.

While the exercise sections in each chapter focus primarily on applying the given lesson, Chapters 7, 8, and 9 offer more comprehensive examples and exercises for applying the entire *storytelling with data* process. **Chapter 7** ("practice more with Cole") contains full-blown case studies presented for you first to solve, followed by my thought process for tackling and completing. **Chapter 8** ("practice more on your own") has additional case studies and robust exercises to practice the process without prescribed solutions. **Chapter 9** ("practice more at work") has tips on how to apply the *storytelling with data* process at work, guides to facilitate group learning, and assessment rubrics that you can use to evaluate your own work and seek feedback from others.

As part of your learning, it's also imperative that you set specific goals. Communicate these to a friend, colleague, or manager. See **Chapter 9** for more on this.

Next, let's talk about how those interested in teaching others to effectively tell stories with data can use this book.

I want to provide feedback, coach, or teach others

You might be a manager or leader who wants to give good feedback on a graph or presentation from your team. Or perhaps you have a role in learning and development and are building training programs around how to communicate effectively with data. You may be a university instructor teaching students this important skill. In all of these scenarios, the chapter recap will provide an overview of the given lesson. After that, you will likely find the most value in the second and third exercise sections: *practice on your own* and *practice at work*. Each chapter ends with discussion questions that can be assigned, incorporated into tests, or used as the basis of group conversations.

The *practice on your own* section within each chapter contains targeted exercises helping those undertaking them practice the lessons outlined in the respective chapter and relevant section of SWD. These can be used as the basis of hands-on exercises in a classroom setting or assigned as homework. Some will also lend themselves well for use as group projects. These examples are provided without prescribed solutions. The problems in these sections can also work as models: consider where you could substitute data or visuals to create unique exercises.

Practice at work's guided exercises can be used directly in a work setting as part of an ongoing program for professionals. They can be assigned, completed, and discussed in a group or classroom setting. Managers looking to develop their team's skills may ask them to focus on specific exercises through their work or projects, or use with individuals as part of a goal-setting or career development process. For those teaching, **Chapter 9** has additional *practice at work* exercises, including facilitator guides and assessment rubrics.

A quick note on tools

Many tools are available for visualizing data. You may use spreadsheet applications like Excel or Google Sheets. Perhaps you are familiar with chart creators such as Datawrapper, Flourish, or Infogram or data visualization software like Tableau or PowerBI. Maybe you write code in R or Python or leverage Javascript libraries like D3.js. Regardless of your tool of choice, pick one or a set of tools and get to know them as best you can so the instrument itself doesn't become a limiting factor for effectively communicating with data. No tool is inherently good or evil—pretty much any can be used well or not so well.

When it comes to undertaking the exercises in this book, you are encouraged to use whatever means for visualizing the data you have at your disposal. These may be tools you use currently, or possibly one or more that you'd like to learn. The visuals that illustrate the *practice with Cole* solutions were all created in Microsoft Excel. That said, this is certainly not your only choice and I welcome you to use other tools. We are also adding solutions built in other tools to our online library for you to explore.

On the topic of tools, there are a couple I highly recommend having on hand while reading this book: a pen or pencil and paper. You may consider dedicating a notebook to use as you work your way through the various exercises. Many direct you to write and sketch. There are important benefits to low-tech physical creation and iteration that we'll explore and practice, which can make the process of working in your technical tools more efficient.

Where to get the data

Downloads for the data throughout this book and for all of the visuals shown in the solutions for the *practice with Cole* exercises can be found at storytellingwith-data.com/letspractice/downloads.

Let's get started

There has never been a time in history where so many people have had access to so much data. Yet, our ability to tell stories with our graphs and visualizations has not kept pace. Organizations and individuals that want to move ahead must recognize that these skills aren't inherent and invest in their development. With a thoughtful approach, we can all tell inspiring and influential stories with our data.

I'm excited to help you take your data storytelling to the next level.

Let's practice!

understand the context

A little planning can go a long way and lead to more concise and effective communications. In our workshops, I find that we allocate an increasing amount of time and discussion on the very first lesson we cover, which focuses on context. People come in thinking they want data visualization best practices and are surprised by the amount of time we spend on—and that they *want* to spend on—topics related more generally to how we plan for our communications. By thinking about our audience, message, and components of content up front (and getting feedback at this early stage), we put ourselves in a better position for creating graphs, presentations or other data-backed materials that will meet our audience's needs and our own.

The exercises in this chapter focus primarily on three important aspects of the planning process:

1. **Considering our audience:** identifying who they are, what they care about, and how we can better get to know them and design our communications with them in mind.

2. **Crafting and refining our main message:** the Big Idea was introduced briefly in *SWD*; here, we'll undertake a number of guided and independent exercises to better understand and practice this important concept.

3. **Planning content:** storyboarding is another concept that was introduced in *SWD*—we'll look at a number of additional examples and exercises related to what we include and how we organize it.

Let's practice **understanding the context!**

First, we'll review the main lessons from *SWD* Chapter 1.

FIRST, LET'S RECAP
The IMPORTANCE of CONTEXT
SWD BOOK CHAPTER 1

TYPES of ANALYSIS

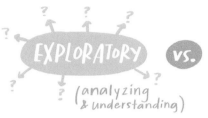
EXPLORATORY
(analyzing & understanding)

VS.

(communicating a specific story)
EXPLANATORY **!**
← *our focus*

WHERE to BEGIN?

① WHO is your AUDIENCE? BE SPECIFIC!

What is their relationship to **YOU**?

What motivates them?

What keeps them up at night?

② WHAT DO YOU NEED them to do? BE EXPLICIT!

CHANGE... CREATE... SUPPORT... IMPLEMENT... EMPOWER...

Don't assume they will connect the dots!

③ HOW WILL DATA HELP make your point? BE DISCERNING!

What data will act as evidence for the case?

THREE MINUTE STORY

THE WHOLE STORY

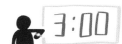

THE ESSENTIALS

(the "So what?")

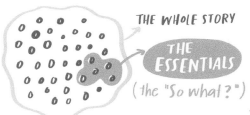

Knowing exactly what you want to communicate reduces reliance on slides and data

BIG IDEA

✷ from Nancy Duarte (Resonate)

A SINGLE SENTENCE that...

the "So what?" boiled down further

1. articulates your point of view

2. conveys what is at stake

3. is one complete sentence

STORY BOARDing

UPFRONT PLANNING to CREATE STRUCTURE

STICKY NOTES help to...

avoid attachment to work done on computer

force concise articulation

easily rearrange the flow

1. BRAINSTORM

2.  EDIT

3.  GET FEEDBACK

PRACTICE with COLE

1.1 get to know your audience

1.2 narrow your audience

1.3 complete the BIG IDEA worksheet

1.4 refine and reframe

1.5 complete another BIG IDEA worksheet

1.6 critique the BIG IDEA

1.7 storyboard!

1.8 storyboard (again!)

PRACTICE on your OWN

1.9 get to know your audience

1.10 narrow your audience

1.11 let's reframe

1.12 what's the BIG IDEA?

1.13 what's the BIG IDEA (this time?)

1.14 how could we arrange this?

1.15 storyboard!

1.16 storyboard (again!)

PRACTICE at WORK

1.17 get to know your audience

1.18 narrow your audience

1.19 identify the action

1.20 complete the BIG IDEA worksheet

1.21 solicit feedback on your BIG IDEA

1.22 create the BIG IDEA as a team

1.23 get the ideas out of your head

1.24 organize your ideas onto a storyboard

1.25 solicit feedback on your storyboard

1.26 let's discuss

When communicating with data, don't do it for yourself – do it for your audience! The following exercises will help you consider your audience, craft your message, and plan your content, setting you up for effective communication.

Exercise 1.1: get to know your audience

Who is my audience? What do they care about? These may seem like obvious questions to ask ourselves when we step back and think about it, but too often we completely skip this step. Getting to know our audience and understanding their needs and what drives them is an important early part of the process for successfully communicating with data.

Let's examine what this looks like in the wild and how we can get to know a new audience.

Imagine you work as a People Analyst (a data analyst within the Human Resources, or HR, function) at a medium-sized company. A new head of HR has just joined the organization (she is now your boss's boss). You've been asked to pull together an overview with data to help the freshly hired head of HR get up to speed with the different parts of the business from a people standpoint. This will include things like interview and hiring metrics, a headcount review across different parts of the organization, and attrition data (how many are leaving and why they are leaving). Some of your colleagues in other groups within HR have already had meet-and-greets with the new leader and given their respective synopses. Your direct manager recently had lunch with the new head of HR.

How could you get to better know your audience (the new head of HR) in this circumstance? **List three things you could do to understand your audience, what she cares about, and how to best address her needs.** Be specific in terms of what questions you would seek to answer. Get out your pen and paper and physically write down your responses.

Solution 1.1: get to know your audience

Since this isn't likely a case where we can ask our audience directly what she cares about, we'll need to get a little creative. Here are three things I could do to set myself up for success when it comes to better understanding my audience and what matters to her most:

1. **Set up time to get a debrief from colleagues who have already met with the new leader.** Talk to those who have had conversations with the new head of HR. How did those discussions go? Do they have any insight on this new leader's priorities or points of interest? Is there anything that *didn't* go well from which you can learn and adapt?

2. **Talk to my manager to get insight.** My manager has lunched with the new leader: what insight did he get about potential first points of focus? I also need to understand what my manager sees as important to focus on in this initial meeting.

3. **Use my understanding of the data and context plus some thoughtful design to structure the document.** Given that I've been working in this space for a while, I have a big picture understanding of the different main topics that someone new to our organization will assumably be interested in and the data we can use to inform. If I'm strategic in how I structure the document, I can make it easy to navigate and meet a wide variety of potential needs. I can provide an overview with the high level takeaways up front. Then I can organize the rest of the document by topic so the new leader can quickly turn to and get more detail on the areas that most interest her.

Exercise 1.2: narrow your audience

There is tremendous value in having a specific audience in mind when we communicate. Yet, often, we find ourselves facing a wide or mixed audience. By trying to meet the needs of many, we don't meet any specific need as directly or effectively as we could if we narrowed our focus and target audience. This doesn't mean that we don't still communicate to a mixed audience, but having a specific audience in mind first and foremost means we put ourselves in a better position to meet that core audience's needs.

Let's practice the process of narrowing for purposes of communicating. We'll start by casting a wide net and then employ various strategies to focus from there. Work your way through the questions and write out how you would address them. Then read the following pages to better understand various strategies for narrowing our audience.

You work at a national clothing retailer. You've conducted a survey asking your customers and the customers of your competitors about various elements related to back-to-school shopping. You've analyzed the data. You've found there are some areas where your company is performing well, and also some other areas of opportunity. You're nearing the point of communicating your findings.

QUESTION 1: There are a lot of different groups of people (at your company and potentially beyond) who could be interested in this data. Who might care how your stores performed in the recent back-to-school shopping season? Cast as wide of a net as possible. **How many different audiences can you come up with who might be interested in the survey data you've analyzed? Make a list!**

QUESTION 2: Let's get more specific. You've analyzed the survey data and found that there are differences in service satisfaction reported by your customers across the various stores. **Which potential audiences would care about this? Again, list them.** Does this make your list of potential audiences longer or shorter than it was originally? Did you add any additional potential audiences in light of this new information?

QUESTION 3: Let's take it a step further. You've found there are differences in satisfaction across stores. Your analysis reveals items related to sales associates as the main driver of dissatisfaction. You've looked into several potential courses of action to address this and determined that you'd like to recommend rolling out sales associate training as a way to improve and bring consistency to service levels across your stores. **Now who might your audience be? Who cares about this data? List your primary audiences.** If you had to narrow to a specific decision maker in this instance, who would that be?

Solution 1.2: narrow your audience

QUESTION 1: There are many different audiences who might care about the back-to-school shopping data. Here are some that I've come up with (likely not a comprehensive list):

- Senior leadership
- Buyers
- Merchandisers
- Marketing
- Store managers
- Sales associates
- Customer service people
- Competitors
- Customers

Eventually, *everyone in the world* may care about this data! Which is great, but not so helpful when it comes to narrowing our audience for the purpose of communicating. There are a number of ways we can narrow our audience: by being clear on our findings, specific on the recommended action, and focused on the given point in time and decision maker. The answers to the remaining questions will illustrate how we can focus in these ways to have a specific audience in mind when we communicate.

QUESTION 2: If service levels are inconsistent across stores, the following audiences are likely to care most:

- Senior leadership
- Store managers
- Sales associates
- Customer service people

QUESTION 3: We want to roll out training—that sparks some questions for me. Who will create and deliver the training? How much will it cost? With this additional clarity, some new audiences have entered the mix:

- Senior leadership
- HR
- Finance
- Store managers
- Sales associates
- Customer service people

The preceding list may all *eventually* be audiences for this information. We've noted inconsistencies with service levels and need to conduct training. HR will have to weigh in on whether we can meet this need internally or if it will require us to bring in external partners to develop or deliver training. Finance controls the budget and we'll have to figure out where to get the money to pay for this. Store managers will need to buy-in so they are willing to have their employees spend time attending the training. The sales associates and customer service people will have to be convinced that their behavior needs to change so that they will take the training seriously and provide consistent high quality service to customers.

But not all of these groups are immediate audiences. Some of the communications will take place downstream.

To narrow further, I can reflect on where we are at in time: today. Before we can do any of the above, we need approval that rolling out training is the right course of action. A decision needs to be made, so another way of narrowing my audience is to be clear on timing as well as who the decision maker (or set of decision makers) is within the broader audience. In this instance, I might assume the ultimate decision maker—the person who will either say, "yes, I'm willing to devote the resources; let's do this," or "no, not an issue; let's continue to do things as we have been"—is a specific person on the leadership team: the head of retail sales.

In this example, we have employed a number of different ways to narrow our target audience for the purpose of the communication. We narrowed by:

1. Being specific about what we learned through the data,

2. Being clear on the action we are recommending,

3. Acknowledging what point we're at in time (what needs to happen now), and

4. Identifying a specific decision maker.

Consider how you can use these same tactics to narrow your audience in your own work. Exercise 1.18 in *practice at work* will help you do just that. But before we get there, let's continue to practice together and turn our attention to a useful resource: the Big Idea worksheet.

PRACTICE *with* COLE

PRACTICE *with* COLE

Exercise 1.3: complete the Big Idea worksheet

The Big Idea is a concept that can help us get clear and succinct on the main message we want to get across to our audience. The Big Idea (originally introduced by Nancy Duarte in *Resonate*, 2010) should (1) articulate your unique point of view, (2) convey what's at stake, and (3) be a complete sentence. Taking the time to craft this up front helps us get clarity and concision on the overall idea we need to communicate to our audience, making it easier and more streamlined to plan content to get this key message across.

In *storytelling with data* workshops, we use the Big Idea worksheet to help craft our Big Idea. Attendees commonly express how unexpectedly helpful they find this simple activity. We'll do a few related exercises so you can practice and see examples of the Big Idea worksheet in action. Let's start by continuing with the example we just worked through for narrowing our audience. As a reminder, the basic context follows.

You work at a national clothing retailer. You've conducted a survey asking your customers and the customers of your competitors about various elements related to back-to-school shopping. You've analyzed the data. You've found there are some areas where your company is performing well, as well as some areas of opportunity. In particular, there are inconsistencies in service levels across stores. Together with your team, you've explored some different potential courses of action for dealing with this and would like to recommend solving through sales associate training. You need agreement that this is the right course of action and approval for the resources (cost, time, people) it will take to develop and deliver this training.

Think back to the audience we narrowed to in Exercise 1.2: the head of retail. **Work your way through the Big Idea worksheet on the following page for this scenario.** Make assumptions as needed for the purpose of the exercise.

the **BIG IDEA** worksheet

Identify a project you are working on where you
need to communicate in a data-driven way.
Reflect upon and fill out the following.

storytelling|||| data®

PROJECT _____

WHO IS YOUR **AUDIENCE**?

(1) List the primary groups or individuals to
whom you'll be communicating.

(3) What does your audience care about?

(4) What action does your audience need to take?

(2) If you had to narrow that to a *single person*,
who would that be?

WHAT IS **AT STAKE**?

What are the *benefits* if your audience acts
in the way that you want them to?

What are the *risks* if they do not?

FORM YOUR **BIG IDEA**

It should:

(1) articulate your point of view,

(2) convey what's at stake, and

(3) be a complete (and single!)
sentence.

PRACTICE *with* **COLE**

FIGURE 1.3a The Big Idea worksheet

Solution 1.3: complete the Big Idea worksheet

the **BIG IDEA** worksheet

Identify a project you are working on where you
need to communicate in a data-driven way.
Reflect upon and fill out the following.

storytelling📊data®

PROJECT *Back-to-school opportunity*

WHO IS YOUR **AUDIENCE**?

(1) List the primary groups or individuals to
whom you'll be communicating.

the executive team

(2) If you had to narrow that to a *single person*,
who would that be?

the head of retail

(3) What does your audience care about?

- *Having a highly profitable
  back-to-school shopping season*
- *Making customers happy because
  happier customers spend more*
- *Beating the competition*

(4) What action does your audience need to take?

*Agree that training is the right way
to deal with inconsistent service levels
and approve the __resources__ it
will take to make that happen
(cost, time, people)*

WHAT IS **AT STAKE**?

What are the *benefits* if your audience acts
in the way that you want them to?

- *better service levels = happier customers*
- *happier customers spend more,
  come back more often,
  tell friends about their
  positive experience*

What are the *risks* if they do not?

- *no action could lead to
  negative word of mouth*
- *people shopping with competitors*
- *reputational risk*
- *lost revenue*

FORM YOUR **BIG IDEA**

It should:

(1) articulate your point of view,

(2) convey what's at stake, and

(3) be a complete (and single!)
sentence.

*Let's invest in sales associate training
to improve the in-store shopping
experience and make the upcoming
back-to-school season the best
revenue generating one yet!*

FIGURE 1.3b Completed Big Idea worksheet

Exercise 1.4: refine & reframe

Consider both your Big Idea from Exercise 1.3 and the one I came up with in Solution 1.3. Answer the following questions.

QUESTION 1: **Compare and contrast.** Are there common points where they are similar? How are they different? Which do you find to be more effective and why?

QUESTION 2: **How did you frame?** Reflect on the Big Idea you originally crafted. Did you frame it positively or negatively? What is the benefit or risk in your Big Idea? How could you reframe it to be the opposite?

QUESTION 3: **How did I frame?** Revisit the Big Idea articulated in Solution 1.3. Is it framed positively or negatively? What is the benefit or risk in this Big Idea? Again, how could you reframe it to be the opposite? How else might you refine?

Solution 1.4: refine & reframe

Given that I don't have your Big Idea as I write this, I'll focus on Question 3, which poses some questions about mine. Here it is again for reference:

Let's invest in sales associate training to improve the in-store shopping experience and make the upcoming back-to-school season the best revenue generating one yet!

How did I frame? What is the benefit or risk? This is currently framed positively, focusing on the benefit of the revenue we stand to gain by investing in sales associate training.

How could you reframe it to be the opposite? I could reframe negatively a couple of different ways. One simple way would be to focus on the same thing at stake—revenue—but change to emphasize the loss that could result from not taking action.

If we don't invest in sales associate training to improve service levels, we will lose customers and have lower revenue for the upcoming back-to-school shopping season.

But revenue isn't the only thing at stake. What if I know that my audience is highly motivated by beating the competition? Then I could try something like this:

We are losing to the competition when it comes to important aspects of our store experience – we will continue to lose unless we invest in sales associate training to improve the customer experience across our stores.

How else can we refine this Big Idea? There's no single right answer. There are a number of different potential benefits (more satisfied customers, greater revenue, beating the competition) and risks (unhappy customers, lower revenue, losing to competition, negative word of mouth, reputational damage). What we assume our audience cares most about will influence how we frame and what we focus on in our Big Idea.

In a real-life scenario, we'd want to know as much about our audience as we can to make smart assumptions. Check out Exercise 1.17 in *practice at work* for guidance on getting to know your audience. Next, let's look at another Big Idea worksheet.

Exercise 1.5: complete another Big Idea worksheet

Let's do another practice run with the Big Idea worksheet.

Imagine you volunteer for your local pet shelter, a nonprofit organization whose mission is to improve the quality of animal life through veterinary care, adoptions, and public education. You help organize monthly pet adoption events, which feed into the organization's broader goal of increasing permanent adoptions of pets by 20% this year.

Traditionally, these monthly events have been held in outdoor spaces in your community (parks and greenways) on Saturday mornings. However, last month's event was different. Due to poor weather, the event was relocated indoors to a local pet supply retailer. Surprisingly, after the event, you observed something interesting: *nearly twice as many pets were adopted* compared to previous months.

You have some initial ideas about the reasons for this increase and think there's value in holding more adoption events at this retailer. You'd like to conduct a pilot program over the next three months to see if the results help confirm your beliefs. To implement this pilot program, you'll need additional support from the pet shelter's marketing volunteers to publicize the events. You've estimated the monthly costs to be $500 for printing and three hours of a marketing volunteer's time. You want to ask the event committee to approve the pilot program at next month's meeting and are planning your communication.

Complete the Big Idea worksheet on the following page for this scenario, making assumptions as necessary for the purpose of the exercise.

PRACTICE *with* COLE

the **BIG IDEA** worksheet

storytelling data®

Identify a project you are working on where you need to communicate in a data-driven way. Reflect upon and fill out the following.

PROJECT _____

WHO IS YOUR **AUDIENCE**?

(1) List the primary groups or individuals to whom you'll be communicating.

(3) What does your audience care about?

(4) What action does your audience need to take?

(2) If you had to narrow that to a *single person*, who would that be?

WHAT IS **AT STAKE**?

What are the *benefits* if your audience acts in the way that you want them to?

What are the *risks* if they do not?

FORM YOUR **BIG IDEA**

It should:

(1) articulate your point of view,

(2) convey what's at stake, and

(3) be a complete (and single!) sentence.

FIGURE 1.5a The Big Idea worksheet

Solution 1.5: complete another Big Idea worksheet

The following illustrates one way to complete the Big Idea worksheet for this scenario.

the BIG IDEA worksheet

storytelling with data®

Identify a project you are working on where you need to communicate in a data-driven way. Reflect upon and fill out the following.

PROJECT _Adoption venue pilot_

WHO IS YOUR AUDIENCE?

(1) List the primary groups or individuals to whom you'll be communicating.

Shelter events planning committee
They'll decide based on a majority vote

(2) If you had to narrow that to a *single person*, who would that be?

Jane Harper, the most influential person on the committee whose opinion would likely affect the outcome

(3) What does your audience care about?

Increasing pet adoptions- in general and specifically toward the organization's 20% increase goal, which will improve ability to fundraise; they are cost-conscious, so low cost options are often supported

(4) What action does your audience need to take?

Approve my pilot program of holding pet adoptions at a local pet supply retailer for the next 3 months and provide additional marketing resources: $500 to print posters + 3 hours/month of a marketing volunteer's time

WHAT IS AT STAKE?

What are the *benefits* if your audience acts in the way that you want them to?

More adoptions (lower euthanization), which will help us achieve the broader 20% goal, and help with future fundraising

What are the *risks* if they do not?

- _Missed opportunity to increase adoptions_
- _More animals don't find homes_
- _Greater euthanization + associated cost_
- _Miss 20% goal_

FORM YOUR BIG IDEA

It should:
(1) articulate your point of view,
(2) convey what's at stake, and
(3) be a complete (and single!) sentence.

Approve our low-cost pilot program that has potential to markedly increase adoptions and result in better future fundraising opportunities.

FIGURE 1.5b Completed Big Idea worksheet

Exercise 1.6: critique the Big Idea

Being able to give good feedback on the Big Idea is important both when we work with others, as well as for critiquing and refining our own work. Let's practice giving feedback on the Big Idea.

Suppose you work for a health care center that has been analyzing recent vaccine rates. Your colleague has been focusing on progress and opportunities related to flu vaccines. He has crafted the following Big Idea for the update he is preparing and has asked for your feedback.

While flu vaccination rates have improved since last year, we need to increase the rate in our area by 2% to hit the national average.

With this Big Idea in mind, write a few sentences outlining your response to the following.

QUESTION 1: What questions might you ask your colleague?

QUESTION 2: What feedback would you provide on his Big Idea?

Solution 1.6: critique the Big Idea

QUESTION 1: The immediate questions I'd have for my colleague would be about their audience: who are they? What do they care about?

QUESTION 2: In terms of giving specific feedback on the Big Idea, let's think back to the components of the Big Idea—it should (1) articulate your point of view, (2) convey what's at stake, and (3) be a complete (and single!) sentence. Let's consider each of these in light of my colleague's Big Idea.

1. **Articulate your point of view.** The point of view is that vaccination rates are low compared to the national average and need to be increased.

2. **Convey what's at stake.** This isn't clear to me currently. I'm going to want to ask some targeted questions to better understand what is at stake for the audience.

3. **Be a complete (and single!) sentence.** Good job on this front. It's often difficult to summarize our point in a single sentence. If anything, we have room to possibly add a little more to the sentence to make it meatier and more clearly convey what is at stake.

In general, the Big Idea in its current form gives me the *what* (increase vaccination rates), but not the *why* (it also doesn't get into the *how*, though there's only so much we can fit into a sentence, and this piece can come into play through the supporting content).

You could argue that the *why* is because we're lower than the national average, but this doesn't feel compelling enough. Is my audience going to be motivated by a national average comparison? Is that even the right goal? Is it aggressive enough? Too aggressive? Can we get more specific by thinking through what will be most motivating for the audience?

It's clear my colleague believes that we should increase flu vaccination rates. But let's consider why our audience should care. What does this mean for them? Are they motivated by competition—maybe we're lower than that other medical center across town, or our area is low compared to the state, or perhaps the national comparison is the right one but can be articulated in a more motivating way? Or maybe my audience is driven by generally doing good—we could get into patient advantages or highlight general community well-being benefits that would be well served by increasing vaccination rates. If we think about positive versus negative framing—which will be best for this scenario and audience?

The conversation I have with my colleague will cause him to explain his thought process, what he knows about his audience, and what assumptions he's making. The dialogue we have will help him both refine his Big Idea as well as be better prepared to talk through this with his ultimate audience. Success!

Exercise 1.7: storyboard!

I sometimes feel like a broken record because I say this so frequently: storyboarding is the most important thing you can do up front as part of the planning process to reduce iterations down the road and create better targeted materials. A storyboard is a visual outline of your content, created in a low-tech manner (before you create any actual content). My preferred tool for storyboarding is a stack of sticky notes, which are both small—forcing us to be concise in our ideas—and lend themselves to being easily rearranged to explore different narrative flows. I typically storyboard in three distinct steps: brainstorming, editing, and seeking and incorporating feedback.

We'll do a couple of practice storyboarding runs so you can both get a feel for it and see illustrative approaches. Let's start with an example you should be familiar with now (we've seen it previously in Exercises 1.2, 1.3, and 1.4). As a reminder, the basic context follows.

You work at a national clothing retailer. You've conducted a survey asking your customers and the customers of your competitors about various elements related to back-to-school shopping. You've analyzed the data. You've found there are some areas where your company is performing well, as well as some areas of opportunity. In particular, there are inconsistencies in service across stores. Together with your team, you've explored different potential courses of action for dealing with this and would like to recommend solving through sales associate training. You need agreement that this is the right course of action and approval for the resources (cost, time, people) it will take to develop and deliver this training.

Look back to the Big Idea that you created in Exercise 1.3 (or if you didn't create one, select one of the Big Ideas from Solutions 1.3 or 1.4). Complete the following steps with a specific Big Idea in mind.

STEP 1: Brainstorm! What pieces of content may you want to include in your communication? Get a blank piece of paper or a stack of stickies and start writing down ideas. Aim for a list of at least 20.

STEP 2: Edit. Take a step back. You've come up with a ton of ideas. How could you arrange these so that they make sense to someone else? Where can you combine? What ideas did you write down that aren't essential and can be discarded? When and how will you use data? At what point will you introduce your Big Idea? Create your storyboard or the outline for your communication. (I highly recommend using sticky notes for this part of the process!)

STEP 3: **Get feedback.** Grab a partner and have them complete this exercise, then get together and talk about it. How are your storyboards similar? Where do they differ? If you don't have a partner who has completed the exercise, you can still talk someone through your plan. What changes would you make to your storyboard after talking through it with someone else? Did you learn anything interesting through this process?

PRACTICE *with* COLE

Solution 1.7: storyboard!

Looking back to Exercise 1.3, my Big Idea was the following:

Let's invest in sales associate training to improve the in-store shopping experience and make the upcoming back-to-school season the best revenue generating one yet!

I'll keep this in mind as I work through the storyboarding steps.

STEP 1: Below is my initial list of potential topics/pieces of content to include from my brainstorming process.

1. Historical context (back-to-school shopping is important)

2. Problem we're trying to solve (historically not data driven)

3. Different ways we envisaged solving the problem

4. Course of action we undertook: survey

5. Survey: customer groups we asked, general demographics, response rates

6. Survey: details on competitors we included

7. Survey: questions we asked, open and close date of survey

8. Data: how our store compares across the various items

9. Data: how this breaks down across stores and regions

10. Data: how we compare to the competition

11. Data: how competitor comparison breaks down by stores & regions

12. Good news: where we're doing best or beating competition (with store breakdown)

13. Bad news: where we're doing worse or lower than competition (with store breakdown)

14. Areas for improvement

15. Potential remedies

16. Recommended course of action: invest in sales training

17. Resources needed (people, budget)

18. What this will solve

19. Projected timeline

20. Discussion to have / decision to be made

STEP 2: Figure 1.7 illustrates how I might curate the preceding list into a storyboard.

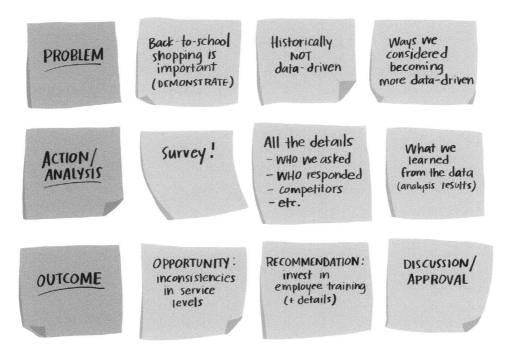

FIGURE 1.7 Back-to-school shopping: a potential storyboard

Does Figure 1.7 illustrate the "right" answer? No. Will you always end up with a perfect grid of sticky notes like this? Not likely. Are there things you would have done differently? Probably. Are there additional changes that I would make to this? Yes. We'll revisit this scenario again a little later to explore how we can further refine this storyboard. But for now, take this as one illustrative storyboard and let's turn our attention to Step 3.

STEP 3: What feedback do you have for me on this storyboard? How is yours similar? Where does it differ? Consider how you can apply this approach to a current project you face. Exercises 1.23, 1.24, and 1.25 in *practice at work* will help you do just that. Before we get there, let's do some additional guided practice storyboarding.

Exercise 1.8: storyboard (again!)

For this exercise, we'll create a storyboard using the pet adoptions pilot program we introduced in Exercise 1.5. As a reminder, the background is as follows:

Imagine you volunteer for your local pet shelter, a nonprofit organization whose mission is to improve the quality of animal life through veterinary care, adoptions, and public education. You help organize monthly pet adoption events, which feed into the organization's broader goal of increasing permanent adoptions of pets by 20% this year.

Traditionally, these monthly events have been held in outdoor spaces in your community (parks and greenways) on Saturday mornings. However, last month's event was different. Due to poor weather, the event was relocated indoors to a local pet supply retailer. Surprisingly, after the event, you observed something interesting: *nearly twice as many pets were adopted this month* compared to previous months.

You have some initial ideas about the reasons for this increase and think there's value in holding more adoption events at this retailer. You'd like to conduct a pilot program over the next three months to see if these results help confirm your beliefs. To implement this pilot program, you'll need additional support from the pet shelter's marketing volunteers to publicize the events. You've estimated the monthly costs to be $500 for printing and three hours of a marketing volunteer's time. You want to ask the event committee to approve the pilot program at next month's meeting and are planning your communication.

Look back to the Big Idea that you created in Exercise 1.5 (or if you didn't create one, revisit the Big Idea from Solution 1.5). Complete the following steps with this specific Big Idea in mind.

STEP 1: **Brainstorm!** In this first step, brainstorm what details might be necessary to include in the eventual presentation. Get a blank piece of paper or a stack of stickies and start writing down ideas. Aim for a list of at least 20. To aid in your brainstorming process, ask yourself: has the organization ever tried a pilot program before? Will the events committee need to understand the risks and benefits of this program? Are they likely to respond favorably or unfavorably? Do you have historical data on the number of adoptions from community spaces? Are you aware whether other shelters have successfully tried this? How will you measure and assess the results from the three-month pilot? What does success look like?

STEP 2: Edit. Examine all the ideas you generated in Step 1. Next, let's plan how to put them to use. Determine which pieces of potential content are essential and which can be discarded. Create your storyboard or the outline for the presentation. To aid in the editing and arranging process, ask yourself: having identified your audience's likely response in Step 1, will you start with the Big Idea or build up to it? How familiar is your audience with the recent success—will you need to communicate this context or is it already well known? Which other details are new to the audience and may require more time or data behind them? Will your audience be accepting of your proposal or will you need to convince them? How can you best do that?

STEP 3: **Get feedback.** Grab a partner and have them complete this exercise, then get together and talk about it. How are your storyboards similar? Where do they differ? If you don't have a partner who has completed the exercise, you can still talk someone through your plan. What changes would you make to your storyboard after talking through it with someone else? Did you learn anything interesting through this process?

PRACTICE *with* COLE

Solution 1.8: storyboard (again!)

Looking back to Exercise 1.5, my Big Idea was the following:

Approve our low-cost pilot program, which has potential to markedly increase adoptions and result in better future fundraising opportunities.

I'll keep this in mind as I work through the storyboarding steps.

STEP 1: Following is my initial list of potential topics to include from my brainstorming process.

1. Historical context: we've always held adoptions at a community space
2. Current state: review benefits and how many were adopted per month
3. Outline how current number of pet adoptions feeds into broader goal of 20% increase
4. Background on why last month's event was held indoors
5. Results: we saw a 2x increase in adoptions
6. Drivers: possible reasons why this happened
7. Drivers: possible reasons why this may continue if we try again
8. Opportunity: introduce 3-month pilot program
9. Analysis: benefits & risk of pilot program
10. Resources needed: explain additional marketing cost of $500
11. Resources needed: consider additional marketing time of 3 volunteer hours
12. Additional requirements: approval from pet supply store manager, comms to employees
13. Additional requirements: logistics for planning & set up in store
14. Data: what other pet shelters have done
15. Recommendation: approve this pilot program
16. Discussion: ways we're working to meet 20% increase goal
17. Timeline & proposed dates
18. How we'll track & measure success for 3 months
19. Implications for fundraising
20. Discussion & decision to be made

STEP 2: Figure 1.8 illustrates how I could curate the preceding list into a storyboard.

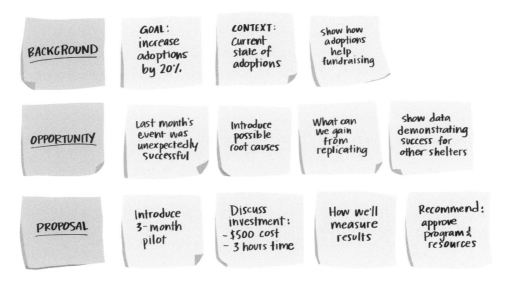

FIGURE 1.8 Pet adoption pilot program: a potential storyboard

STEP 3: What feedback do you have for me on this storyboard? How is yours similar? Where does it differ? How can you apply this approach to a current project you face? Refer to exercises 1.23, 1.24, and 1.25 for guidance on storyboarding at work.

You've practiced narrowing your audiences, crafting your Big Idea, and storyboarding with me. Next, you'll find more low-risk practice for you to tackle on your own.

PRACTICE with COLE

PRACTICE on your OWN

It is by continuing to practice that truly understanding your audience and integrating important low-tech planning will feel constructive and become part of your regular routine. Let's undertake additional exercises to help form these good habits.

Exercise 1.9: get to know your audience

Let's say you work at a consulting company. You have a new client, the director of marketing at a prominent pet food manufacturer. You are one level removed from your audience: rather than interfacing with them directly, you provide analysis and reports to your boss, who presents this work to the client, discusses it with them, and then communicates any feedback or additional needs to you.

How can you better get to know your audience in this case? **List three things you could do to better understand your audience and what they care about.** How does having the intermediate audience of your manager potentially complicate things? How might you use this to your advantage? What other considerations do you need to make in order to be successful in this scenario?

Write a paragraph or two to answer these questions.

Exercise 1.10: narrow your audience

Next, you'll practice narrowing the audience. Read the following, then work your way through the various questions posed to determine how you can narrow your audience for purposes of communicating given different assumptions.

Imagine you work for a regional medical group. You and several colleagues have just wrapped up an evaluation of Suppliers A, B, C, and D for the XYZ Products category. Your analysis examined historical costs by facility, patient and physician satisfaction, and cost projections going forward. You are in the process of creating a presentation deck with this information.

QUESTION 1: There are a lot of different groups of people (at your company and potentially beyond) who may be interested in this data. Who can you think of who is apt to care how the various suppliers compare when it comes to historical usage, patient and physician satisfaction, and cost projections? Cast as wide of a net as possible. **How many different audiences can you come up with who might be interested in this information? List them!**

QUESTION 2: Let's get more specific. The data shows that historical usage has varied a lot by medical facility, with some using primarily Supplier B and others using primarily Supplier D (and only limited historical use of Suppliers A and C). You've also found that satisfaction is highest across the board for Supplier B. **Which potential audiences might care about this? Again, list them.** Does this make your list of potential audiences longer or shorter than it was originally? Did you add any additional potential audiences in light of this new information?

QUESTION 3: Time to take it a step further. You've analyzed all of the data and realized there are significant cost savings in going with a single or dual supplier contract. However, either of these will mean changes for some medical centers relative to their historical supplier usage. You need a decision on how to best move forward strategically in this space. **Now who might your audience be? Who cares about this data? List your primary audiences.** If you had to narrow to a specific decision maker, who would that be?

PRACTICE on your OWN

Exercise 1.11: let's reframe

One component of the Big Idea is what is at stake for your audience. As we've discussed, this can be framed either in terms of *benefits* (what does your audience stand to gain if they act in the way you recommend?) or in terms of *risks* (what does your audience stand to lose if they don't act accordingly?). It is often useful to explore both the positive *and* negative framing as you think through which might work best for your specific situation.

Consider the following Big Ideas and answer the accompanying questions to practice identifying and reworking how each is framed.

BIG IDEA 1: *We should increase incentives to complete our email survey so we can collect better quality data and gain a robust understanding of our customers' pain points.*

(A) Is this Big Idea currently positively or negatively framed?

(B) What is the benefit or risk in this Big Idea?

(C) How could you reframe it to be the opposite?

BIG IDEA 2: *We stand to miss our earnings per share target if we don't reallocate resources to support emerging markets now that revenue from our traditional line of business has plateaued.*

(A) Is this Big Idea currently positively or negatively framed?

(B) What is the benefit or risk in this Big Idea?

(C) How could you reframe it to be the opposite?

BIG IDEA 3: *Last quarter's digital marketing campaign resulted in the traffic and sales increases we expected: we should maintain current spend levels to achieve this year's sales goal.*

(A) Is this Big Idea currently positively or negatively framed?

(B) What is the benefit or risk in this Big Idea?

(C) How could you reframe it to be the opposite?

PRACTICE on your OWN

Exercise 1.12: what's the Big Idea?

We've undertaken a number of exercises to get you comfortable working your way through the Big Idea worksheet and also seeing potential solutions (Exercises 1.3 and 1.5). These next couple of exercises are similar—we pose a scenario and ask you to complete the Big Idea worksheet—but there's no illustrative answer. Rather, it's up to you to critique and refine what you've created.

You are the Chief Financial Officer (CFO) for a national retailer. You are responsible for managing the financial well-being of the company and your duties include analyzing and reporting on the company's financial strengths and weaknesses and proposing corrective actions. Your team of financial analysts just completed a review of Q1 and have identified that the company is likely to end the fiscal year with a loss of $45 million if operating expenses and sales follow the latest projections.

Because of a recent economic downturn, an increase in sales is unlikely. Therefore, you believe the projected loss can *only* be mitigated by controlling operating expenses and that management should implement an expense control policy ("expense control initiative ABC") immediately. You will be reporting the Q1 quarterly results at an upcoming Board of Directors meeting and are planning your communication—a summary of financial results in a PowerPoint deck—that you will present to the board with your recommendation.

Your goals for the presentation are twofold:

1. For the Board of Directors to understand the long-term implications of ending the year at a net loss, and

2. Get agreement from the daily operating managers (CEO and executives) to implement "expense control initiative ABC" immediately.

Complete the Big Idea worksheet on the following page for this scenario, making assumptions as necessary for the purpose of the exercise.

PRACTICE on your OWN

the **BIG IDEA** worksheet

Identify a project you are working on where you
need to communicate in a data-driven way.
Reflect upon and fill out the following.

storytelling |ı‖ı| data®

PROJECT _____

WHO IS YOUR **AUDIENCE**?

(1) List the primary groups or individuals to
whom you'll be communicating.

(3) What does your audience care about?

(4) What action does your audience need to take?

(2) If you had to narrow that to a *single person*,
who would that be?

WHAT IS **AT STAKE**?

What are the *benefits* if your audience acts
in the way that you want them to?

What are the *risks* if they do not?

FORM YOUR **BIG IDEA**

It should:

(1) articulate your point of view,

(2) convey what's at stake, and

(3) be a complete (and single!)
sentence.

PRACTICE on your OWN

FIGURE 1.12 The Big Idea worksheet

Exercise 1.13: what's the Big Idea (this time)?

Let's do another practice run with the Big Idea worksheet.

Imagine you're a rising university senior serving on the student government council. One of the council's goals is to create a positive campus experience by representing the student body to faculty and administrators and electing representatives from each undergraduate class. You've served on the council for the past three years and are involved in the planning for this year's upcoming elections. Last year, student voter turnout for the elections was 30% lower than previous years, indicating lower engagement between the student body and the council. You and a fellow council member completed benchmarking research at other universities and found that universities with the highest voter turnout had the most effective student government council at effecting change. You think there's opportunity to increase voter turnout at this year's election by building awareness of the student government council's mission by launching an advertising campaign to the student body. You have an upcoming meeting with the student body president and finance committee where you will be presenting your recommendation.

Your ultimate goal is a budget of $1,000 for the advertising campaign to increase awareness of why the student body should vote in these elections.

STEP 1: Considering this situation, complete the following Big Idea worksheet, making assumptions as needed for the purpose of this exercise. (Don't overlook Steps 2 and 3 that follow it.)

PRACTICE on your OWN

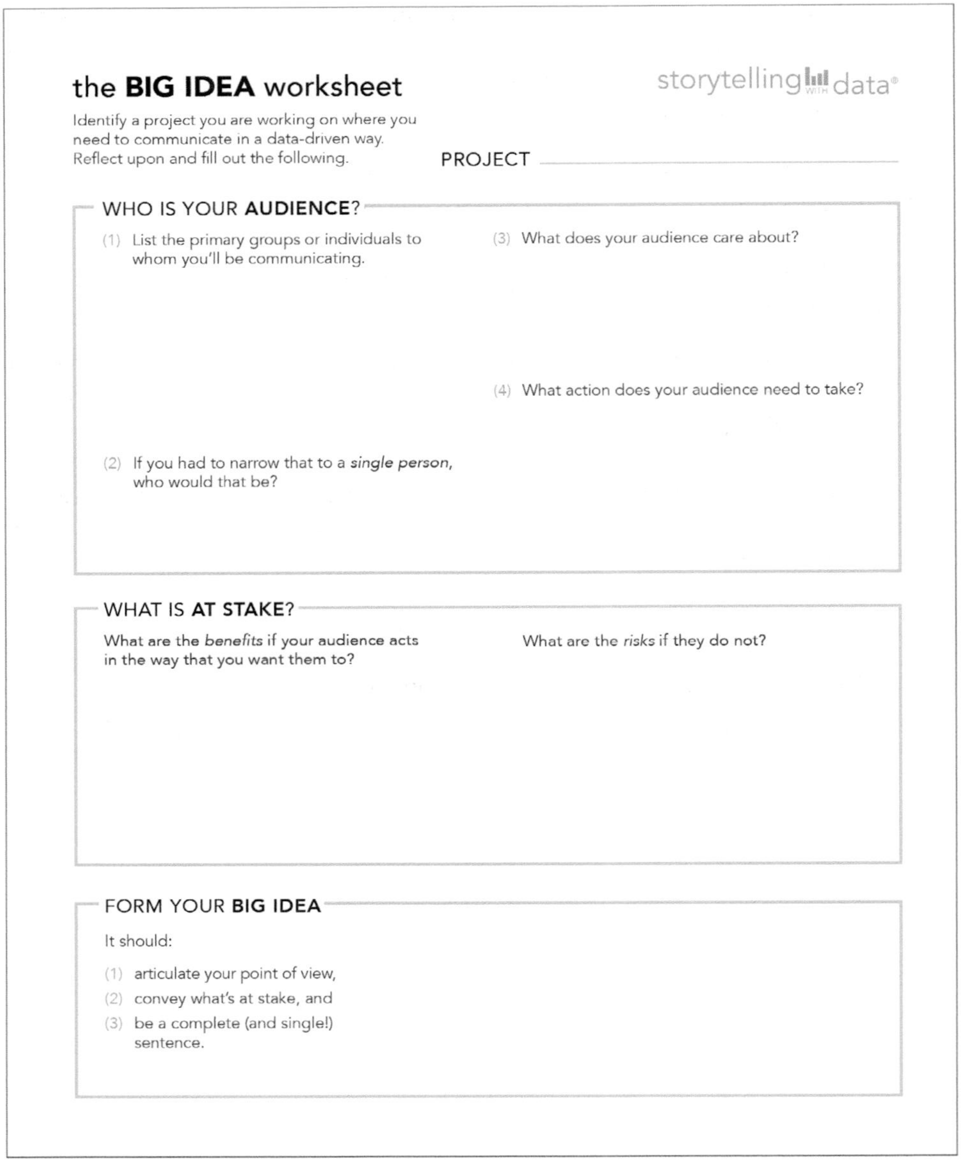

PRACTICE on your OWN

the **BIG IDEA** worksheet

storytelling ▥ data®

Identify a project you are working on where you need to communicate in a data-driven way. Reflect upon and fill out the following.

PROJECT _____

WHO IS YOUR **AUDIENCE**?

(1) List the primary groups or individuals to whom you'll be communicating.

(3) What does your audience care about?

(4) What action does your audience need to take?

(2) If you had to narrow that to a *single person*, who would that be?

WHAT IS **AT STAKE**?

What are the *benefits* if your audience acts in the way that you want them to?

What are the *risks* if they do not?

FORM YOUR **BIG IDEA**

It should:

(1) articulate your point of view,

(2) convey what's at stake, and

(3) be a complete (and single!) sentence.

FIGURE 1.13   The Big Idea worksheet

STEP 2: Let's suppose you've just learned that your intended audience—the student body president—will not be attending the upcoming meeting due to a scheduling conflict. The vice-president will cover the meeting and approve or deny your budget request. In light of this, answer the following:

(A) You don't know the vice-president well. What could you do to get to know her better? Identify one thing you can do *immediately*—before the meeting—to better understand what she cares about and one thing you'll do *over your tenure on the council* to better understand the vice-president's needs for future communications.

(B) Revisit your framing of the Big Idea. Did you write it with a positive or negative focus? What may cause you to change to the opposite framing given this new audience?

STEP 3: You'd like to solicit feedback on your Big Idea. You are deciding between two different people from whom to potentially get feedback: (1) your roommate or (2) a fellow council member. Answer the following:

(A) What would be the advantages or disadvantages of each?

(B) How do you anticipate the conversations would be different?

(C) Who would you ultimately choose to solicit feedback from? Why?

PRACTICE on your OWN

Exercise 1.14: how could we arrange this?

There are many ways we can organize the content that we present. Storyboarding allows us to plan the order and consider different arrangements in light of who our audience is and what we hope to achieve when we communicate with them. Look at the potential components of a storyboard in Figure 1.14 (which are presented in no particular order) and answer the following questions.

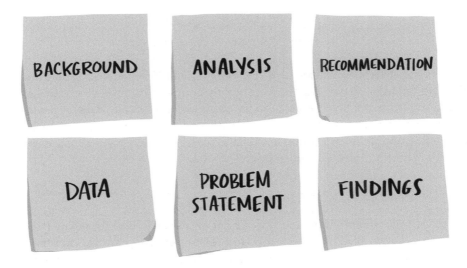

FIGURE 1.14 Potential components of a storyboard

QUESTION 1: How would you arrange these components into a storyboard? (What would you start with? What would you end with? How would you order the topics in between?) What drives your decisions on how to order the content?

QUESTION 2: Let's say you made some assumptions about the data as part of your analysis. At what point in your planned arrangement would you include this? Why is that?

QUESTION 3: Assume you are presenting to a highly technical audience and anticipate there will be a lot of questions and discussion about the data and your analysis. Does this change how you would order your content? Are there additional elements you would include or remove?

QUESTION 4: Imagine you have a solid understanding of the data, but that there is important context that your audience will need to contribute in order for everyone to understand the full picture. Does this affect how you would arrange your content? Where and how would you invite audience input? Would you add or remove any elements?

QUESTION 5: Assume you are presenting to senior leadership. You recognize that you'll only get a short amount of time (perhaps even shorter than your allotted time slot on the agenda). Does this change how you would order the content? Why or why not?

Exercise 1.15: storyboard!

For this exercise, we'll create a storyboard using the CFO's Q1 financial update introduced in Exercise 1.12. As a reminder, the background is as follows:

You are the Chief Financial Officer for a national retailer. You are responsible for managing the financial well-being of the company and your duties include analyzing and reporting on the company's financial strengths and weaknesses and proposing corrective actions. Your team of financial analysts just completed a review of Q1 and have identified that the company is likely to end the fiscal year with a loss of $45 million if operating expenses and sales follow the latest projections.

Because of a recent economic downturn, an increase in sales is unlikely. Therefore, you believe the projected loss can *only* be mitigated by controlling operating expenses and that management should implement an expense control policy ("expense control initiative ABC") immediately. You will be reporting the Q1 quarterly results at an upcoming Board of Directors meeting and are planning your communication—a summary of financial results in a slide deck—that you will present to the board with your recommendation.

Your goals for the presentation are twofold:

1. For the Board of Directors to understand the long-term implications of ending the year at a net loss, and

2. Get agreement from the daily operating managers (CEO and executives) to implement "expense control initiative ABC" immediately.

Look back to the Big Idea that you created in Exercise 1.12 (if you didn't create one, spend a few moments doing so now!). Complete the following steps with this Big Idea in mind.

STEP 1: **Brainstorm!** In this first step, brainstorm what details you might possibly include in the eventual presentation. Get a blank piece of paper or a stack of sticky notes and start writing down ideas. Aim for a list of at least 20. To aid in the brainstorming process, ask yourself a few questions: Is this the first time you've introduced your Big Idea to this audience? Do you anticipate they will respond favorably or unfavorably? How frequently have they seen the data you'll show

PRACTICE on your OWN

them—is it a regular update or will you need to allow time to educate them on unfamiliar terms or methodology? Do you anticipate needing to get buy-in from the decision maker on your recommendations? If so, what data points need to be included to help with this process?

STEP 2: **Edit.** Examine all the ideas you generated in Step 1. Identify which are essential and which can be discarded. Create your storyboard or the outline for the presentation. To aid in the editing and arranging process, ask yourself: having identified your audience's likely response in Step 1, will you start with the Big Idea or will you lead up to it at the end? Which details has the audience seen regularly that can possibly be discarded? What details are new to the audience and may require more time or data behind them? Are there pieces that can be combined?

STEP 3: **Get feedback.** Grab a partner and have them complete this exercise, then get together and talk about it. How are your storyboards similar? Where do they differ? If you don't have a partner who has completed the exercise, you can still talk someone through your plan. What changes would you make to your storyboard after talking through it with someone else? Did you learn anything interesting through this process?

PRACTICE on your OWN

Exercise 1.16: storyboard (again!)

For this exercise, we'll critique and revise a storyboard using the university elections example from Exercise 1.13. As a reminder, the background is as follows:

Imagine you're a rising university senior serving on the student government council. One of the council's goals is to create a positive campus experience by representing the student body to faculty and administrators and electing representatives from each undergraduate class. You've served on the council for the past three years and are involved in the planning for this year's upcoming elections. Last year, student voter turnout for the elections was 30% lower than previous years, indicating lower engagement between the student body and the council. You and a fellow council member completed benchmarking research at other universities and found that universities with the highest voter turnout had the most effective student government council at effecting change. You think there's opportunity to increase voter turnout at this year's election by building awareness of the student government council's mission by launching an advertising campaign to the student body. You have an upcoming meeting with the student body president and finance committee where you will be presenting your recommendation.

Your ultimate goal is a budget of $1,000 for the advertising campaign to increase awareness of why the student body should vote in these elections.

QUESTION 1: Your fellow council member created the following storyboard (Figure 1.16) for the communication to the student body president and has asked for your feedback. Critique the storyboard with these questions in mind:

(A) How is it currently ordered (chronological, leading with Big Idea, something else)?

(B) What points would you combine? What would you add? What would you remove?

(C) How would you suggest revising the storyboard based on your critique?

FIGURE 1.16 University elections colleague's storyboard

QUESTION 2: You've now learned that the vice-president will be presiding over the meeting and will be deciding whether to approve your $1,000 advertising campaign. She is a busy woman and you know from others who have presented to her before that she will be hyper-focused when you are presenting but frequently has an overbooked schedule, often causing her to cut meetings short. In light of this primary audience change, reexamine your revised storyboard from Question 1C. What factors would cause you to make changes to the flow? Would you add or remove components?

QUESTION 3: Revisit the revised storyboard you created in 1C and answer the following questions:

(A) Why did you decide to put the call to action in its current location?

(B) In creating this storyboard, what were the advantages of using sticky notes over software?

(C) What benefits did you get from creating this storyboard?

You've practiced with me and on your own. Next, let's talk through how you can apply the strategies we've covered in your work.

PRACTICE on your OWN

PRACTICE
at
WORK

Let's put this important planning process into action; a little time spent up front helps streamline the rest of your work, reducing iterations and keeping you on track. Consider a current project and undertake the forthcoming exercises.

Exercise 1.17: get to know your audience

When communicating, it can be useful to start by identifying your primary audience and reflecting on what is important from their perspective. Even if you don't know your audience, there are ways to get clarity on what drives them. Can you talk to them and ask questions to better understand their needs? Do you know people who are similar to your audience? Do you have colleagues who have successfully (or unsuccessfully) communicated to your audience and might have a perspective to offer? What assumptions can you make about what your audience cares about or motivates them, the biases they may have, whether they will find data important and if so, which, or how they may react to what you need to convey? As we've discussed, being clear on this can put you in a better position to successfully communicate.

If you have a mixed audience where different segments or people care about different things, it can be useful to create groups of similar audiences and work through this exercise for each of them. In cases where you identify overlap in their needs, this can be a useful place from which to communicate.

If you are making assumptions about your audience—and we nearly always are!—talk through these with a colleague or two. Do they agree with you? Have them help you identify and pressure-test your assumptions. Ask them to play devil's advocate and take an opposing viewpoint, so you can practice responding to this. The more you can do to anticipate how things could go wrong and prepare for that, the better off you'll be.

Pick a project where you need to communicate something to somebody. **Identify specific actions you can take to better get to know your audience and understand what is important to them.** What assumptions are you making about your audience when you do this? How big of a deal will it be if those assumptions are wrong? How else can you prepare for the audience to whom you'll be communicating? List specific actions, then undertake them!

PRACTICE at WORK

Exercise 1.18: narrow your audience

As we've discussed, it can be useful to have a specific audience in mind when we communicate. This allows us to really target our communication. The following exercise will help you think through how you can narrow your audience.

STEP 1: Consider a project where you need to communicate in a data-driven way. What is the project?

STEP 2: Start by casting a wide net: **list all of the potential audiences** who may care about what you will be sharing. Write them down! How many can you come up with?

STEP 3: Do you have them all? I bet there are more. See if you can add to the list you just made.

STEP 4: Next, let's narrow. Read through the following questions and list the audience(s) that will care most in light of each of these things.

(A) What did you learn through the data? Which audience(s) will care about this?

(B) What is the action you are recommending? Who needs to take this action?

(C) What point are we at in time—what needs to happen *now*?

(D) Who is the ultimate decision maker or group of decision makers?

(E) In light of all of the above, who is the primary audience(s) to whom you need to communicate?

PRACTICE at WORK

Exercise 1.19: identify the action

When we communicate for explanatory purposes, we should always want our audience to do something—take an action. Rarely is it as simple as, "We found x; therefore you should do y." Rather, there are often nuances that come into play in determining how explicit we should be with the next step we want our audience to take. In some situations, we may need input from them to help determine an appropriate course of action. In other cases, we want them to come up with the next step on their own. In any event, we—as the communicators—should be very clear on what we think that action should be.

Consider a current project where you need to communicate something to an audience. List out the potential actions they *could* take based on the data you share. What is the primary action you want them to take? Be specific—suppose you will say the following sentence to your audience:

"After reading my deck or listening to my presentation, you should

_____."

If you're having trouble, scan the following list and contemplate whether any of these might apply or spark ideas:

accept | agree | approve | begin | believe | budget | buy | champion | change
collaborate | commence | consider | continue | contribute | create | debate
decide | defend | desire | determine | devote | differentiate | discuss | distribute
divest | do | empathize | empower | encourage | engage | establish | examine
facilitate | familiarize | form | free | implement | include | increase | influence | invest
invigorate | keep | know | learn | like | maintain | mobilize | move | partner | pay for
persuade | plan | procure | promote | pursue | reallocate | receive | recommend
reconsider | reduce | reflect | remember | report | respond | reuse | reverse | review
secure | share | shift | support | simplify | start | try | understand | validate | verify

PRACTICE at WORK

Exercise 1.20: complete the Big Idea worksheet

Identify a project you are working on where you need to communicate in a data-driven way. Reflect upon and fill out the following. A fresh copy of the Big Idea worksheet can be downloaded at storytellingwithdata.com/letspractice/bigidea.

FIGURE 1.20 The Big Idea worksheet

PRACTICE at WORK

Exercise 1.21: solicit feedback on your Big Idea

After you've crafted your Big Idea, the next critical step is to talk through it with someone else.

Grab a partner, your completed Big Idea worksheet, and 10 minutes. If they aren't familiar with the Big Idea concept, have them read through the relevant section of *SWD* ahead of time, or simply tell them the three components (it should articulate your point of view, convey what's at stake, and be a complete and single sentence). Prep your partner that you want candid feedback that will help you improve the overarching message you want to get across to your audience. Have them ask you a ton of questions so they can understand what you want to communicate and help you achieve clarity through the words that you use.

Read your Big Idea to your partner. From there, you can let the conversation take its natural course. If you're feeling stuck, refer to the following questions.

- What is your overarching goal? What would success look like in this situation?

- Who is your intended audience?

- Is there any specialized language (words, terms, phrases, acronyms) that are unfamiliar or should be defined?

- Is the action clear?

- Have you framed what you want to happen from your perspective or from your audience's point of view? If the former, how could you reframe for the latter?

- What is at stake? Will this be compelling for your audience? If not, how can you change it? "So what?" is always a good question to ask related to this—why should your audience care? What matters to them?

- Are there other words or phrases that may enable you to more easily get your point across?

- Can your partner repeat your main message back to you in their own words?

- "Why?" is probably the best question your partner can ask—and continue to ask to get you to articulate your logic in a way that will help you refine your Big Idea.

Revise your Big Idea during or following the conversation with your partner. If anything still feels rough or unclear, or if you'd simply like an additional perspective, repeat this exercise with someone new.

See Exercise 9.7 in Chapter 9 for a facilitator's guide on how to run a formal Big Idea group session. Next, let's talk about how you can use the Big Idea on team projects.

PRACTICE at WOR

Exercise 1.22: create the Big Idea as a team

Are you working on a project as part of a team? Here's a great exercise to undertake to make sure everyone is aligned and working towards the same overarching goal.

1. Give each person a copy of the Big Idea worksheet (download from storytellingwithdata.com/letspractice/bigidea) and have them individually work their way through it and craft their Big Idea with the given project in mind.

2. Book a room with a whiteboard or start a shared document and write out each of the Big Ideas. Ask each person to read theirs aloud.

3. Discuss. Where are there commonalities across the various statements? Is there anyone who seems out of alignment? What words or phrases best capture the essence of what you want to communicate?

4. Create a master Big Idea, pulling pieces from the individual ones and further augmenting and refining as needed.

This exercise helps ensure that everyone is on the same page and creates buy-in as people see components of their Big Idea flowing into the master Big Idea. It can also spark some awesome conversations that help everyone become clear on and confident about what needs to happen.

Exercise 1.23: get the ideas out of your head!

Let's put into practice a good first step in the storyboarding process: brainstorming. Consider a project where you need to create an explanatory communication like a slide deck. Get a stack of sticky notes and a pen. Find a quiet workspace with a large empty table or whiteboard. Set a timer for 10 minutes. Start the timer and see how many ideas you can get out of your head and onto stickies. You can imagine that each small square reflects a piece of potential content in your eventual deck. That said, don't filter your thoughts—rather, let it be a cathartic process (there are no bad ideas during this step). Don't worry about order or how the ideas fit together at this point in the process. Simply see how many sticky notes you can fill up in a set amount of time.

Tip: do this low-tech exercise after you've spent enough time with the data to know what you want to communicate with it, but *before* you start creating content with your computer. This exercise is best done after you've created, solicited feedback on, and refined the Big Idea for the given project (see Exercises 1.20 and 1.21).

If you find you're still on a roll writing down ideas when your timer goes off, feel free to add more time. After you've completed this exercise, move on to Exercise 1.24.

Exercise 1.24: organize your ideas in a storyboard

You've completed Exercise 1.23—the ideas are out of your head in writing on sticky notes—now it's time to organize them. Step back and think about what overarching structure can help you tie everything together in a way that will make sense to someone else. It may be helpful to make additional stickies for meta topics or themes as you organize your ideas. Where can you group things together? What might you eliminate?

Speaking of eliminating, start a discard pile. For each sticky note you consider, ask yourself: does this help me get my Big Idea across? If you can't come up with a good reason to include it, move it to the discard pile.

Here are some specific questions to contemplate as you're determining what order could work best for your situation:

- How will you present to your audience: are you there live, over the phone or through a webinar, or sending something out that will be consumed on its own?

- What order will work well for getting your content across to your audience? Does it make sense to start with the action you want from them, build up to it, or something in between?

- What context is essential? Does your audience need to know it up front, or does it better fit later? How quickly should you answer "So what?"

- Do you already have established credibility with your audience, or do you need to build it? If so, how will you do that?

- Were there assumptions made in your work? When and how should you introduce those? What if your assumptions are wrong? Does that materially change the message?

- Do you need input from your audience? How and where can you best get that?

- At what point does data fit in? Does the data confirm expectations or run counter to them? What data or examples will you integrate and where?

- How can you best create common ground, get buy-in, and prompt action?

There is no single right path, but the answers to the preceding questions will help you think through different options that could work well for your given circumstance. If there is a non-message impacting data or other content that you can't bear to get rid of, push it to the background—either physically by putting it later in the document (perhaps in the appendix) or visually by de-emphasizing it and putting emphasis on the most important components of what you need to communicate.

We'll look at additional strategies for ordering content when we discuss Story in Chapter 6. In the meantime, move on to Exercise 1.25 and get feedback on your storyboard.

PRACTICE at WORK

Exercise 1.25: solicit feedback on your storyboard

After creating your storyboard, talk through it with someone else. There are a couple of benefits to this. First, simply talking through it can be helpful. Doing so forces you to articulate your thought process, which can help illuminate alternate approaches. Second, sharing with someone else may introduce new perspectives or ideas that help you improve your storyboard.

This can be free-form: create your storyboard and then simply talk through it with a partner. Let the questions and conversation take their natural course. If you're feeling stuck, or don't have a partner handy and want to simulate this exercise, ask yourself the following questions:

- How are you presenting to your audience? Are you creating something they will consume on their own, or will you (or someone else) be presenting the material?

- Do the overall order and flow make sense?

- What is your Big Idea? Where will you introduce it?

- Does your audience care about all of these pieces?

- If there are pieces your audience cares less about but you still need to include, how can you keep their attention during this part?

- Where could things go wrong? How can you prepare for that?

- How will you transition from one topic or idea to the next?

- Is there anything that could be cut? Added? Rearranged?

If it makes sense to get stakeholder or manager feedback at this point, do it! This can be a great early check-in point to get confirmation that you're on the right track or redirect your efforts—before you've invested a ton of time.

When you spend time up front identifying and getting to know your audience, crafting the main message, and storyboarding content, you emerge with a plan of attack. This both reduces iterations and helps you be more targeted with your communications. The resulting materials are typically shorter than they otherwise would have been. This leaves you more time to create quality content: slides and graphs. We'll turn our attention there in the next chapter.

PRACTICE at WORK

Exercise 1.26: let's discuss

Consider the following questions related to Chapter 1 lessons and exercises. Discuss with a partner or group.

1. What audiences do you communicate to regularly? What do the various audiences have in common? How are they different? How can you take the needs of your audience into account when communicating with data?

2. Do you face a mixed audience when communicating with data? What are the main groups that make up this audience? Do you have to communicate to all of them at once? Are there any ways to narrow for purposes of communication? How can you set yourself up for success? Do others have related experience or learnings to share?

3. Reflect on the Big Idea and the practice of distilling your message down to a single sentence. How did you find the related exercises in this chapter? In what situations does it make sense to take the time to craft the Big Idea in your work? Have you tried this on the job? Was it helpful? Did you encounter any challenges?

4. Why are sticky notes good tools for storyboarding? Do you have other useful or recommended methods for planning content for your communications?

5. What tip or exercise did you find most useful in *SWD* or this book on the planning process for communicating effectively? Which strategies have you employed? Were you successful? What learnings will you put into practice going forward?

6. Was there anything covered in this section that didn't resonate or that you don't think will work in your team or organization? Why is that? Do others agree or disagree?

7. Are there things you believe your work group or team should do differently related to the planning process for communicating? How can you make that happen? What challenges do you anticipate related to this and how can you overcome them?

8. What is one specific goal you will set for yourself or your team related to the strategies outlined in this chapter? How can you hold yourself (or your team) accountable to this? Who will you turn to for feedback?

PRACTICE *at* WORK

choose an effective visual

Once you've taken time to understand the context and planned your communication in a low-tech fashion, as we practiced in Chapter 1, comes the question: when I have some data I need to show, how do I do that in an effective way? This is the topic we'll tackle next.

There is no single "right" answer when it comes to how to visualize data. Any data can be graphed countless different ways. Often, it takes iterating—looking at the data one way, looking at it another way, and perhaps even another—to discover a view that will help us create that magical "ah ha" moment of understanding that graphs done well can do.

Speaking of iterating, we have some forthcoming exercises that will encourage you to do just that. Through the exercises in this chapter, we'll create and evaluate a number of different types of graphs, helping us understand both the advantages and limitations of different individual pictures of the data. Our go-tos will mainly be the usual suspects—lines and bars—but we'll look at some twists on graph types introduced in *SWD* as well.

Let's practice **choosing an effective visual!**

First, we'll review the main lessons from *SWD* Chapter 2.

SWD BOOK **CHAPTER 2**

FIRST, LET'S RECAP
CHOOSING an EFFECTIVE VISUAL

SIMPLE TEXT

Just because you have numbers doesn't mean you need a graph!

TABLE

What is the main point I want to make?

	A	B	C
CATEGORY 1	15%	22%	42%
CATEGORY 2	40%	36%	20%
CATEGORY 3	35%	17%	34%
CATEGORY 4	30%	29%	58%

OFTEN THERE ARE MORE EFFICIENT WAYS

Avoid using tables in live presentations because people stop listening & start reading

HEAT MAP

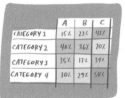

	A	B	C
CATEGORY 1	15%	22%	42%
CATEGORY 2	40%	36%	20%
CATEGORY 3	35%	17%	34%
CATEGORY 4	30%	29%	58%

EYES CAN EASILY PICK OUT BIG DIFFERENCES IN COLOR INTENSITY, but smaller ones don't stand out

Can work well when beginning to explore data and deciding where to dig further

SCATTER PLOT

Good for encoding data simultaneously on two axes to identify what relationships exist

LINE

RULE: The lines that connect the dots have to make sense! Most effective with continuous data, often <u>time</u>

SLOPE GRAPH

↑
A FANCY WORD FOR A LINE GRAPH WITH ONLY 2 POINTS

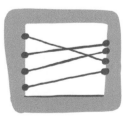

Useful to focus on change between two points in time or difference between groups

BAR CHARTS

Great for categorical data

Easy for our eyes - comparing heights to a consistent baseline

Rule: Must have a zero baseline. No exceptions!

VERTICAL

HORIZONTAL

Good when category names are long

STACKED

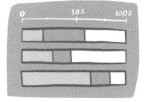

OFTEN MISUSED... EASIER TO COMPARE TOTAL & FIRST SERIES, BUT SEGMENTS UP THE STACK DON'T LINE UP

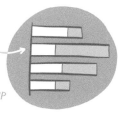

100% STACKED

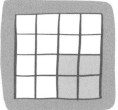

TWO BASELINES FOR COMPARISON

WATER-FALL

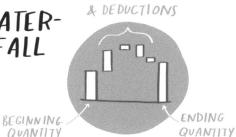

ADDITIONS & DEDUCTIONS

BEGINNING QUANTITY

ENDING QUANTITY

Often used in finance to show variance to budget

SQUARE AREA

(AKA WAFFLE CHART)

THE GRID IS IMPORTANT BECAUSE WE TEND TO OVERESTIMATE AREAS

Good for showing numbers of very different magnitudes, or as an alternative to a pie chart

PRACTICE with COLE

2.1 improve this table

2.2 visualize!

2.3 let's draw

2.4 practice in your tool

2.5 how would you show this data?

2.6 visualize the weather

2.7 critique

2.8 what's wrong with this graph?

PRACTICE on your OWN

2.9 let's draw

2.10 practice in your tool

2.11 improve this visual

2.12 which graph would you choose?

2.13 what's wrong with this graph?

2.14 visualize and iterate

2.15 learn from examples

2.16 participate in #SWDchallenge

PRACTICE at WORK

2.17 draw it!

2.18 iterate in your tool

2.19 consider these questions

2.20 say it out loud

2.21 solicit feedback

2.22 build a data viz library

2.23 explore additional resources

2.24 let's discuss

We'll start with basic tables and explore how visualizing data in graphs helps us more quickly see what's going on – as well as how different visuals cause us to identify new things and make varying design choices when graphing our data.

Exercise 2.1: improve this table

Frequently, when we first aggregate our data, we put it into a table. Tables allow us to scan rows and columns, reading the data and comparing the numbers. Let's look at an example table and explore both how we can improve it and take things a step further to visualize the data it contains.

Figure 2.1a shows the breakdown of new clients by tier for the recent year. Use this table to complete the following steps.

New client tier share

Tier	# of Accounts	% Accounts	Revenue ($M)	% Revenue
A	77	7.08%	$4.68	25%
A+	19	1.75%	$3.93	21%
B	338	31.07%	$5.98	32%
C	425	39.06%	$2.81	15%
D	24	2.21%	$0.37	2%

FIGURE 2.1a Original table

STEP 1: Review the data in Figure 2.1a. What observations can you make? Do you have to make any assumptions when interpreting this data? What questions do you have about this data?

STEP 2: Consider the layout of the table in Figure 2.1a. Let's assume you've been told this information must be communicated in a table. Are there any changes you would make to the way the data is presented or the overall manner in which the table is designed? Download the data and create your improved table.

STEP 3: Let's assume the main comparison you want to make is between how accounts are distributed across the tiers compared to how revenue is distributed— and that you have the freedom to make bigger changes (it's not required to be a table). How would you visualize this data? Create a graph in the tool of your choice.

Solution 2.1: improve this table

STEP 1: When I encounter this table, I start reading and scanning down columns and across rows. In terms of specific observations, I might start by noticing that the majority of accounts are in Tiers B and C, while Tiers A and A+—though they don't make up a huge number (or percentage) of accounts—do make up a meaningful amount of revenue. In terms of questions, I wonder if the tiers are in order: I would think A+ belongs above A and am confused that they don't appear that way in the table (perhaps due to alphabetical sorting?).

I wish there was a "Total" row at the bottom, because in the absence of this I find myself wanting to add up numbers. In fact, it's when I start to do that when I notice some bigger issues. The third column (% Accounts)—which I assume means percent of total accounts—sums to 81.16%. The final column (% Revenue)—which I assume means percent of total revenue—sums to 95%. So now I'm unsure whether these really are percent of total or something else. If they are, then there must be some "Other" or "Non-tier" category that I'd want to include in order to have the full picture.

When I focus on the numbers themselves, two digits of significance (places past the decimal point) seem like a lot for the % Accounts column given the scale of the numbers. When showing data like this, you should be thoughtful about the appropriate level of detail. There isn't necessarily a single "right" answer, but you want to avoid too many digits of significance. This can make the numbers themselves harder to interpret and recall and may convey a false sense of accuracy. Is the difference between 7.08% and 7.09% meaningful? If not, we can drop a digit by rounding. Here, given the scale of the numbers and differences between them, I would round to whole numbers across all except the fourth column depicting revenue. There we are already summarizing in millions and it seems like we would lose important differences between the dollar volumes by rounding to a whole number, so there I'd round to one digit past the decimal point.

Figure 2.1b is an improved table that addresses the preceding points.

New client tier share

Tier	# of Accounts	% Accounts	Revenue ($M)	% Revenue
A+	19	2%	$3.9	21%
A	77	7%	$4.7	25%
B	338	31%	$6.0	32%
C	425	39%	$2.8	15%
D	24	2%	$0.4	2%
All other	205	19%	$0.9	5%
TOTAL	1,088	100%	$18.7	100%

FIGURE 2.1b Slightly improved table

STEP 2: There are additional improvements I can make to this table. When tables are designed well, the actual design fades to the background so that we focus on the numbers in a way that makes sense. I recommend against shading every other row and instead am an advocate for white space (and limited light borders) to set apart columns and rows as needed. Speaking of white space, I typically avoid center-aligned text in graphs (because it creates hanging text and jagged edges that look messy) in favor of left- or right-aligning text. In the case of tables, however, I do sometimes opt for center alignment because of the separation this creates between columns (another common practice in tables is to right-align numbers or align by decimal point, which allows you to easily eyeball relative size). I can group the accounts-related columns and revenue-related columns with a single title (and under that, number and percent), which will reduce some redundancy of titles and also give me more space to be specific about what the columns represent. Doing so also allows me to make the columns narrower so the table overall takes up less space. These are some specific tips—I'll also put forth a couple of more general ones: consider the zigzagging "z" and where your eyes are drawn.

Consider the zigzagging "z": Without other visual cues, your audience will typically start at the top left of your visual (for example, your table) and do zigzagging "z's" across to take in the information. When we think about applying this to how we design our tables, it means you want to put the most important data at the top and at the left—when you can do so in the context of the overall data in a way that makes sense. In other words, if there are super-categories or data that needs to be taken into account together, keep them in the order that makes sense. In this particular example, I'd sort my tiers starting with the top (that is indeed A+) and decreasing as we move down the table. Going left to right, I'm happy enough with the way it is structured. I want to keep the distribution of accounts and percent of accounts next to each other since those relate to each other. If revenue were more important than accounts, I could move the two revenue columns leftwards, but I can also use other ways to focus attention there. Let's discuss that next.

Where are your eyes drawn? Similarly to how we focus attention thoughtfully in graphs as part of explanatory analysis (something we'll explore in detail in Chapter 4), we can also focus our audience's attention in tabular data to establish hierarchy of information. This can be especially useful in instances where you can't put the most important stuff leftward or at the top (because other constraints dictate the ordering). Despite this, you can still indicate relative importance to your viewers. Look back to Figure 2.1b: where are your eyes drawn? Mine go to the very first row where the column titles are Tier, # of Accounts, and so on. This isn't even the data! Rather than use up ink and draw attention there, I can be conscious about where I want to direct attention in the data and take intentional steps to get my audience to look there. This can be done through sparing use of color or by outlining a specific cell or column or row. Adding visual aspects to some of the data in the table is another way to draw attention there: colors and pictures grab our attention when they are used judiciously.

PRACTICE *with* COLE

If we assume the primary comparison we'd like our audience to make is between the distribution of % Accounts compared to % Revenue, I could apply heatmapping (using relative intensity of color to indicate relative value) to just those two columns. See Figure 2.1c.

New client tier share

TIER	ACCOUNTS		REVENUE	
	#	% OF TOT	$M	% OF TOT
A+	19	2%	$3.9	21%
A	77	7%	$4.7	25%
B	338	31%	$6.0	32%
C	425	39%	$2.8	15%
D	24	2%	$0.4	2%
All other	205	19%	$0.9	5%
TOTAL	1,088	100%	$18.7	100%

FIGURE 2.1c Table with heatmapping

As another approach, I could embed horizontal bar charts in place of the heatmapping. See Figure 2.1d. This does work quite well to direct attention to those columns and allows us to see how the shape of the distribution varies across the two. However, the specific comparison between % Accounts and % Revenue for a given tier is harder, since these bars aren't aligned to a common baseline. Tip: If you are working in Excel, conditional formatting is available that will allow you to create heatmapping or embedded bars in a table with ease.

New client tier share

TIER	ACCOUNTS		REVENUE	
	#	% OF TOT	$M	% OF TOT
A+	19		$3.9	
A	77		$4.7	
B	338		$6.0	
C	425		$2.8	
D	24		$0.4	
All other	205		$0.9	
TOTAL	1,088	100%	$18.7	100%

FIGURE 2.1d Table with embedded bars

STEP 3: Let's take it a step further and focus on the data that is in the bars in Figure 2.1d and review some different ways we could graph it. When I hear a term like "percent of total," it makes me think of parts of a whole—which might cause us to look to the pie chart. In this case, since we are interested in both % of Accounts and % of Revenue, we could depict this with a pair of pies. See Figure 2.1e.

New client tier share

% of Total **Accounts**   % of Total **Revenue**

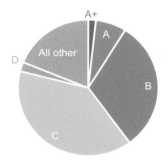 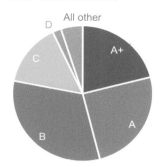

FIGURE 2.1e   A pair of pies

I'm not a big fan of pies—I sometimes joke that there's one thing worse than a single pie: two pies!

Let me back up, though, and say that pies can work well if we want to make the point that one piece of the whole is very small, or another piece of the whole is very big. The challenge for me is that pies break down pretty quickly if we want to say anything more nuanced than that. This is because our eyes' ability to accurately measure and compare areas is limited, so when the segments are similar in size, it is difficult for us to assess which is bigger or by how much. If that's a comparison that is important, we'll want to represent it differently.

In this instance, the primary comparison we want our audience to make is between the various segments in the pie on the left and those in the pie on the right. This is difficult for two reasons: the area challenge mentioned above and the spatial separation between pies. This is further compounded by the fact that the segments are in different places on the right as a result of how the data differs between the breakdown on the left compared to the right. Basically, if any of the data is different between the pies (which it should be if we have something interesting to say about it!) then all the pieces are in different places across the two pies—making them hard to compare. In general, you want to identify the primary comparison you want your audience to make and put those things as physically close together and align to a common baseline to make that comparison easy.

Let's start by aligning each measure to its own baseline, with a view similar to the bars embedded in the table previously. See Figure 2.1f.

New client tier share

TIER | % OF TOTAL **ACCOUNTS** | % OF TOTAL **REVENUE**

FIGURE 2.1f Two horizontal bar charts

In Figure 2.1f, it's very easy for us to compare the % of Total Accounts across tiers. It's also easy to compare the % of Total Revenue across tiers. I can attempt to compare accounts to revenue, but this is harder because they aren't aligned to a common baseline. If I want to allow for that as well, then I could pull both of these series into a single graph. See Figure 2.1g.

New client tier share

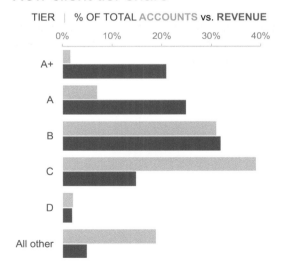

FIGURE 2.1g Horizontal dual series bar chart

With the arrangement in Figure 2.1g, the easiest comparison for me to make is, for a given tier, the % of Total Accounts compared to the % of Total Revenue. These elements are both the closest together and they are aligned to a common baseline. Bingo!

We could also flip this graph on its side into a vertical bar chart, or column chart. See Figure 2.1h.

New client tier share

% OF TOTAL ACCOUNTS vs. REVENUE

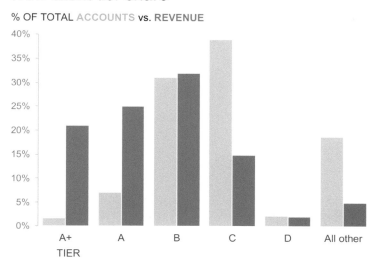

FIGURE 2.1h A vertical bar chart

When we depict data in this manner, the primary comparison our eyes are making is the endpoints of the paired bars relative to each other and to the baseline. Let's draw some lines to further highlight this comparison. See Figure 2.1i.

New client tier share

% OF TOTAL ACCOUNTS vs. REVENUE

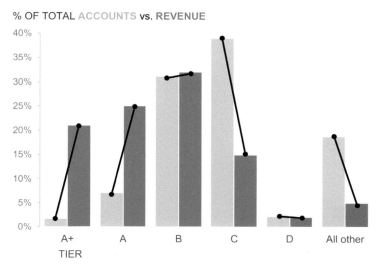

FIGURE 2.1i Let's draw some lines

Now that we've drawn the lines, we don't need the bars anymore. I've removed those in Figure 2.1j.

New client tier share

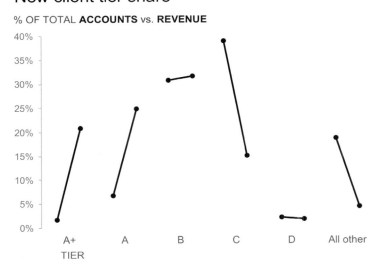

FIGURE 2.1j Take away the bars

Next, I'll collapse all of these lines and label everything directly. This yields the slopegraph shown in Figure 2.1k.

New client tier share

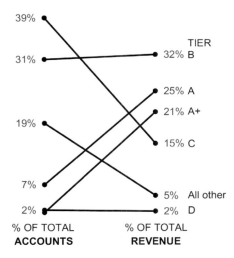

FIGURE 2.1k A slopegraph

Slopegraph is really just a fancy word for a line graph that only has two points in it. By drawing lines between the % of Total Accounts and % of Total Revenue for a given tier, we can quickly see where the two measures differ. Revenue as a proportion of total is quite a lot lower for Tier C and All other (indicated by lines sloping downwards), while revenue as a proportion of total is much higher for tiers A+ and A. In other words, though A+ and A make up a very small proportion of accounts (9% combined), together they account for nearly 50% of revenue!

We've looked at a number of ways to visualize this data. You likely made your own observations along the way about what worked well and what did not. What I've illustrated isn't exhaustive; I could have added a dot plot to the mix or calculated revenue per account and visualized that. That said, we don't typically have to go through every possible view of the data to find one that works. Perhaps both absolute values and percent of total are important, in which case the table might be the easiest way to show these different measures after all. If we can narrow our focus to a specific comparison or two, or a specific point we want to make, that will help us choose a way to show the data that will facilitate this.

Any data can be graphed countless different ways. This exercise illustrates how moving through different representations of our data allows us to more (or less) easily see different things. Allow yourself time to iterate and complete the additional exercises that will give you more practice at this important junction in the process!

PRACTICE *with* COLE

Exercise 2.2: visualize!

Let's look at another table. The following shows the number of meals served each year as part of a corporate giving program. Spend a moment looking at the data. What is interesting about it?

Meals served over time

Campaign Year	Meals Served
2010	40,139
2011	127,020
2012	168,193
2013	153,115
2014	202,102
2015	232,897
2016	277,912
2017	205,350
2018	233,389
2019	232,797

FIGURE 2.2a Table showing meals served over time

Notice how much work it is to process a column of numbers like this. We read data that is presented to us in tabular form, which—though this may seem like a simple way to show the numbers—actually takes a ton of brainpower! When I scan these numbers, I see the jump from 2010 to 2011, and another between 2013 and 2014. You probably did, too. But if you're like me, it means you started at the top of the table and got there by scanning down the second column—comparing each new number to the one(s) before it.

Let's practice easing how hard our brains must work by making the data more visual. Download this data. Create the following visuals in the tool of your choice.

STEP 1: Apply **heatmapping** to the second column of values.

STEP 2: Create a **bar graph**.

STEP 3: Create a **line graph**.

STEP 4: Choose: **which of the visuals you've created do you like best**? Are there any other ways you would graph this data?

Solution 2.2: visualize!

Pretty much anything we do to visualize the data originally shown in table form in Figure 2.2a is going to make it more quickly understandable. Let's check out a few ways we can ease the processing.

STEP 1: First, let's apply some **heatmapping**. Most graphing applications have built-in functionality that will allow you to do this with ease. You can pick colors and choose how to apply them to the data. For example, I've created the following in Excel by applying conditional formatting to the second column of values. I indicated a 3-color scale, with lowest value white, 50th percentile light green and maximum value green. In some situations, you could add a legend to make it clear how to interpret the colors. In this case, I just want to give a general sense that more intense color represents bigger values and vice versa. Eyeballing it, this sense is intuitive given the numbers and relative intensity within the same hue.

Meals served over time

Campaign Year	Meals Served
2010	40,139
2011	127,020
2012	168,193
2013	153,115
2014	202,102
2015	232,897
2016	277,912
2017	205,350
2018	233,389
2019	232,797

FIGURE 2.2b   Table with heatmapping

In Figure 2.2b, I'm perhaps more inclined to notice how much lower the number of meals served in 2010 was—it's totally white—less than a third of the next closest number! I can also quickly observe that 2016 had the greatest number of meals served without having to read the numbers. The relative intensity of color helps me more quickly interpret the relative quantitative values.

Related to this, I should point out that our eyes are pretty good at picking out big differences in intensity, but we have a harder time with more minor differences. This means that if there is something interesting about all of those medium shades of green, that's a little harder to quickly grasp and I might want to find a way to more fully visualize the values. Let's do that next.

STEP 2: Figure 2.2c shows a **bar graph** I could make based on this data. I chose to keep the y-axis for reference. Almost instantly, we can get a general sense of magnitude of the various bars. I thickened the bars from the default graph so there is less of a gap between them, which makes it easier for my eyes to follow along the tops of the bars and compare them to each other. I like the idea of bars.

We do have a continuous variable on the x-axis (time), but we can categorize it into years, which may make sense if we want to focus on a specific year at a time and have clear demarcation between the years.

Meals served over time

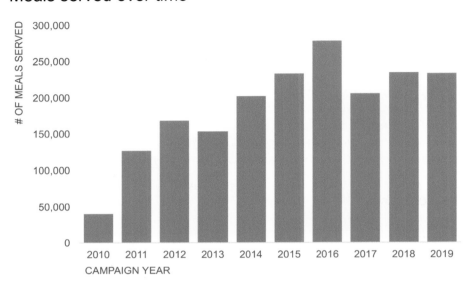

FIGURE 2.2c Bar chart

STEP 3: We can also show this data as a **line graph**; see Figure 2.2d. In this iteration, I decided to omit the y-axis and instead labeled only the beginning and end data points. This makes it easy (and obvious) for my audience to compare the number of meals served in 2010 to 2019. The rest of the values would have to be visually estimated. If there are other values you thought your audience would be particularly interested in (for example, the high point in 2016), you could also add data markers and labels to those points specifically.

When I remove the y-axis, I'll often use the subtitle space for the axis title. Here, given the graph title, you could probably argue that the subtitle is redundant and perhaps unnecessary. I'd rather be explicit so there is no question for my audience about what they are viewing. That said, another reasonable person might make a different decision.

I've used green in the visuals in this exercise, mainly to make it clear that—while I often default to blue—blue certainly isn't our only choice when it comes to using color in our visuals. We'll talk more about color as part of the exercises in Chapter 4.

Meals served over time
OF MEALS SERVED

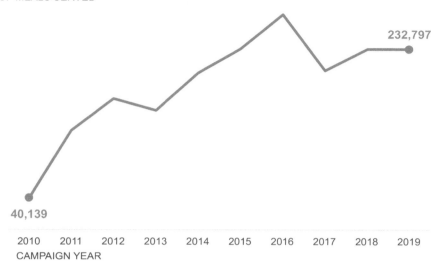

40,139

2010   2011   2012   2013   2014   2015   2016   2017   2018   2019
CAMPAIGN YEAR

FIGURE 2.2d Line graph

You inevitably made different design choices with your heatmap, bar graph, and line chart, and that's totally fine. The examples here and throughout are meant to be illustrative, not prescriptive. We'll look more specifically at aspects of design in Chapter 5.

STEP 4: Which do I like best? When I look back over the visuals I created, I'm surprised at my own answer to this one. Going into it, I thought for sure I'd prefer the line. It's the cleanest and it takes up the least amount of ink. But seeing them together, and taking the limited context into account, I actually prefer the bar chart (Figure 2.2c). If there is a clear start and end to the program within each year, I'd provide this segmented picture. That said, I do think the overall trend is easier to see with the line graph. Additionally, if there were context that I wanted to annotate via text on the graph, I'd likely choose the line, which has more space to accommodate this.

As we saw in solution 2.1, this is another illustration that there is no single right approach for visualizing data. Two different people faced with the same data visualization challenge may opt for different approaches. Of utmost importance is that we are clear about what we want to enable our audience to see and choose a view that will help facilitate that.

PRACTICE with COLE

Exercise 2.3: let's draw

One of the best tools we all have at our disposal when visualizing data is a blank piece of paper. If I'm ever feeling stuck or am looking for a creative solution, I get out a fresh sheet and start sketching. You don't need to be an artist to reap the important benefits of drawing. When working on paper, we remove the constraints of our tools (or what we know how to do with our tools). We are also less likely to form attachment to our work (the way we do after we've taken the time to create it with our computer). There's also simply something about empty space waiting to be filled that can help spark creativity.

Let's do a quick practice exercise using this important instrument: paper. The following graph (Figure 2.3a) shows capacity and demand measured in number of project hours over time. It is currently graphed as a horizontal bar chart. But is this the only way to show this data? Certainly not!

Get a blank piece of paper and set a timer for 10 minutes. How many different ways can you come up with to potentially visualize this data? Draw them! (Don't worry about plotting every specific data point exactly—make it quick and dirty to get an overall sense of what each visual could look like.) When the timer goes off, look over your sketches. Which do you like best and why?

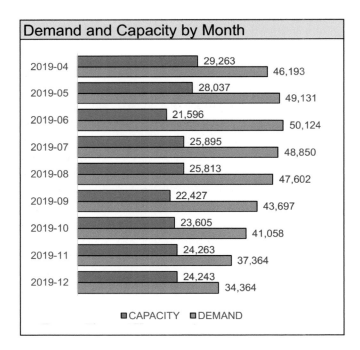

FIGURE 2.3a Let's draw this data!

Solution 2.3: let's draw!

After 10 minutes, my paper is filled with six different ways to depict the data. See Figure 2.3b.

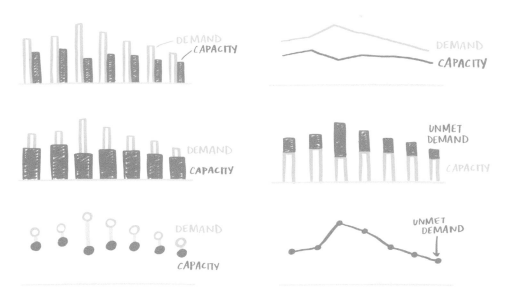

FIGURE 2.3b My data drawings

Starting at the top left, my initial sketch simply turns the horizontal bars upright so that time can move from left to right along the x-axis in a way that is intuitive. My second graph (top right) turns the bars into lines. I find it easier to focus on the gap with this view. But I wanted to do some more playing with bars of various forms, so my third iteration (middle left) goes back to those. I made Demand thinner and behind Capacity, in hopes that this would make it clear how much we're meeting out of the potential of what could be met. As a twist on that, we could stack the bars, which I've done in the middle right picture. The stacked series becomes the Unmet Demand (note that this stacked version only works if Demand is always greater than or equal to Capacity—it would get tricky if Demand were to fall below Capacity). My penultimate view (bottom left) re-envisions the bars as dots and connects them to bring attention to the difference (this would still work if Demand falls below Capacity so long as we've made the Demand circles distinct from those representing Capacity, for example, by coloring them differently). My final illustration simply plots the trend of Unmet Demand. With this last one, we lose the context of the overall magnitude of Demand and Capacity, but depending on our goals, that may be okay.

When it comes to which I like best, I prefer the stacked bars (middle right) if Demand is always higher than Capacity, as it is for the data we're graphing. That said, I think any of these views could potentially work. There are definitely other ways to show this data as well. Compare your drawings to mine. Did you come up with any similar graphs? Where do our ideas differ? Which do you like best out of the full group (yours plus mine)?

Let's continue working with this data and determine how we can make one of the sketches come to life in our tools! Move on to Exercise 2.4.

Exercise 2.4: practice in your tool

Consider the sketches created as part of Exercise 2.3—both the ones you drew and the ones I sketched. Pick one (or more for extra credit!), download the data, and create in the tool of your choice.

Solution 2.4: practice in your tool

I'm an overachiever, so I created all of the views I drew by hand in Excel. See Figures 2.4a - 2.4f.

Basic bars. First is the basic bar graph, or column chart. See Figure 2.4a. I've intentionally filled in Capacity and left Demand as an outline to try to visually differentiate what we're able to meet compared to the unmet capacity. I don't love this graph—and I think I like it less than I did in my drawn version. I appreciate the idea of just having the outline for Capacity, yet I find the outline plus the white space between the bars visually jarring. I also feel this is the view out of all of them that directs the least amount of attention to the gap between Capacity and Demand, which seems like an important aspect of this data.

In this case I chose to use the subtitle space for my legend. I'll sometimes do this if there isn't an obvious place to label the data directly. As an alternative, I could try directly labeling the first or last set of bars and using those as my legend.

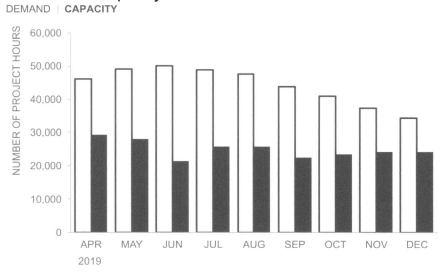

Demand vs capacity over time
DEMAND | **CAPACITY**

FIGURE 2.4a Basic bars

Line graph. The line graph is a cleaner design compared to the bars, because it simply takes up less ink. I chose to label the lines (and also added data labels) at the ends of the lines, eliminating any confusion over which series is which and reducing the work of going back and forth between a legend and the data. I like that the line allows us to focus on either Capacity or Demand, and it also makes the comparison of them really easy, so we can see the gap between the lines and quickly identify where it is growing and where it is shrinking. I bolded the Capac-

PRACTICE with COLE

ity line so our attention would go there first, then see the context of the greater Demand. See Figure 2.4b.

Demand vs capacity over time

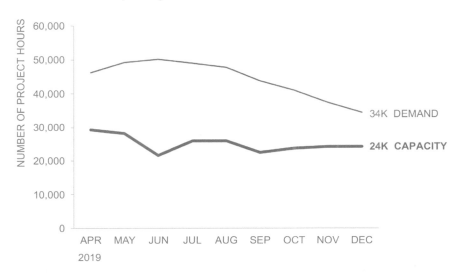

FIGURE 2.4b Line graph

Overlapping bars. We go back to bars in Figure 2.4c, which shows an atypical approach: making the bars overlap. I've made the Capacity series slightly transparent so that it is clear that the Demand series starts at zero and isn't meant to be interpreted as being stacked.

I like this iteration better than I anticipated when I sketched it on paper. That said, I could imagine an audience might find it confusing or off-putting since it doesn't look like a typical bar chart. If I wanted to use this graph, it would be a good one to show to a couple people and get feedback to see whether others find it confusing or if it could get the job done.

Demand vs capacity over time
DEMAND | **CAPACITY**

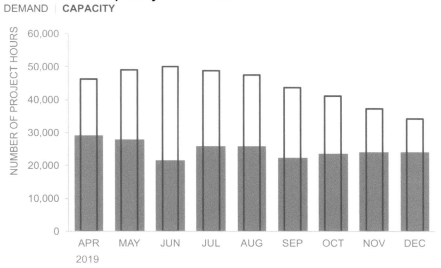

FIGURE 2.4c Overlapping bars

Stacked bars. With stacked bars, I kept Capacity plotted at the baseline, but then changed the second series to Unmet Demand so it could be stacked on top. I switched my emphasis to Unmet Demand, making it blue and rendering Capacity in a light grey. I like this view.

Demand vs capacity over time
CAPACITY | **UNMET DEMAND**

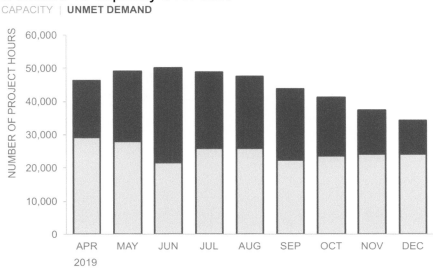

FIGURE 2.4d Stacked bars

PRACTICE *with* COLE

Dot plot. This is another view that could catch my audience off guard. It feels intuitive to me, but I have to recognize that pretty much any way I graph this data is going to feel intuitive because I've spent time with the data: I know what it represents and what I want my audience to take away. It may not be as obvious to them, however. Again, soliciting feedback would be a good way to test and assess.

While I'm not sure I love this one, I am impressed at my own Excel wizardry used to create it. The circles are actually data markers on two line graphs (one for Demand, another for Capacity) where I've chosen not to show the actual line and made the data markers huge so I'd have room to center the data label within each point. The shaded region that connects the dots is Unmet Demand, which is a stacked bar that sits on top of a second inclusion of the Capacity series (unfilled so you don't see the bottom series in the stack). This is what I call brute force Excel at its finest!

Demand vs capacity over time

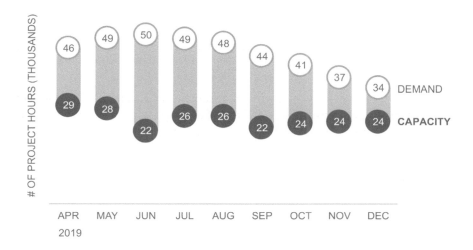

FIGURE 2.4e   Dot plot

Graph the difference. My final view is a simple line graph that plots the Unmet Demand (Demand minus Capacity). This is my least favorite of all (or maybe I'd rate it as tied for last with the basic bars), as it feels like too much context is omitted when we go from the two data series to plotting the difference. See Figure 2.4f.

Unmet demand over time

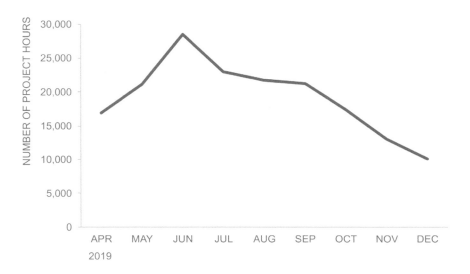

FIGURE 2.4f Graph the difference

How did the visual(s) you made in your tool turn out? Which out of all of them do you like best and why?

In absence of any context, I'd choose the Stacked Bar in Figure 2.4d. I like that it's easy to see both how Unmet Demand and Capacity are changing over time and I appreciate how this view makes it easy to focus attention on the decreasing Unmet Demand.

We will revisit this data in context of the broader dashboard it originated from in Chapter 6.

Exercise 2.5: how would you show this data?

The following table shows attrition rate for a 1-year associate training program for a given company. Spend a moment familiarizing yourself with it, then answer the following questions.

Year	Attrition Rate
2019	9.1%
2018	8.2%
2017	4.5%
2016	12.3%
2015	5.6%
2014	15.1%
2013	7.0%
2012	1.0%
2011	2.0%
2010	9.7%
AVG	7.5%

FIGURE 2.5a Attrition over time

QUESTION 1: How many different ways can you come up with to show this data? Draw or create in the tool of your choice.

QUESTION 2: How would you show the average in the various views you've created?

QUESTION 3: Which of the visuals you've created do you like best and why?

Solution 2.5: how would you show this data?

QUESTIONS 1 & 2: There are many potential ways we could show this data, depending on our audience and our goals. I came up with six different potential visuals and integrated the Average into each. Let's review and discuss each of these.

Simple text. Just because we have numbers doesn't mean we need a graph! In some situations we can simply communicate a number or two. For example, I could summarize all of this data by saying, "The attrition rate for this program has averaged 7.5% over the past ten years." This doesn't give us any sense of the range over time, or basis for comparison, which in some cases would be simplifying too much. If that's important, perhaps I could say something like, "The attrition rate has varied from 1% to 15% over the past decade, and was 9.1% in 2019." Or if I want to focus on more recent data, which may be more relevant, I could say, "The attrition rate for this program has increased in recent years, from 4.5% in 2017 to 9.1% in 2019."

Each time you create a visual, come up with a sentence that answers the question, "So what?" (Exercises 6.2, 6.7, 6.11, 7.5, and 7.6 will ask you to do this explicitly.) You may find that you can communicate with that sentence, eliminating the need for the graph altogether. When you do have more data you need to communicate, consider what context is helpful and how you can visualize it. Let's look at some ways to graph the data next.

Dot plot. I can use points to illustrate attrition rate (y-axis) by year (x-axis). I incorporated the average by adding a line to the graph, which allows us to easily see when we've been above and below average over time. See Figure 2.5b.

Attrition rate over time

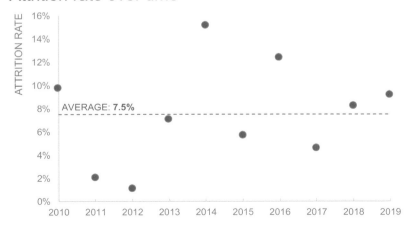

FIGURE 2.5b Dot plot

Line graph. Rather than plot the points, I could visualize the lines that connect them so we can more easily see the trend over time. Figure 2.5c illustrates this. I retained the thin dotted line for the Average, but moved my labeling of it (and also abbreviated) so that it would better fit given this new layout of the data. I also chose to put a data marker and label on the final data point. This makes the comparison between the most recent point of data and the average an obvious one for my audience.

Attrition rate over time

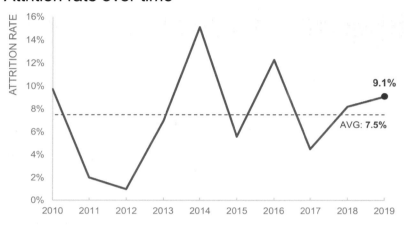

FIGURE 2.5c Line graph

I tried a second iteration on the line graph, using shaded area for the Average, rather than a line. See Figure 2.5d. I prefer the original line view in Figure 2.5c, but I could envision scenarios with different data that might cause me to choose another approach.

Attrition rate over time

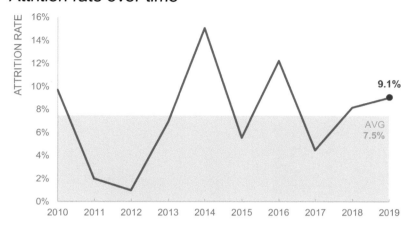

FIGURE 2.5d Line graph with shaded area depicting average

Area graph. After trying out area for the Average, I decided to switch it up and depict the Attrition Rate with area and revert back to a line for the Average. See Figure 2.5e. I chose a lighter blue for the Average line so it would show up both against the empty white background as well as when it overlaps the area encoding attrition rate. In each visual, I've labeled the Average differently—this is mainly due to the space available and the shape of it. Alternate views of the data may cause you to make other design modifications like this as well.

I don't love this one. It takes up a lot of ink for what we're trying to show and makes it seem like there's something important about the area under the curve, which isn't the case here. I don't use a lot of area graphs in general.

Attrition rate over time

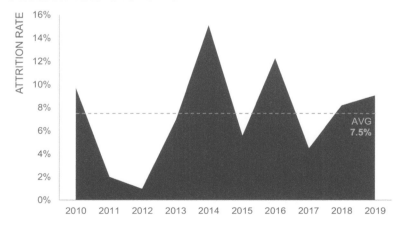

FIGURE 2.5e Area graph

Bar graph. Finally, I tried plotting this data as a bar chart. See Figure 2.5f. I preserved the Average as a line, labeling it again differently from prior views given the layout of the overall graph.

Attrition rate over time

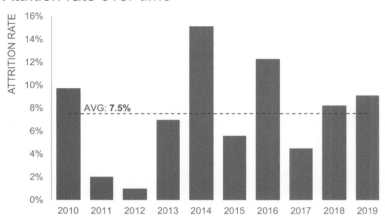

FIGURE 2.5f Bar graph

QUESTION 3: Which do I like best? I'm happy with the preceding bar chart, but I like the line graph in Figure 2.5c best of all. Connecting the dots via lines makes it easy to see the trend in Attrition Rate over time. I can easily compare it to the Average. It doesn't use a lot of ink, which leaves me space to add commentary if it makes sense to do so.

Exercise 2.6: let's visualize the weather

I'm a big fan of bar charts. They are easy to read—our eyes and brains are great at comparing lengths when aligned to a common baseline, which is what the bar chart does for us. We take in the information in bar charts by comparing the relative heights of the bars to each other and the baseline, so it's easy to see which is biggest and by how much. Also the familiarity of bar charts can be useful when communicating: since most people already know how to read them, they can focus their brainpower on what to do with the data rather than try to figure out how to read the graph.

Let's take a look at an example bar chart. See Figure 2.6a, which shows the weather forecast for the next six days measured by the expected daily high in degrees Fahrenheit.

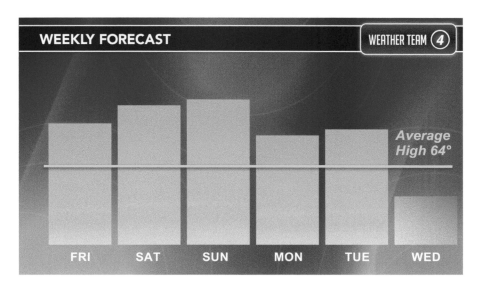

FIGURE 2.6a The weather forecast

QUESTION 1: Imagine you are preparing for a Sunday afternoon at the park. What temperature would you estimate for the high on Sunday?

QUESTION 2: You are planning your children's clothes for the coming week and trying to decide what type of jacket or coat they'll need midweek. What temperature might you estimate for the high on Wednesday?

QUESTION 3: What other observations can you make from this data?

Solution 2.6: visualize the weather

While the temperature may appear to be somewhere in the 90s on Sunday and in the 40s on Wednesday, that's not actually the case. Let's take a closer look.

It turns out that Sunday is 74 degrees while Wednesday is 58 degrees. How is that possible? The initial graph in Figure 2.6a does not have a y-axis that starts at zero. Rather, it begins at 50. This distorts the data, making it so we can't accurately compare the temperature day to day. See Figure 2.6b, which adds both the y-axis and data labels to the original graph.

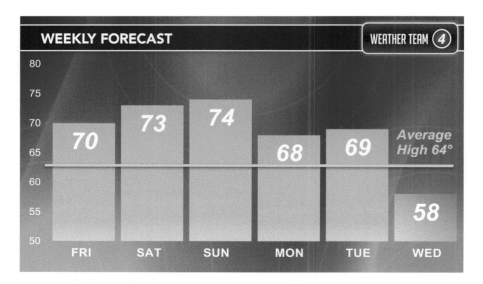

FIGURE 2.6b   Bar charts must have a zero baseline!

Let's redesign the graph to start the y-axis at zero. Figure 2.6c shows the side-by-side. Notice the difference this makes in interpreting the data.

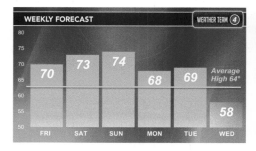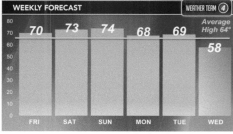

FIGURE 2.6c   Let's compare the two graphs

What looked like a large deviation from the average on the left of Figure 2.6c looks comparatively a lot smaller on the right. With this view, you'd likely make a different decision when it comes to how thick the kids' coats should be on Wednesday!

There aren't a lot of hard-and-fast rules when it comes to visualizing data. But there are a few, and we've just witnessed one of them broken: bar charts must have a zero baseline. Because of the way our eyes compare the endpoints of the bars to each other and the baseline, we need the context of the full bar there in order to make that an accurate visual comparison.

There are no exceptions.

That said, this is not a rule that applies to all graphs. With bars, you can't chop or zoom because of the way we compare the ends of the bars relative to each other and the axis. But with points (scatterplots or dot plots) or lines (line graphs, slope-graphs), we focus primarily on the relative positions of the points in space, and in the case of line graphs, the relative slopes of the lines that connect the points. Mathematically, as we zoom, the relative positions and slopes remain constant. You still want to take context into account and avoid overzooming and making minor changes or differences look like a big deal. Though sometimes minor changes or differences are a big deal, so if you find yourself needing to change the axis to highlight this, reach for points or lines, not bars.

On a related note, I've heard the idea raised that a zero baseline for weather doesn't make sense, since temperatures can be negative, and zero (particularly on a Fahrenheit scale) isn't meaningful. In the case of a short-term weather forecast, like we looked at here, the bars are fine so long as we do have a zero baseline allowing us to compare the day by day expectations accurately. On the other hand, if we take the case of climate change, for example, a couple degrees change in global temperatures—which is nearly impossible to see in bars with a zero baseline—is meaningful. This isn't a good argument for changing to a non-zero baseline bar chart, but rather for not using bars to illustrate this data. We could shift to a line graph or graph the change in temperature instead of absolutes to bring focus to the small but meaningful differences. As always, we should step back and think critically about what we want to show, then choose an appropriate visual to facilitate this.

PRACTICE with COLE

Exercise 2.7: critique!

Speaking of points (mentioned in the solution to the previous exercise), let's take a look at some next, in the context of critiquing a less than ideal graph.

See Figure 2.7a, which is a dot plot showing the bank index over time for a number of national banks. Assume you work at Financial Savings.

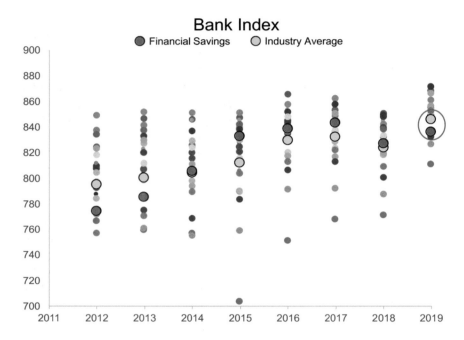

FIGURE 2.7a Bank index

QUESTION 1: What questions do you have about this data?

QUESTION 2: If you were designing the graph, what changes would you make? How would you visualize this data?

Solution 2.7: critique!

QUESTION 1: This graph seems to incite many more questions than it answers! My first question is: what exactly is the metric being plotted? I might assume "Bank Index" is some type of customer satisfaction score, and that the higher the number, the better. But what if this is really something like bank teller errors? I'd interpret that data very differently.

My next question is, do we need all of the data? We can see at the top that the red and yellow data points represent our company (Financial Savings) and the Industry Average, respectively (these also seem like odd color choices, though I guess they are bright in an attempt to stand out against all of the other color in this graph). I assume all of these dots roll up into the average (which is another question I have: is that the case?). This begs yet another question: do we need all of those individual data points or would showing only Financial Savings and the Industry Average work? When you consider getting rid of data, you always want to think through what context you lose when doing so. Here, by summarizing with the average, we'd lose line of sight to the spread across competitors. Depending on our goals, this may or may not be important.

In terms of other questions, I'm also curious what the red circle in 2019 is meant to highlight. I appreciate the thought process behind it: someone looked at this data and thought "I'd like you to look here" and drew a red circle. This presents a couple of challenges, however. First, there's so much competing for our attention in the graph with all the various colored dots that we might not even notice the red circle. Second, when we do notice it, it isn't immediately clear what it is trying to point out to us.

My final questions are: So what? What does this data show us? What's the story?

QUESTION 2: Let's shift from asking questions to redesigning how we show this data. It turns out the metric being graphed is branch satisfaction, where the higher the number, the better. I'll assume that we care most about how Financial Savings compares to the Industry Average. Simply making that decision means I can declutter this graph a ton and focus on the data points for Financial Savings and the Industry Average.

Speaking of data points, this data is over time. We can plot it as points, but I'd be apt to connect the points and display this data in a line graph. Lines will help us more easily see the change over time and can also help highlight interesting things when it comes to how these lines interact with each other: if one is always above the other, the lines will help us see the gap. If that's not the case, lines will help us see when one series crosses the other, which will be interesting as we try to answer the question, "So what?"

Figure 2.7b shows my makeover of this visual.

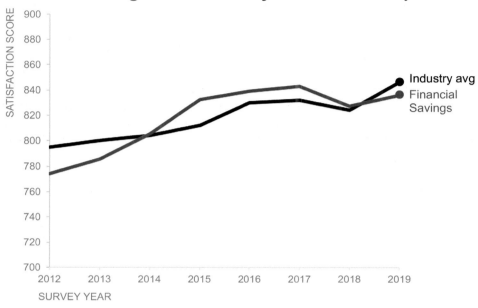

FIGURE 2.7b Revamped graph

Decluttering and changing the graph to lines helps us focus on the data. I've titled and labeled everything directly, so there's no need to make assumptions or hunt around for how to interpret the data. I used the title space to answer the question, "So what?"

With an additional understanding of what's driving the ups and downs in satisfaction for our business and the industry, I could take this even further. In a live meeting or presentation, I could build it line by line or time point by time point, which would allow me to focus my audience's attention as I talk through relevant context. If it needs to stand on its own, I could put text directly on the graph to annotate what's causing the changes we see. We'll look at a number of examples that employ these strategies as we get further along. We'll revisit this example and look at a scenario where we keep all of the original data in Chapter 4.

Next, let's redesign another graph.

Exercise 2.8: what's wrong with this graph?

Sometimes, we design a graph with the best of intentions, but inadvertently make things difficult for our audience. Let's take a look at an example where this is the case and discuss how we can improve it.

Continuing in the banking industry, next let's imagine you work as an analyst in consumer credit risk management. For those who may not be familiar—when people take out loans, some portion of those people don't repay them. These loans move through various levels of delinquency: 30-days past due, 60-days past due, and so on. Once they become 180 days past due, they are categorized as "Non-Performing Loans." After reaching this stage of delinquency, despite col-lection activities, many still don't repay and this results in a loss. Banks have to reserve money for these potential losses.

Now that we're past credit risk 101, let's talk about the data. You've been asked to create a graph showing how Non-Performing Loan (NPL) volume compares to the Loan Loss Reserves over time. Look at Figure 2.8a. **Take note of how your eyes move as you process this information. What is confusing about this graph? How would you improve it?**

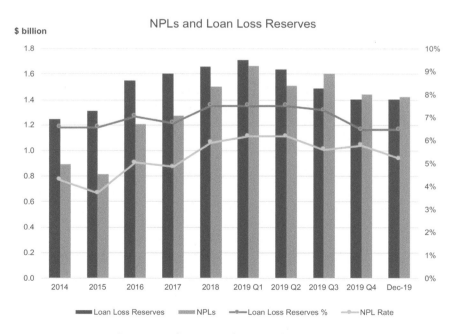

FIGURE 2.8a   What is confusing in this graph?

PRACTICE *with* COLE

Solution 2.8: what's wrong with this graph?

In considering how I process this data, I start out by doing a lot of back and forth between the bars, the lines, and the legend at the bottom of the graph to try to interpret the data. I scan the y-axes to see what those are. After some reading and thinking about it, I figured out that the lines—Loan Loss Reserves % and NPL Rate—are meant to be read against the secondary y-axis on the right-hand side of the graph. This means the bars—Loan Loss Reserves and NPLs—should be read against the primary y-axis on the left. This seems more difficult than it needs to be.

Going back to the Loan Loss Reserves % and NPL Rate: I'm not sure what the denominator is. I might assume that it's the total loan portfolio—but I'd rather this be made clear so I don't have to assume! I'm also unsure these lines add any value—they aren't adding any new information. There may be additional context that would cause me to make a different decision, but in the absence of that I'm going to focus on the volume—the dollars—and not confuse things by also showing the rate. As a bonus, this decision will eliminate the secondary y-axis (I recommend against the use of dual y-axes in general; for alternate approaches to the secondary y-axis, refer to Chapter 2 in *SWD*).

It's only after all this that I start paying attention to the x-axis and notice the biggest issue: we have **inconsistent time intervals**. Upon first glance (and several thereafter—perhaps you didn't even catch this problem), I started reading the x-axis to see it is in units of years and then assumed that continues to be the case as we move from left to right. When we read each label, however, we find that after 2018, the time interval changes to quarters, and after Q4 it seems we've broken out December on its own. This is not good!

I can appreciate the thought process that presumably led to this. December is probably the most recent month. Showing years for historical context is helpful, but then it's nice to also show greater granularity (e.g. quarterly, monthly) for the more recent time periods.

Sometimes inconsistent time intervals are a reality—we might be missing data or simply have something that occurs inconsistently over time. In that situation, we need to denote that visually and make it clear to our audience. The same bar or line shouldn't be used to represent a year and a quarter, as this can too easily lead to incorrect interpretation and false observations.

We have a couple of options for overcoming this challenge. If we have all of the quarterly data, I'd be apt to just plot that. Bars will get messy simply because there would be so many of them, but given that we're getting rid of the two data series that were originally depicted by lines, we could swap the original bars and plot the volume with lines. Or if for some reason we don't want to or can't show the quarterly data, and leave it all in one graph, one option would be to space the

PRACTICE with COLE

x-axis such that each year takes up the same width that the four quarters together take up. If I did this, I would exclude year 2019 so there isn't redundancy between that and the four quarters that are broken out separately.

As another alternative, we could split this data into two graphs: one to show the annual data for 2014 through 2019, and then a second to break out the quarterly data just for 2019. This would allow me to title each explicitly and make the difference in time components clear. I would also compress the quarterly data more than the annual data to help visually reinforce the shorter time periods. The makeover incorporating these changes is shown in Figure 2.8b.

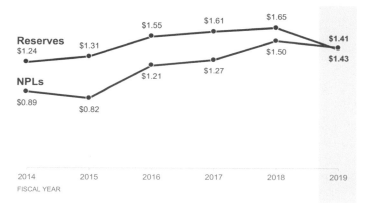
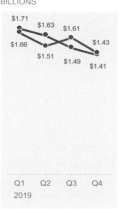

FIGURE 2.8b An alternative view

In this case, I chose to label the data directly so we can compare the volume of NPLs to that of Reserves without the work of having to estimate it from an axis. I maintained two decimal places of significance so there wouldn't be instances where two points of different heights shared the same value (for example, the third and fourth points on the Reserves line would both round to $1.6M, which could cause confusion since the heights are visibly different) and so we can easily interpret the smaller but meaningful differences in the recent quarterly numbers. I used shading to tie the final data point in the first graph (2019) to the quarterly breakout for 2019 in the right graph. It is very important in showing the data like this to ensure that the y-axis minimum and maximum are set to be the same amount across the two graphs, so that the audience can compare the quarterly data points to the annual ones according to their relative height.

With this visual, I've taken away a lot of things that were making us do work in the original. Instead of trying to understand the graph, we can focus on the data. I can see that the gap between NPLs and our Loan Loss Reserves has narrowed markedly over time. Both were increasing through 2018, but decreased in 2019. 2019 marks the first time that NPL volume exceeds the Loan Loss Reserves. On a

PRACTICE with COLE

quarterly basis, this happened in Q3 and Q4. This seems pretty important, so we should probably take some action!

Now that you've practiced with me, it's time to tackle some additional examples on your own.

PRACTICE on your OWN

Grab a pencil and paper! Let's draw some more, iterate in our tools, and improve less-than-ideal visuals through additional exercises.

Reminder:
The data and graphs can be downloaded at storytellingwithdata.com/letspractice/downloads

Exercise 2.9: let's draw

As illustrated in Exercise 2.3, some of our best tools for figuring out how to show our data are a blank piece of paper and pen or pencil. Let's practice using these important instruments!

The following data shows the average time to close a deal (measured in days) for direct and indirect sales teams across four products for a given company. Spend a moment to familiarize yourself with this data.

Get a blank piece of paper and set a timer for 10 minutes. How many different ways can you come up with to potentially visualize this data? Draw them! (Don't worry about plotting every specific data point exactly—quick and dirty to get an overall sense of what each visual could look like will suffice.) When the timer goes off, look over your sketches. Which do you like best and why?

Average time to close deal (days)

Product	Direct Sales	Indirect Sales	Total Sales
A	83	145	128
B	54	131	127
C	89	122	107
D	90	129	118

FIGURE 2.9a Average time to close deal

As part of this, what assumptions are you making about this data? What additional context do you wish you had?

Exercise 2.10: practice in your tool

STEP 1: Refer back to the sketches you created as part of Exercise 2.9. Pick one (or more for extra credit!), download the data, and create in the tool of your choice.

STEP 2: After creating your graph(s), pause and reflect upon the following.

QUESTION 1: What was helpful about sketching?

QUESTION 2: Did you find anything about the drawing process annoying or frustrating?

QUESTION 3: Was creating a graph in your tool different after first sketching it?

QUESTION 4: Can you envision using this approach (draw options first, then create in your tool) in the future? In what situations?

Write a few sentences summarizing your thoughts.

Exercise 2.11: improve this visual

Imagine you work for a regional health care center and want to assess the relative success of a recent flu vaccination education and administration program across your medical centers.

You have a dashboard where related metrics are reported and your colleague pulled the following visual from it. Take a moment to study Figure 2.11 and answer the following questions.

PRACTICE on your OWN

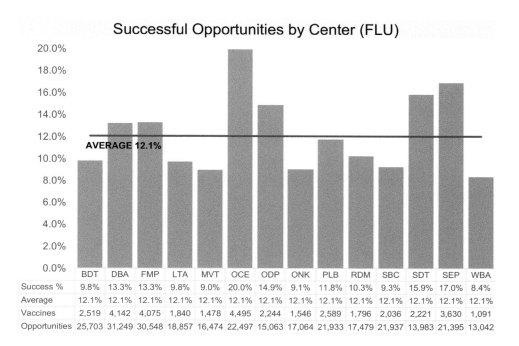

Figure title: Successful Opportunities by Center (FLU)

AVERAGE 12.1%

	BDT	DBA	FMP	LTA	MVT	OCE	ODP	ONK	PLB	RDM	SBC	SDT	SEP	WBA
Success %	9.8%	13.3%	13.3%	9.8%	9.0%	20.0%	14.9%	9.1%	11.8%	10.3%	9.3%	15.9%	17.0%	8.4%
Average	12.1%	12.1%	12.1%	12.1%	12.1%	12.1%	12.1%	12.1%	12.1%	12.1%	12.1%	12.1%	12.1%	12.1%
Vaccines	2,519	4,142	4,075	1,840	1,478	4,495	2,244	1,546	2,589	1,796	2,036	2,221	3,630	1,091
Opportunities	25,703	31,249	30,548	18,857	16,474	22,497	15,063	17,064	21,933	17,479	21,937	13,983	21,395	13,042

FIGURE 2.11 Original visual from dashboard

QUESTION 1: How is the data sorted? How else could we sort it? In what circumstances would you make a different decision about how to order the data?

QUESTION 2: There is currently a horizontal line to show the average. How do you feel about this? How else could you show the average?

QUESTION 3: What if there were a target—how might you incorporate it? Assume the target is 10%. How would you show this? Now assume the target is 25%. Does this change what you would show or how you would show it?

QUESTION 4: The graph contains a data table. Do you find this effective? What are the pros and cons of embedding a data table within a graph? Would you keep it or eliminate it in this case?

QUESTION 5: The graph currently shows the proportion who received the vaccination. What if you wanted to focus on the opportunity—the proportion who did not receive the vaccination—how could you visualize this?

QUESTION 6: How would you graph this data? Download it and create your ideal view in the tool of your choice.

PRACTICE on your OWN

Exercise 2.12: which graph would you choose?

Any set of data can be graphed many ways and varying views allow us to see different things. Let's look at a specific instance of numerous graphs plotting the same data.

You are visualizing data from your employee survey and want to show how employees responded this year compared to last year to the retention item "I plan to be working here in one year." Figures 2.12a through 2.12d depict four different views of the exact same data. Spend some time examining each, then answer the following questions.

OPTION A: **pies**

"I plan to be working here in one year"

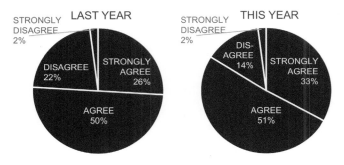

FIGURE 2.12a Pies

OPTION B: **bars**

"I plan to be working here in one year"

LAST YEAR | **THIS YEAR**

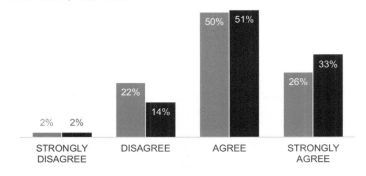

FIGURE 2.12b Bars

PRACTICE on your OWN

OPTION C: **divergent stacked bars**

"I plan to be working here in one year"

FIGURE 2.12c Divergent stacked bars

OPTION D: **slopegraph**

"I plan to be working here in one year"

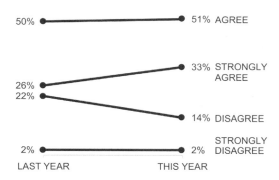

FIGURE 2.12d Slopegraph

QUESTION 1: What do you like about each graph? What can you easily see or compare?

QUESTION 2: What is difficult about the given view? Are there limitations or other considerations of which to be aware?

QUESTION 3: If you were tasked with communicating this data, which option would you choose and why?

QUESTION 4: Grab a friend or colleague and talk through the various options together. Do they agree with your preferred view, or is there a preference for another? Did your discussion highlight anything interesting that you hadn't previously considered?

PRACTICE on your OWN

Exercise 2.13: what's wrong with this graph?

Consider Figure 2.13, which shows response and completion rates for an email marketing campaign where email recipients were asked to complete a survey.

STEP 1: List three things that are not ideal about this graph. What makes it challenging?

STEP 2: For each of the three things you've listed, describe how you would overcome the given challenge.

STEP 3: Download the data. Create your visual that puts into practice the strategies you've outlined.

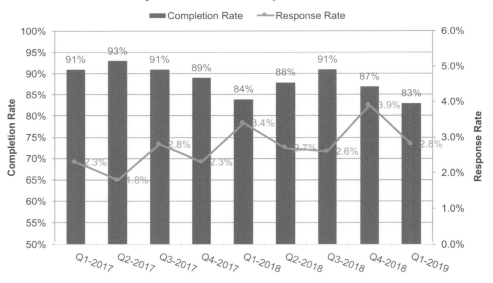

FIGURE 2.13 What's wrong with this graph?

Exercise 2.14: visualize & iterate

As we've seen through a number of examples so far, visualizing data—when done well—can help us spark a magical "ah ha" moment of understanding in our audience. But often it takes iterating—looking at the data numerous ways—both to better understand the nuances of the data and what we want to highlight, as well as to figure out a way that will work for our audience. Let's practice visualizing and iterating.

Imagine you work at a medical device company and are looking at data that shows patient-reported pain levels when a component of a certain device is turned on and when it is turned off. Figure 2.14 shows the data.

Patient-reported pain

PAIN LEVEL	DEVICE SETTING	
	ON	OFF
IMPROVED	58%	36%
UNCHANGED	32%	45%
WORSENED	10%	19%
TOTAL	100%	100%

FIGURE 2.14 Let's visualize & iterate

STEP 1: Make a list: how many potential methods can you come up with to visualize this data? What different graphs might work? List as many as you can.

STEP 2: From the list you've made, create at least four different views of this data (draw or realize in the tool of your choice).

STEP 3: Answer the following related questions:

QUESTION 1: What do you like about each visual? What is easy to compare?

QUESTION 2: What considerations or limitations should you take into account with each?

QUESTION 3: Which view would you use if you were communicating this data?

PRACTICE on your OWN

Exercise 2.15: learn from examples

A great deal can be learned from the data visualizations that others create—both the good and the not so good. When you see a nice graph, pause and reflect: what makes it effective? What can you learn from it that you can apply in your own work? When you see a not-so-good example, do the same thing: stop and examine what was not done well and how you can avoid similar issues in your own work. Let's practice learning from examples.

Find a graph from the media that's done well and another that is less than ideal. Answer the following questions for each of these examples.

QUESTION 1: What do you like about it? What makes it effective? Make a list!

QUESTION 2: What do you not like about the example? What limits its effectiveness? How would you approach it differently?

QUESTION 3: What learnings from this process can you generalize to guide your future work?

Exercise 2.16: participate in #SWDchallenge

One of the best ways to learn is to do. The #SWDchallenge is a monthly challenge where readers of our blog practice and apply data visualization and storytelling skills. You can take part, too! Think of it as a safe space to try something new: test out a new tool, technique, or approach. Everyone is encouraged to participate and all backgrounds, experience levels, and tools are welcome.

We announce a new topic at storytellingwithdata.com at the beginning of each month. Participants have a set amount of time to find data and create and share their visual and related commentary. Historically, the focus has been on different graph types, but we sometimes change it up with a tip to try or a specific topic. This is meant to be a fun reason to flex your skills and share your work with others.

All submissions received by the deadline are shared in a recap post later in the given month. The monthly challenges and recap posts are archived at storytellingwithdata.com/SWDchallenge.

There are a number of exercises you can undertake related to this challenge. Visit storytellingwithdata.com/SWDchallenge and tackle one (or more!) of the following:

- **Participate!** Take part in the live challenge by creating and sharing your work. Or choose a past one as inspiration to flex your data visualization skills. This can be done on your own, with a partner, or as a small team. Share your creations on social media, tagging #SWDchallenge.

- **Emulate!** Pick a recap post from the archives and review submissions. Select a visual you like and work to recreate it in the tool of your choice. Are there any aspects you would tackle differently than the original author?

- **Critique!** Select a recap post from the archives and examine submissions. Pick three you believe are effective and describe what is done well. Consider how you could generalize the learnings to apply to your own work. Pick three designs you believe are not ideal and reflect on the issues you see and how you could overcome them. What common challenges can you generalize from this that you can overcome in your own work?

- **Run your own challenge!** Get a group of colleagues or friends together, pick a past challenge (or create your own), and run your own version: everyone has a set amount of time to find data and create their visual. Share them with each other. Get together to discuss, giving everyone the opportunity to share their creation and receive feedback from others. Examine what you learn from this process that you can apply to future work. See Exercise 9.4 for more on how this fun process can help cultivate a feedback culture.

PRACTICE on your OWN

Next, let's explore how we can put the various lessons learned related to choosing an effective visual to use at work, including questions to ask yourself and how to get feedback.

Get a project in mind and tackle the following exercises!

Exercise 2.17: draw it!

Consider a current project where you need to visualize data. Grab a blank piece of paper and a pen or pencil. Set a timer for 10 minutes and see how many ideas you can sketch out for how to potentially show your data.

When the timer goes off, step back and take inventory of what you've created. Which view(s) do you like best? Why is that?

Show your sketches to someone else. Explain to them what you want to communicate. Which visuals(s) do they like best? Why is that?

If you ever feel stuck or are looking for an innovative approach and having trouble coming up with one on your own, grab a conference room with a whiteboard and a creative colleague or two. Talk them through what you want to show. Start drawing—and redrawing. Debate as you mock up the different views: what works well? What is lacking? Which visuals(s) are worthy of creating in your tools? Can you do it on your own, or if not, what or who can help you realize your ideas?

Exercise 2.18: iterate in your tool

Allowing yourself time and flexibility to iterate through different views of your data allows you both to better understand the nuances and determine which way of showing the data might help you achieve that magical "ah ha" moment of understanding that you seek in your audience.

Take some data you'd like to visualize. Open your favorite graphing tool and start creating different visuals. How many ways can you come up with to look at the data? Set a timer for 30 minutes and iterate to create different views of the data in your graphing application.

When the timer goes off, assess for each: what are the pros and cons? What do you want to enable your audience to see? Which iteration(s) will facilitate this? If unsure, jump to Exercise 2.21, which provides some tips for soliciting feedback from others.

Exercise 2.19: consider these questions

When you create a graph, it's not surprising that it makes sense to you. You are familiar with the data, and you know what to look at and what is important. Don't assume this is necessarily true for your audience. After you've made your graph, ask the following questions to help determine whether further iteration is necessary.

- **What are you trying to show?** What do you want to enable your audience to do with your data? Does the visual you've created facilitate this? What takeaways are easiest to see? What comparisons are easiest to make? What things are harder to do given the way you are showing the data?

- **How important is it?** Is this a critical issue or merely something that people might find interesting? What are the stakes? Is it a scenario where quick and dirty is okay? What level of perfection is warranted? What level of accuracy is required?

- **Who is your audience?** Is your audience familiar with the data you are presenting or is it new? Does it fit in with their preconceived notions, or may it challenge a held belief? Does your audience expect the data to be presented in a certain way? What are the pros and cons of following the norm in this situation compared to doing something new or unexpected? What questions will your audience have and how can you anticipate and be prepared to seamlessly address them?

- **Is your audience familiar with the type of graph?** Anytime we use something less familiar to our audience, we are introducing a hurdle: we either have to get them to listen to us long enough to tell them how to read the graph, or get them to spend enough time with it to figure it out on their own. If you're using something less familiar, have a good reason for it. Does this view let your audience easily see something that would otherwise be difficult, or create a new insight that isn't possible with more familiar ways of graphing the data? Consider also: how much time do you want to spend talking about the graph—how much of your audience's brainpower do you want them to spend trying to understand the graph versus what the data in the graph shows?

- **How are you presenting the information?** Will you be there live in person to talk through the data, set context, and answer questions, or are you sending something around that has to be processed on its own? Especially in the case where you aren't there, you need to take intentional steps to make it clear to your audience what the graph represents, how to read it, and how you want them to process your data.

PRACTICE *at* WORK

Exercise 2.20: say it out loud

After you've created your graph or your slide, practice talking through it out loud. If you'll be presenting the data in a live setting (a meeting or presentation), put it on the big screen and practice discussing it as you would in a meeting. Even in the instance when you will send it off for your audience to process the data on their own, there can be important benefits to talking through your graphs.

First, set up how to read the graph, what it shows, and what each axis represents. Then talk through the data and what important observations can be made. What you say may reveal pointers on how to iterate. If you find yourself saying things like, "This isn't important" or "Ignore that," these are cues for elements you can push to the background (or in some instances, eliminate entirely). Similarly, when you hear how you direct attention when talking through the data, consider how you can achieve this visually through the way you design the graph.

In the case where you will be presenting the data live, practicing out loud will also help make the ultimate delivery smoother. First, do this on your own. Once you feel good about that, practice talking through it with someone else and get their feedback. The next exercise (Exercise 2.21) provides more pointers for getting good graph feedback.

Want to learn more benefits to saying it out loud? Listen to Episode 6 of the *storytelling with data* podcast (storytellingwithdata.com/podcast), which focuses on this topic.

Exercise 2.21: solicit feedback

You've created a graph and you think it's pretty awesome. The challenge is that you know your work better than probably anybody else and since you're the one who created the graph, of course it's going to make sense to you. But will it work for your audience?

Or what about the scenario where you've iterated in your tool—you've created several different views of the data but aren't entirely sure which one will work best?

In each of these cases, I recommend soliciting feedback from others.

Create your visual or set of graphs and find a helpful friend or colleague. It can be someone without any context. Have them talk you through their thought process for taking in the information, including:

PRACTICE at WORK

- What do they pay attention to?
- What questions do they have?
- What observations do they make?

This conversation can help you understand whether the visual you've created is serving its intended purpose, or if it isn't, give you pointers on where to concentrate your iterations. Ask questions. Discuss your design choices and talk about what is working effectively and what might not be as obvious to someone who is less close to the data. Seeking feedback from various sources can also be beneficial: think about when it would be helpful to get feedback from someone in a totally different role than your own.

Also, watch initial facial responses: there is a microsecond that passes before people censor their physical reactions. If you see any furrowing of brows or pursing of lips—any general face-scrunching—these are micro-cues that something may not be working quite right. Pay attention to these cues and work to refine your visuals. If people are having a hard time with your graph, don't assume it's them. Consider what you can do to make the information easier to take in: perhaps you can more clearly title or label, use sparing color to focus attention, or choose a different graph type to get your point across more easily.

You'll find additional guidance for giving and receiving effective feedback in Exercise 9.3.

Exercise 2.22: build a data viz library

Collect and build a library of the effective data visualization examples created and used at work. You can do this on your own, or this can be an excellent undertaking for a team or organization. Be thoughtful how you organize the content for easy searchability (for example, by graph type, topic, or tool). Make files available to download so others can see the specifics of how they were made and modify for use in their own work. You can also add effective examples that you encounter externally from the media, blogs, or #SWDchallenge.

Make effective data visualization a team goal. To ensure continued focus, host a regular friendly competition, where individuals can nominate their own or their colleagues' examples of effective data visualization. Each month or quarter, choose winners and archive their work in the shared library. This can be a great ongoing source of inspiration: if someone is feeling stuck, they have something to turn to and flip through for possible ideas. It is also an excellent resource for new hires, so they have examples of effective data visualization in your work environment, helping set the right expectations for their own work.

PRACTICE at WORK

Exercise 2.23: explore additional resources

There are many additional resources out there when it comes to choosing an effective graph or getting inspiration from other people's creations. Practicing, getting feedback, and iterating are keys to success. That said, here are a few chart choosers I'm aware of that you may find helpful when it comes to figuring out what graphs might work for your specific needs:

- **Chart Chooser** (Juice Analytics, labs.juiceanalytics.com/chartchooser). Use their filters to find the right chart type for your needs, download as Excel or PowerPoint templates and insert your own data.

- **The Chartmaker Directory** (Visualizing Data, chartmaker.visualisingdata. com). Explore the matrix of chart type by tool and click the circles to see solutions and examples.

- **Graphic Continuum** (PolicyViz, policyviz.com/?s=graphic+continuum). The poster includes more than 90 graphic types grouped into six categories. Also check out the related Match It Game and Cards.

- **Interactive Chart Chooser** (Depict Data Studio, depictdatastudio.com/ charts). Explore the interactive chart chooser using filters.

Check out the following collections to browse other people's work for inspiration. For each graph you encounter, pause to reflect on what works well (or not so well) and consider how you can use (or avoid!) similar aspects in your own work:

- **Information Is Beautiful Awards** (informationisbeautifulawards.com). These annual awards celebrate excellence and beauty in data visualizations, infographics, interactives, and informative art. The archives contain hundreds of data visualizations.

- **Reddit: Data Is Beautiful** (reddit.com/r/dataisbeautiful). A place for visual representations of data: graphs, charts, and maps.

- **Tableau Public Gallery** (public.tableau.com/s/gallery). Stunning data visualization examples from across the web created with Tableau Public. In particular, check out the Greatest Hits Gallery using the drop-down menu.

- **The R Graph Gallery** (r-graph-gallery.com). Looking for inspiration or help? Here you will find hundreds of distinctive graphics made with the R programming language, including code.

- **Xenographics** (xeno.graphics). Xeno.graphics is a repository of novel, innovative, and experimental visualizations to help inspire, fight xenographphobia and popularize new chart types.

PRACTICE at WORK

Exercise 2.24: let's discuss

Consider the following questions related to Chapter 2 lessons and exercises. Discuss with a partner or group.

1. How is the way that we process tables different from how we process graphs? What are the pros and cons of presenting data in tabular form? In what circumstances does it make sense to use a table? In what scenarios should you avoid a table?

2. One common decision when graphing data is whether to have a y-axis that is titled and labeled or omit the axis and label the data directly. What considerations should you make when determining which is better for a given situation?

3. When is it okay to have a non-zero baseline when graphing data?

4. Why is paper a good tool for graphing data? Were the exercises in this chapter that asked you to draw helpful? Will you use this low-tech method in your work going forward? Why or why not?

5. What is the purpose of graphing a given set of data multiple ways? Why is it important to iterate and look at different views of your data? When will you take the time to do this going forward? When does it not make sense to spend time on this?

6. The examples in *SWD* and in this book are mostly basic charts: a lot of lines and bars. When does it make sense to use a graph that is more novel or less familiar? What are the pros and cons of using a graph that your audience may not have previously encountered? What steps can you take in this situation to help ensure success?

7. Are there any cases where data has historically been graphed a certain way by your team or your organization that you believe should be changed? How might you drive this change? What sort of resistance or pushback do you anticipate? How can you address this?

8. What is one specific goal you will set for yourself or your team related to the strategies outlined in this chapter? How can you hold yourself (or your team) accountable to this? Who will you turn to for feedback?

PRACTICE at WORK

identify &
eliminate clutter

Every element we put in our graphs or on the pages and slides that contain them adds cognitive burden—each one consumes brainpower to process. We should take a discerning look at the elements we allow into our visual communications and strip away those things that aren't adding enough informative value to make up for their presence.

This lesson is simple but the impact is huge: get rid of the stuff that doesn't need to be there. We'll illustrate and experience the power of doing so through a handful of targeted exercises in this chapter.

Let's practice **identifying and eliminating clutter!**

First, we'll review the main lessons from *SWD* Chapter 3.

SWD BOOK
CHAPTER 3

FIRST, LET'S RECAP
CLUTTER is your ENEMY

CLUTTER   VISUAL ELEMENTS *that* TAKE UP SPACE
and DON'T AID *our* UNDERSTANDING

**COGNITIVE
LOAD**   The MENTAL EFFORT *that's* REQUIRED
to LEARN NEW INFORMATION

Every element we put
on a page or screen
puts cognitive burden
on our audience ...

So we should take
care not to include
things that aren't
adding information

**LACK of
VISUAL
ORDER** ⟷   (*Another type of* **CLUTTER**)

LEVERAGE WHITE SPACE
and ALIGN ELEMENTS

Aim for clean horizontal
and vertical elements,
avoid diagonal

NON-STRATEGIC USE of CONTRAST

CLEAR CONTRAST is a SIGNAL, INDICATING WHERE to LOOK

Don't make too many things different, or key points will get lost

GESTALT PRINCIPLES

DESCRIBE HOW we SUBCONSCIOUSLY ORDER what we SEE in the WORLD

We can use this understanding of how people see to help identify & eliminate **CLUTTER**

PROXIMITY

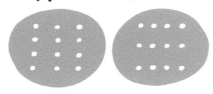

SIMILARITY

ENCLOSURE

CLOSURE

CONTINUITY

CONNECTION

PRACTICE with COLE

3.1 which Gestalt principles are in play?

3.2 how can we tie words to the graph?

3.3 harness alignment & white space

3.4 declutter!

PRACTICE on your OWN

3.5 which Gestalt principles are in play?

3.6 find an effective visual

3.7 create alignment and use white space

3.8 declutter!

3.9 declutter (again!)

3.10 declutter (some more!)

PRACTICE at WORK

3.11 start with a blank piece of paper

3.12 do you NEED that?

3.13 let's discuss

We'll start by familiarizing ourselves with the Gestalt Principles of Visual Perception, then explore how we can use them to declutter and make our visual communications easier for our audience to process.

Exercise 3.1: which Gestalt principles are in play?

The Gestalt principles describe ways in which we subconsciously bring order to the things we see. *SWD* introduced six of these principles: proximity, similarity, enclosure, closure, continuity, and connection. We can use the Gestalt principles to make our visual communications easier for our audience to process by helping make the connections between the different elements we show more obvious. (If you aren't familiar with these principles and don't have *SWD* handy, we'll review them in detail through the solution to this exercise.)

Consider the following visual, which illustrates actual and forecast market size (measured by total sales) over time for a class of pharmaceutical drugs. **Which of the Gestalt principles mentioned above can you identify? Where and how are each used?**

Market size over time

FIGURE 3.1 Which Gestalt principles are in play?

Solution 3.1: which Gestalt principles are in play?

I've made use of each of the six Gestalt principles in Figure 3.1. Let's briefly discuss.

Proximity: Proximity is used in a number of ways. The physical closeness of the y-axis title and labels indicates to us that those elements are to be understood together. The close proximity of the data labels to the data markers makes it clear that those relate to each other.

Similarity: Similarity of color (orange and blue) is used to visually tie sparing words in the text at the top to the data points in the graph that those words describe.

Enclosure: The light grey shading on the right side of the graph employs the enclosure principle both to differentiate the forecast from the actual historical data and also to link that part of the line to the words at the bottom that lend additional detail. The lines between 2018 and 2019 on the x-axis also have an enclosing effect.

Closure: The overall visual makes use of the closure principle. I didn't put a border around the graph. I didn't need to—the closure principle says we perceive a set of individual elements as a single, recognizable unit. So the graph appears as part of a whole. If we look at this on an element-by-element basis, this is true for each of the individual text boxes as well.

Continuity: The dotted line depicting the forecast data on the right-hand side of the graph employs the continuity principle. This allows us to make this part of the line visually distinct, but still enables us to "see" it as a line. Because dotted lines themselves add clutter (since they are many dashes compared to a single solid line), I recommend reserving their use for when there is uncertainty to depict, as is the case with the forecast.

Connection: The connection principle is used in the line graph itself, connecting all of the monthly data points and making the overall trend easier to see. Each axis employs this principle as well, visually connecting dollars on the y-axis and time on the x-axis.

There may be additional uses of the principles that I've not mentioned directly. How many of those that I've outlined above did you identify? How might you make use of similar strategies in the future? We'll look at additional applications of the Gestalt principles through the remaining exercises in this chapter and beyond.

Expanding to other lessons covered in Chapter 3 of *SWD*, reflect on how the strategic use of contrast, alignment, and white space contributed to the effectiveness of the visual in Figure 3.1. Speaking of these design elements, we'll do an exercise looking at these more closely soon. But first, let's look at how we can use Gestalt principles to tie words to the data we show.

Exercise 3.2: how can we tie words to the graph?

When we communicate with data for explanatory purposes, often the final result is a slide deck, where each page contains both words and visuals. I frequently encounter client examples that have a graph on one side and words on the other or words at the top and a graph or two underneath. Often, both the words and visuals are important: the words help lend context or describe something and the graph helps us to see it.

The challenge is that this often creates a lot of work for the audience. When we read the text, we are left on our own to search in the data for where we should be looking in the graph(s) for evidence of what is being said. We have to figure out for ourselves how the words relate to the graph and vice versa.

Don't make your audience do this kind of work: do it for them!

To help, we can use the Gestalt principles to visually tie the text to the data. Let's practice. Consider the following visual. **Which Gestalt principles could we make use of to tie the words at the right to the graph at the left?** List them and either describe or draw how you would make use of each. Which would you employ if you were communicating this data?

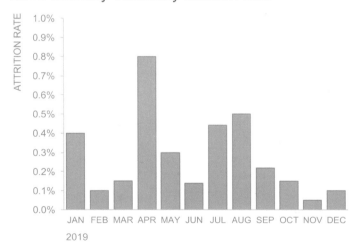

2019 monthly voluntary attrition rate

Highlights:

In April there was a reorganization. No jobs were eliminated, but many people chose to leave.

Attrition rates tend to be higher in the Summer months when it is common for associates to leave to go back to school.

Attrition is typically low in November and December due to the holidays.

FIGURE 3.2a How can we visually tie the words to the graph?

Solution 3.2: how can we tie words to the graph?

When the audience reads the text at the right, there are no visual cues to help them know where to look in the graph for evidence of what is being said. They have to read, think about it, and search in the graph. This is a straightforward example—if we spend some time, we can figure it out. But I don't want my audience to have to "figure it out"; I want to identify this work that the visual in Figure 3.2a implicitly asks my audience to undertake and instead design my visual in a way that minimizes or eliminates the work to make things easy on my audience. Tying related things through Gestalt principles allows me to do this.

I will illustrate ideas for making use of four of the Gestalt principles to tie my data to the text: proximity, similarity, enclosure, and connection. Let's discuss each of these and take a look at how we can apply them.

Proximity. I can put the text physically close to the data it describes. This tends to be a good approach as long as you can do so without interfering with the ability to read the data. See Figure 3.2b.

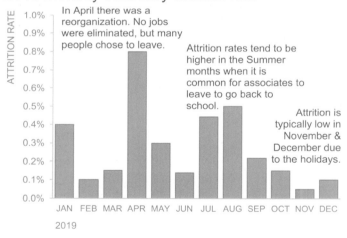

FIGURE 3.2b Proximity

Because of the close proximity of the text to the data it describes, this takes away some of the work. That said, we still have to make some assumptions or read the x-axis to orient ourselves to exactly which data points are being described. If we wanted to illustrate this more quickly, we might somehow make those individual data points distinct. See Figure 3.2c.

2019 monthly voluntary attrition rate

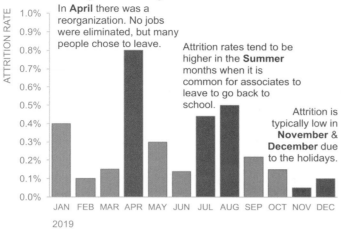

FIGURE 3.2c Proximity with emphasis

In Figure 3.2c, both the darker grey for the points of interest and the sparing bold in the text allow us to quickly understand as we read the various observations described in the text which data points illustrate these takeaways. When we put text directly on the graph, however, it can sometimes make it harder to see what's going on in the data. At other times, text directly on the graph can feel cluttered or you simply may not have the room for it. In those instances, look to one of the following solutions.

Similarity. We can keep the text at the right, but employ similarity of color to tie the words to the graph. See Figure 3.2d.

2019 monthly voluntary attrition rate

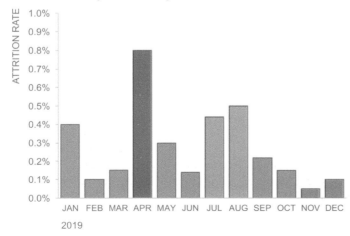

FIGURE 3.2d Similarity

PRACTICE with COLE

When I process the information in Figure 3.2d, my eyes do a lot of bouncing back and forth. I start at the top left, then my eyes scan to the right, pausing on the red bar and then over to the first block of text at the right and the red "April." Then I continue reading downward and encounter the orange "Summer," which prompts me to bounce leftward to the orange bars. Then finally, I pause on the blue bars and then read the text that describes them. This feels pretty natural to me and I employ this strategy frequently. Still, let's look at some other options.

Enclosure. We can physically enclose the text with the data it describes. See Figure 3.2e.

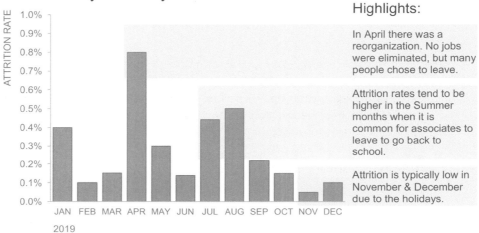

2019 monthly voluntary attrition rate

Highlights:

In April there was a reorganization. No jobs were eliminated, but many people chose to leave.

Attrition rates tend to be higher in the Summer months when it is common for associates to leave to go back to school.

Attrition is typically low in November & December due to the holidays.

FIGURE 3.2e Enclosure

In Figure 3.2e, the light shading is meant to connect the data points to the text. If the data were shaped differently, this method may not work so well. For example, if the September bar had value 0.8%, this would be confusing because it would cross both the first and second grey shaded areas, and could cause us to think we should relate it to one of those, when really none of the text is about that particular data point.

Though I like how this looks, another drawback compared to the previous use of similarity of color is that we don't have any visual cues to help us talk about this data. If I will be presenting this graph live, it can be useful to be able to say things like "Look at the red bar, which shows…" or "The blue bars indicate where…". I could solve this by adding color to my shaded regions. See Figure 3.2f.

2019 monthly voluntary attrition rate

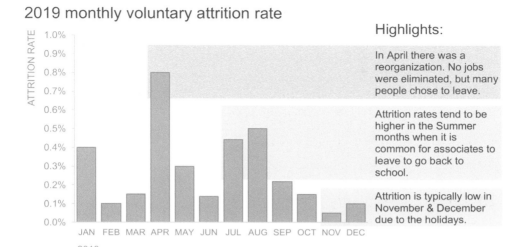

FIGURE 3.2f Enclosure with color differentiation

I could take this a step further and use similarity of color for sparing data and words in addition to the shaded regions to make it clear which text relates to which data points. See Figure 3.2g.

2019 monthly voluntary attrition rate

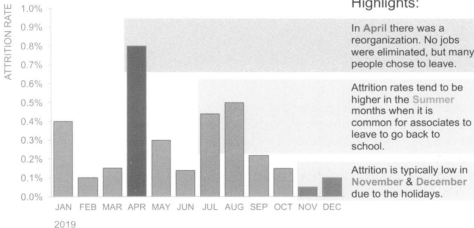

FIGURE 3.2g Enclosure plus similarity

PRACTICE with COLE

Connection. Another way we could tie the words to the data is by physically connecting them. Figure 3.2h illustrates this.

2019 monthly voluntary attrition rate

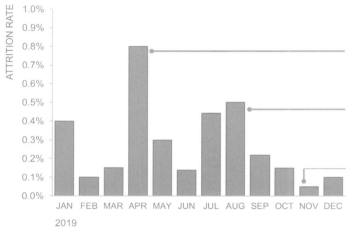

Highlights:

In April there was a reorganization. No jobs were eliminated, but many people chose to leave.

Attrition rates tend to be higher in the Summer months when it is common for associates to leave to go back to school.

Attrition is typically low in November & December due to the holidays.

FIGURE 3.2h Connection

This works well given the layout of the data and varying heights of bars. This method will look the cleanest when you have only a few lines and are able to orient them horizontally (diagonal lines look messy and are attention grabbing, so if you find yourself needing to use diagonal lines, I would recommend using similarity rather than connection). Notice that the lines themselves don't need to draw any attention—they can be thin and light, so they are there for reference, but aren't distracting from our data.

There is still some processing I have to do, though, with the view in Figure 3.2h. I have to read the middle block of text to know that it applies to not only the August bar, but also to the July bar that precedes it. Similar processing is needed for December and the final takeaway. I could ease this work by layering on similarity of color. See Figure 3.2i.

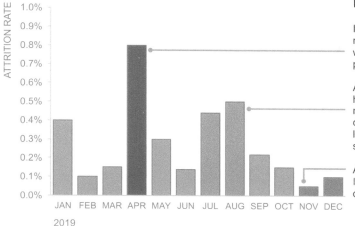

2019 monthly voluntary attrition rate

Highlights:

In **April** there was a reorganization. No jobs were eliminated, but many people chose to leave.

Attrition rates tend to be higher in the **Summer** months when it is common for associates to leave to go back to school.

Attrition is typically low in **November & December** due to the holidays.

PRACTICE *with* **COLE**

FIGURE 3.2i Connection plus similarity

Figure 3.2i makes it clear through both connection and similarity which text relates to which data.

In choosing among these options (and you may very well have come up with additional options), I tend to favor the simple similarity of color illustrated in Figure 3.2d. The preceding view in Figure 3.2i is a close second for me. How were the ideas you came up with similar or different from mine? After reading my explanation, does your decision about how you'd communicate this data stay the same?

As with most of what we've been discussing, there is no single right answer. Different people will make different choices. Of utmost importance is that you make it easy for your audience. When you show text and data together, make it clear to your audience when they read the text, where they should look in the data for evidence of what's being said, and when they look at the data, where they should look in the text for additional detail. The Gestalt principles can help you achieve this.

Exercise 3.3: harness alignment & white space

We've looked at Gestalt principles for organizing what we see. We should also eliminate visual clutter. When elements aren't aligned and white space is lacking, things feel cluttered. The concept is similar to cleaning up a messy room: put everything in its place and magic happens—the same items are present but now there is a harmonious sense of order.

Let's do a quick exercise to illustrate how we can undertake a similar endeavor with our graphs. These seemingly minor components of our visual designs can have major impacts on the overall look and feel of what we create as well as the perceived ease with which our audience can consume it.

See Figure 3.3a, which is a slide showing data about physicians writing prescriptions (writers) for a pharmaceutical drug (Product X) across three different promotions (A, B, and C). The slopegraph compares the percent of total across the three promotion types between repeat writers (those physicians who have prescribed Product X before) at the left and new writers (those prescribing it for the first time) at the right. The details in this case aren't so important. It's probably also worthy of note that we could debate whether this is the best way to show this data, but let's not worry about that—rather, let's focus on how we might better arrange the current components.

What changes would you make when it comes to alignment and white space to improve this visual? Are there other changes you would suggest? Write them down.

If you'd like, you can download this visual and implement the changes you've outlined.

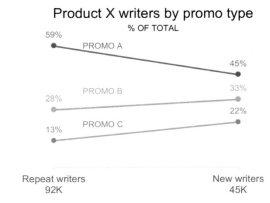

There were 45K new writers in the past year.
The distribution across promo types looks different than repeat writers.

Product X writers by promo type
% OF TOTAL

59%   PROMO A

                                    45%

       PROMO B   33%
28%

                        22%
       PROMO C
13%

Repeat writers   New writers
92K   45K

Though Promo A makes up the biggest segment overall, they contribute less to new writers than to repeat writers.
Both Promo B and Promo C brought in higher proportion of new writers compared to repeat writers.
How should we use this data for our future promotion strategy?

FIGURE 3.3a How might we better use alignment & white space?

Solution 3.3: harness alignment & white space

The visual in Figure 3.3a feels sloppy. It appears as if elements were simply thrown onto the slide. A couple of minutes and quick changes to alignment and use of white space can bring a sense of order and make the information easier to assimilate.

First, let's discuss alignment. Currently, the text on the slide is all center-aligned. I tend to avoid center alignment because it can leave things hanging in space. Additionally, when the text flows onto multiple lines, it creates jagged edges that look messy. I'm an advocate of left or right-aligning text boxes to create clean vertical and horizontal lines across the elements. Doing so allows us to makes use of the Gestalt principle of closure—as we create framing, it helps tie the elements of the slide together. In this case, I'll left-align the takeaways at the top, the graph title, and the left x-axis labels (Repeat writers, 92K). I'll pull the data labels within the graph to be labeled at the left for Repeat writers and at the right for New writers. I'll also pull the Promo A, Promo B, Promo C descriptions out of the middle of the graph and orient those on the right, lining them up horizontally with the data labels for those points (I could have also put these to the left of the left labels—which I choose typically depends where I want my audience to focus). Finally, I left-aligned the text at the right.

I left-justified most of the text (the only exception is the New writers and 45K x-axis label, which I've right-justified to provide framing on the right side of the graph). Which you choose between left or right alignment (or in rare instances, center alignment) depends on the layout of the elements on the rest of the page. The idea is to create clear vertical and horizontal lines. Sometimes right-justified text will also work well, and you'll see this in a number of examples throughout this book. I did try right-aligning the text at the right side of the page, but it created some jagged trapped white space in the middle of the page that I didn't like, so I reverted to left alignment.

The other change I made was in regards to white space. I pulled the graph title up so there would be a little space between it and the graph. I reduced the width of the graph both to allow room to label the various data series at the right as well as to have some space between that and the text box at the right. Probably the biggest (and fastest to implement) change in this area was simply adding line breaks to the text on the right, making it easier to scan and a little nicer to view.

PRACTICE with COLE

You can see all of these changes implemented in Figure 3.3b.

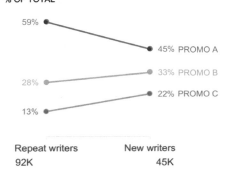

There were 45K new writers in the past year.
The distribution across promo types looks different than repeat writers.

Product X writers by promo type
% OF TOTAL

59% ●
45% PROMO A

33% PROMO B
28% ●
22% PROMO C
13% ●

Repeat writers   New writers
92K   45K

Though Promo A makes up the biggest segment overall, it contributes less to new writers than to repeat writers.

Both Promo B and Promo C brought in higher proportions of new writers compared to repeat writers.

How should we use this data for our future promotion strategy?

FIGURE 3.3b   Better employment of alignment & white space

Compare Figure 3.3b to Figure 3.3a. How does this ordered graph feel compared to the original? I appreciate the sense of structure in Figure 3.3b that was initially lacking.

You may have made some different decisions in your redesign, and that's okay. The main point is to be thoughtful in your use of alignment and white space. These small things can have a big impact!

We'll look at more examples illustrating the benefit of paying attention to detail in our visual design in Chapter 5.

Exercise 3.4: declutter!

A frequent source of clutter in data visualization comes from unnecessary graph elements: borders, gridlines, data markers, and the like. These can make our visuals appear overly complicated and increase the work our audience has to undertake in order to understand what they are viewing. As we eliminate the things that don't need to be there, our data stands out more. Let's take a closer look at the benefit that decluttering can have on our data visualizations.

See Figure 3.4a, which shows time to close deals, measured in days, for direct and indirect sales teams over time.

What visual elements could you eliminate? What other changes would you make to what is shown or how it's shown to reduce cognitive burden? Spend a moment considering this and make some notes. How many changes would you make to this visual?

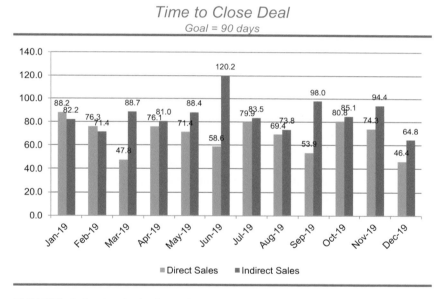

FIGURE 3.4a Let's declutter!

Solution 3.4: declutter!

I identified *15* changes I'd like to make to the Time to Close Deal graph. If your list falls short of this, refer back to Figure 3.4a and take another minute or two to see what else you might modify before you read through my ideas.

Ready? Let me walk you through what I would do—step by step—and my thought process behind each choice.

1. Remove heavy lines. The heavy horizontal lines between title and graph and at bottom graph border are unnecessary. The closure principle tells us we already see the graph as part of a whole—we don't need these partial enclosures to make that clear. Use white space instead to set the title and graph apart from other elements as needed.

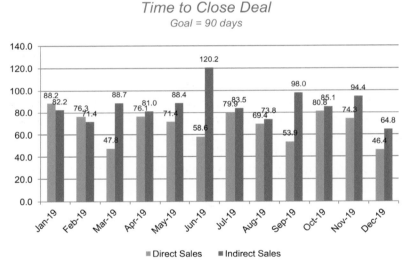

FIGURE 3.4b Remove heavy lines

2. Remove gridlines. Gridlines are gratuitous! It's amazing to me how much the simple steps of removing the chart border and gridlines do to make our data stand out more. See Figure 3.4c.

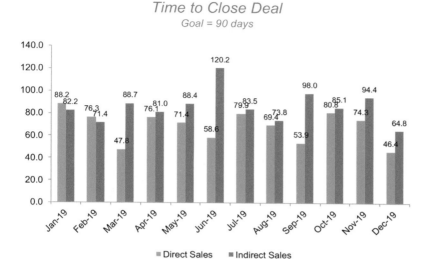

FIGURE 3.4c Remove gridlines

3. Drop trailing zeros from y-axis labels. This is one of my pet peeves! The zeros after the decimal place carry no information—get rid of them. I'm also going to change the frequency of my y-axis labels. While labeling every 20 makes sense given the scale of the numbers, we're plotting days, so something like every 30 would make more sense (approximating a month). I started with that, but the axis looked overly sparse, so I opted for every 15 days. Let's also add a y-axis title so we know what we're looking at. I advocate titling axes directly so that your audience isn't left questioning or having to make assumptions to decipher the data.

FIGURE 3.4d Drop trailing zeros from y-axis labels

PRACTICE *with* COLE

4. Eliminate diagonal text on x-axis. Diagonal text looks messy. Worse than that, studies have shown it's slower to read than horizontal text (vertical text, by the way, is even slower). If efficiency of information transfer is one of your goals when communicating with data—which I'd argue it should be—aim for horizontal text whenever possible.

I see this issue often with diagonal x-axis labels, where the years are repeated with every date—which is both redundant and also space constraints frequently force the date to be diagonal. We can avoid this by using month abbreviations for the primary x-axis label, and then use year as supercategory x-axis label or title the axis with the year. In this case, I've simply titled the x-axis with the year (2019) to make the date range clear.

FIGURE 3.4e Eliminate diagonal text on x-axis

5. Thicken the bars! Another pet peeve is when the white space between the bars is bigger than the bars themselves. Let's thicken those. This also makes use of the connection Gestalt principle, where with reduced distance between the bars, my eyes start to try to draw lines between the bars (if moving from bars to lines was on your list of recommendations, don't worry, it's on mine, too—we'll get there soon!).

Time to Close Deal
Goal = 90 days

FIGURE 3.4f Thicken the bars!

6. Pull data labels into ends of bars. Now that we've thickened the bars, we have space to pull the data labels into the bars. This is a cognitive trick. Looking back to the previous iteration (Figure 3.4f), when we had a data label outside the end of each bar, each bar and label acted as two discrete elements. Now that we've thickened the bars, we can have room to embed the data labels, taking what were previously two distinct elements and turning them into a single element. This reduces the perceived cognitive burden, without reducing any of the actual data that we are showing.

Previously, we had a decimal of significance on each data label. This will always be context-dependent, but in this case given the scale of the numbers, we don't need that specificity (also be cautious of the aforementioned false precision that having too many decimal places can convey). Here, we have an added benefit: reducing precision allows us to more cleanly fit the labels into the ends of the bars. I've made the labels white (versus the previous black), simply because I like the contrast you get with white-on-color. See Figure 3.4g.

PRACTICE with COLE

FIGURE 3.4g Pull data labels into ends of bars

7. Eliminate data labels. In the previous step, I rounded and pulled the data labels into the ends of the bars. Note, though, that we don't need both the y-axis *and* every data point labeled—this is redundant. This is a common decision point when it comes to visualizing data: do I preserve the axis, label the data directly, or some combination of the two? The main thing you want to consider when making this decision is the degree of importance of the specific numeric values. If it's critical that your audience know that time to close a deal for Direct Sales went from exactly 74 days in November to exactly 46 days in December, then you could label the data directly and get rid of the y-axis altogether. If, on the other hand, you want your audience to focus on the shape of the data, or general trends or relationships, then I'd recommend preserving the axis and not cluttering the graph with the data labels.

In this case, I'll assume the shape and general trends are more important than the precise numeric values. Because of this, I'm going to keep the y-axis and remove the data labels from each bar.

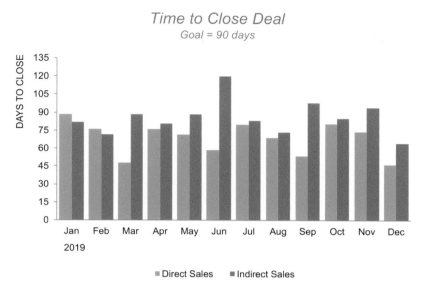

FIGURE 3.4h Eliminate data labels

8. Make it a line graph. If you've been thinking this entire time: "This is data over time, so shouldn't it be a line graph?" I'm with you. Check out the impact of moving from bars to lines. We're using less ink, so the overall design feels cleaner. This is also a big win from a cognitive burden standpoint: we've taken what was previously twenty-four bars and replaced them with just two lines.

FIGURE 3.4i Make it a line graph

9. Label the data directly. Look back to Figure 3.4i and locate the legend. Your eyes do a bit of scanning to find it, right? This is work. It's perhaps more notice-able now that we've taken a number of steps to reduce the other issues that were causing cognitive burden. This is the kind of work that we want to identify and take upon ourselves—as the designers of the information—so our audience doesn't have to exert effort to figure out what they are seeing.

We can use the Gestalt principle of proximity to put the data labels right next to the data they describe. This eliminates any searching to figure out how to read the data.

FIGURE 3.4j Label the data directly

10. Make data labels the same color as the data. While we leverage proximity—putting the data labels right next to the data they describe—let's also make use of similarity, recoloring the data labels to match data they describe. It's another visual cue to our audience to indicate that these things are related.

FIGURE 3.4k Make data labels the same color as the data

11. Upper-left-most orient graph title. Without other visual cues, your audience will start at the top left of your page, screen, or graph, and do zigzagging "z's" to take in the information. Because of this, I advocate upper-left-most justifying graph and axis titles and labels. This means your audience sees how to read the data before they get to the data itself. As we discussed in Exercise 3.3, I tend to avoid center alignment of text because it leaves things hanging out in space (revisit Figure 3.4k and look at the graph title positioning). When you have text that goes onto multiple lines, this creates jagged edges that look messy. While I was changing the positioning of the title, I also eliminated the italics, which were unnecessary.

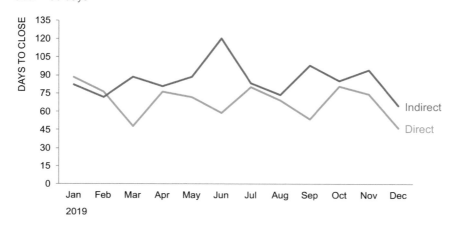

FIGURE 3.4l Upper-left-most orient graph title

12. Remove title color. Up until now, the graph title has been blue. Did you find yourself trying to tie that to the Indirect trend in the data? That's the Gestalt principle of similarity at play: we naturally try to associate things of similar color. In this case, that is a false association. Let's eliminate it by taking color out of the title entirely (we'll look at an alternative approach where we do use some color in the title to make use of this natural association momentarily).

Time to close deal
Goal = 90 days

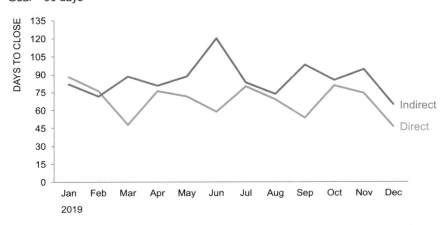

FIGURE 3.4m Remove title color

13. Put the goal in the graph. Originally, the subtitle told us that the goal for time to close a deal is 90 days. If we want to be able to relate this to the data (are we above goal? below goal?)—which would make sense here—let's put that information in the graph directly so we can visually compare the data and don't have to really think about it.

Time to close deal

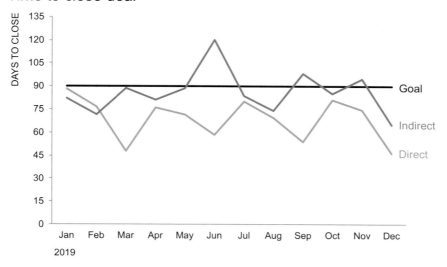

FIGURE 3.4n Put the goal in the graph

14. Iterate to best visualize *Goal.* The Goal line is quite pronounced in the preceding graph. Let's take a look at some different views. This is a good example of how allowing yourself time to iterate and look at things a number of different ways can be useful at many points during the process. I like using dotted lines for goals or targets, but when the line is thick, this introduces visual clutter. When I make the line thinner, it deemphasizes it—so it's there and easy to see, but isn't drawing undue attention. I also like all caps for short phrases, such as GOAL, because they are easy to scan and create nice rectangular shapes (versus mixed case, which doesn't have clean lines at the top since letters such as l are taller than letters such as a).

Iterating on **goal** line

FIGURE 3.4o Iterating: different formatting for Goal line

Let's look at a bigger version of that final iteration.

Time to close deal

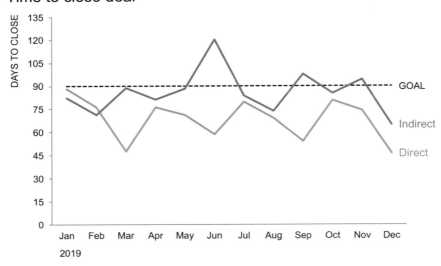

FIGURE 3.4p My favorite of the Goal line iterations

15. Remove color. Given that we have sufficient spatial separation between the lines in this graph, we don't need to use color as a categorical differentiator the way we have up to this point. I'll make everything grey. Color will come back into play when we focus attention—let's do that next.

Time to close deal

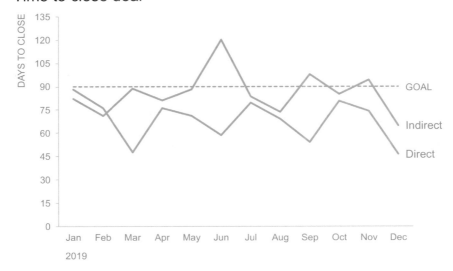

FIGURE 3.4q Remove color

Focus attention. We're jumping ahead, but now that we've come this far it only feels right that we carry this one through to the end. I'll stop numbering my steps at this point, since I'm no longer decluttering. In the preceding view, I pushed everything to the background—made it all grey. This forces me to be thoughtful about *where* and *how* I direct my audience's attention. There are a number of things we could point out in this data. Let's assume for a moment that we want to draw attention to the Indirect data series in this graph.

Figure 3.4r illustrates one way I could achieve that.

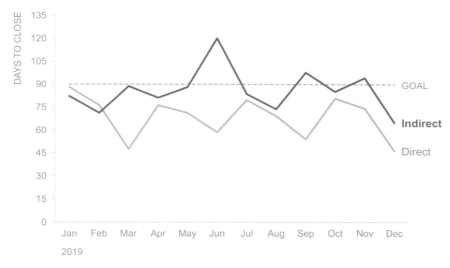

FIGURE 3.4r Focus attention

Notice how my words above the graph are tied visually to the Indirect trend within the graph through similar use of color. This is akin to how we perhaps tried to tie the original blue title in the initial graph to the blue trend, only this time I'm doing it on purpose and it makes sense. By reading those words at the top of the graph, my audience will already know what to look for in the data before they get there. Also, if we think of this from a scannability standpoint, if I only look at this for a couple of seconds, the colored words and line draw my attention and I clearly and quickly get the takeaway that time to close indirect deals varies.

PRACTICE *with* COLE

Focus attention elsewhere. I can use this same strategy and some highlighted data points to make a different point. See Figure 3.4s.

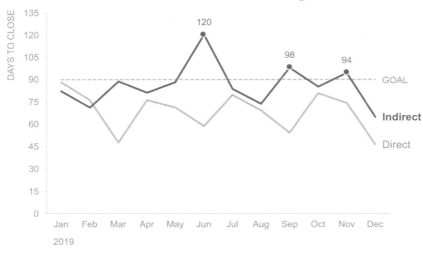

FIGURE 3.4s Focus attention elsewhere

Introduce a bit more color to really direct attention. I could take the preceding example a step further by introducing another color. I tend to avoid green for "good" and red for "bad," because of the inaccessibility for colorblind audience members. Bright orange can have a similar negative connotation to red and stands out quite nicely given the other colors we have in play (this particular shade of blue was chosen because it matched the client's branding).

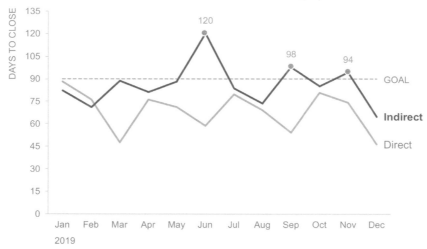

FIGURE 3.4t Introduce a bit more color to really direct attention

Focus attention on yet another takeaway. If the times where we've missed goal *aren't* the crux of the point we want to make, we could direct attention to a meta-takeaway: we're beating our goal most of the time across both Indirect and Direct sales. We can use words and color to make this point clear. In this view, with the end markers and data labels, one obvious comparison for our audience to make is how Indirect and Direct time to close deals compared to each other and the goal in December.

Time to fill: beating goal the majority of time

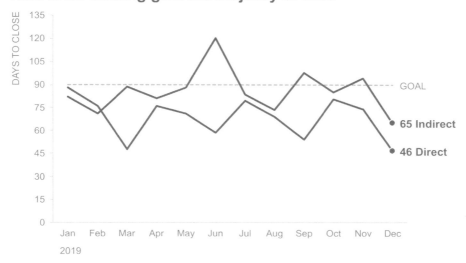

FIGURE 3.4u Focus attention on yet another takeaway

We'll look at more strategies for focusing attention in Chapter 4.

Next, let's shift gears and have you undertake some practice on your own.

PRACTICE On your OWN   Little changes can combine to have big impact—reducing cognitive burden and making our visuals easier with which to interact. We'll continue our practice of identifying and removing clutter next.

Exercise 3.5: which Gestalt principles are in play?

As we've discussed and seen illustrated through a number of examples so far, Gestalt principles help us organize what we see, providing cues to what clutter we can eliminate and relating elements to each other in various ways. Consider the six principles we've covered—proximity, similarity, enclosure, closure, continuity, and connection—and review the following visual.

Which Gestalt principles are being used in Figure 3.5? Where and how? What effect does each achieve?

Wallet share by growth type

Growth Type	# of Accounts	Gain Share Opportunity ($M)	Keep Share Opportunity ($M)
Growing Fast	407	$1.20	$16.50
Growing	1,275	$8.10	$101.20
Stable	3,785	$34.40	$306.30
Dropping	1,467	$6.50	$107.20
Dropping Fast	623	$0.40	$27.70
Total	7,557	$50.60	$558.90

Stable and Dropping represent:

69% of total accounts   **81%** of gain share opportunity   **74%** of keep share opportunity

FIGURE 3.5 Which Gestalt principles are in play?

Exercise 3.6: find an effective visual

Find an example graph that you believe is effective. This can be from your work, someone else's work, the media, storytellingwithdata.com, or other sources. **Are any Gestalt principles being used?** I'll bet there are. Which and how? List them! What do the Gestalt principles you identify help achieve? What else do you like about the graph? What makes it effective?

Write a paragraph or two outlining your evaluation. See the following for reference.

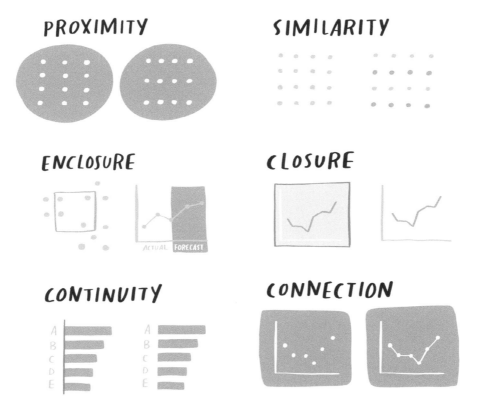

Exercise 3.7: alignment & white space

Alignment and white space—these are elements of the visual design, that when done well, we don't even notice. However when they *aren't* done well, we feel it in the resulting visual. It may seem disorganized or connote lack of attention to detail, distracting from our data and message.

Consider Figure 3.7, which shows consumer sentiment based on survey results about various potential beverage line extensions for a food manufacturing company. Complete the following steps.

STEP 1: Reflect on what specific changes you would recommend when it comes to the effective use of alignment and white space. List them.

STEP 2: Think back to the other lessons covered in this chapter (making use of Gestalt principles, decluttering, employing contrast). What other steps would you take to declutter or otherwise improve this visual?

STEP 3: Download the data and make the changes you've recommended to the existing graph, or import the data into your preferred tool and create a clutter-free visual that aligns elements and makes use of white space.

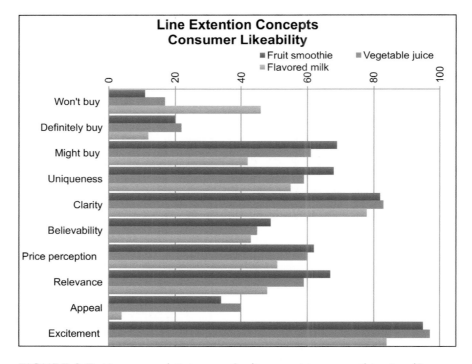

FIGURE 3.7 How can white space & alignment improve this visual?

PRACTICE on your OWN

Exercise 3.8: declutter!

As we've seen through a number of the examples we've looked at already, there can be great value in identifying and removing things in our visuals that don't need to be there. Each element we take away helps our data stand out more *and* frees up space so we can add things that matter. Let's continue to practice this important skill of identifying clutter and removing it from our visual designs. We'll do a few of these so you can have the opportunity to identify a number of different types of clutter.

Consider Figure 3.8, which shows customer satisfaction score over time. **What unnecessary visual elements could you eliminate?** What other changes would you make to reduce cognitive burden? Make some notes about the changes you would make to declutter this graph.

To take it a step further, download the data and make the changes you've recommended to the existing graph, or import the data into your preferred tool and create a visual that is clutter-free.

FIGURE 3.8 Let's declutter!

Exercise 3.9: declutter (again!)

Clutter takes a lot of different forms. Let's look at another example graph that can be improved.

Check out Figure 3.9, which shows the monthly number of cars sold by a national chain of dealerships. **What unnecessary visual elements could you eliminate? What other changes would you make to reduce cognitive burden?** Make some notes about the changes you would make to declutter this graph.

To take it a step further, download the data and make the changes you've recommended to the existing graph, or import the data into your preferred tool and create a visual that is clutter-free.

PRACTICE on your OWN

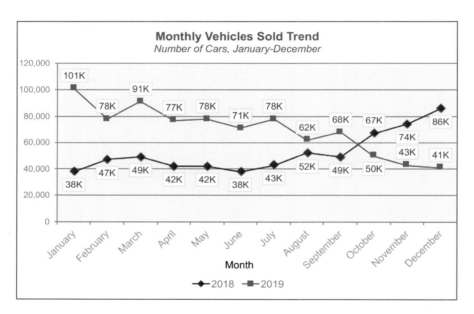

FIGURE 3.9 Let's declutter!

Exercise 3.10: declutter (some more!)

Here is another opportunity to identify and eliminate clutter. See Figure 3.10, which shows the percent of customers of a given bank having automated payments by different products. **What unnecessary visual elements could you eliminate?** What other changes would you make to reduce cognitive burden? Make some notes about the changes you would make to declutter this graph.

To take it a step further, download the data and make the changes you've recommended to the existing graph, or import the data into your preferred tool and create a visual that is clutter-free.

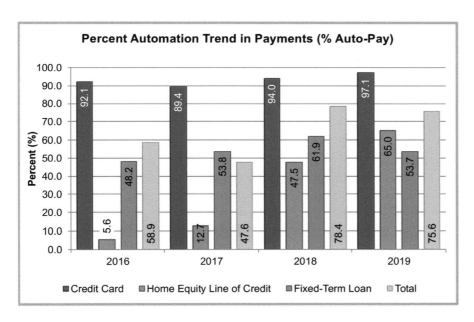

FIGURE 3.10 Let's declutter!

PRACTICE at WORK

Just a couple quick tips to employ and questions to consider will wrap up our decluttering practice. Don't let unnecessary elements get in the way of effective communication!

Exercise 3.11: start with a blank piece of paper

Often, the culprit behind the clutter in our visuals is our tool. When we draw, each stroke of the pen or pencil takes effort. We don't tend to put forth that effort unless it's worth it, which means it's harder for non-information-carrying elements to work their way into our designs.

In the same way we used drawing to brainstorm and iterate through different views of our data in Chapter 2, there are benefits to drawing from a decluttering standpoint, too.

Consider a project where you need to communicate with data. Spend some time getting familiar with the data and what you want to communicate. **Get yourself a blank piece of paper and sketch your visual.** Consider whether you've included anything that's not necessary. Once you have it right on paper, determine what tools or experts you have at your disposal to make your ideas real.

PRACTICE at WORK

Exercise 3.12: do you need that?

Once we've taken the time to put something together, it can become difficult to look at it with fresh eyes and determine what we should eliminate. After creating a visual, pause and ask yourself the following questions. Or take an existing visual from a regular report or dashboard and assess how it could be improved through decluttering.

- **What visual clutter can you eliminate?** Are there any unnecessary elements distracting from your data or message? You can usually get rid of borders and gridlines. Is anything unnecessarily complicated? How might you simplify? What feels like work? How can you remedy? What other changes can you make to reduce cognitive burden?

- **Is there redundant information you could streamline?** It's important to clearly title and label everything, but look for redundancy that can be eliminated. For example, decide whether an axis or data labels will best meet your needs—you typically won't need both. Units should be clearly displayed, but may not need to be attached to every data point. Use effective titling to help streamline.

- **Is all of the data you are showing necessary?** Go through each piece of data in your graph or presentation and ask yourself whether you need it. If you plan to remove any data, consider what context you lose with it. In some cases, this still makes sense. As part of this, think about: what is the right time frame to show? What are the important comparison points? Are they all equally important? Reflect on what aggregation or frequency makes sense—sometimes rolling daily data into weekly or monthly data into quarterly (for example) can simplify and make it easier to see overarching trends.

- **What could you push to the background?** Not all elements in a chart or on a page are equally important. Where can you make use of grey to push non-message-impacting components to the background and employ strategic contrast to help direct attention?

- **Seek feedback.** Recruit a colleague to look at your visual and ask probing questions that will force you to talk through what you are showing. If you ever find yourself saying things like, "Ignore this" or they ask you questions about points that you thought were clear, these are verbal cues that you can use to further refine your visual, pushing less important elements to the background or getting rid of them entirely. Make changes and then go through the process with someone else. Iterate based on feedback to help push your work from good to great.

PRACTICE at WORK

Exercise 3.13: let's discuss

Consider the following questions related to Chapter 3 lessons and exercises. Discuss with a partner or group.

1. Why is it important to identify and eliminate clutter? What are common types of clutter that you will remove from your visual communications going forward? When does it *not* make sense to spend time decluttering?

2. Review the Gestalt principles. Which of these would you like to use more in your work? How will you do so? Are there any that don't make sense or where you are unclear how you could use them in your work?

3. Is there any common clutter that your graphing application routinely adds to your visuals? How can you streamline your process of decluttering to be more efficient in your tools?

4. We've looked at some examples where data over time is plotted as bars. What are the benefits from a clutter standpoint of showing this data as a line graph? When would it make sense to do this? In what scenarios would you keep the bars?

5. What is one tip you picked up from the lessons in this chapter that you plan to employ going forward? Where and how will you make use of it? Can you foresee exceptions where you *wouldn't* put into practice the given strategy?

6. Lining up elements, preserving white space, and employing strategic contrast: are these just about making things pretty, or is there more to it than that? Does this sort of attention to detail matter? Why or why not?

7. Can you imagine any situations where clutter is desirable? When and why?

8. What is one specific goal you will set for yourself or your team related to the strategies outlined in this chapter? How can you hold yourself (or your team) accountable to this? Who will you turn to for feedback?

PRACTICE at WORK

focus
attention

Where do you want your audience to look? It's a simple question, yet one we frequently don't give much thought to when we are creating graphs and the pages that contain them. We can take intentional steps in our visuals to make it clear to our audience where they should pay attention and in what general order. This can be achieved by using preattentive attributes—such as color, size, and position—strategically. Not everyone sees the same thing when they look at data, but by taking thoughtful design steps, you can help your audience focus on the right things.

Let's practice **focusing attention**!

First, we'll review the main lessons from *SWD* Chapter 4.

FIRST, LET'S RECAP

FOCUS *your* AUDIENCE'S ATTENTION

YOU SEE with YOUR BRAIN

A SIMPLIFIED PICTURE of HOW YOU SEE

THREE TYPES of MEMORY

ICONIC ✳

SHORT TERM

LONG TERM

Super short term - fractions of a second before forwarding

✳ Picks up on pre-attentive attributes!

People can hold on to about 4 chunks of info at a time

Things either disappear into oblivion or they get forwarded into long-term memory

What we are trying to access in our audience

Story helps here, we'll talk more about it soon

PREATTENTIVE ATTRIBUTES

SIGNAL WHERE to LOOK and create VISUAL HIERARCHY to help ease the processing of information

ORIENTATION   SHAPE   LINE LENGTH   LINE WIDTH

SIZE   CURVATURE   ADDED MARKS   ENCLOSURE

HUE   INTENSITY   SPATIAL POSITION   MOTION

BE AWARE

SPECIFIC ATTRIBUTES to REMEMBER

SIZE — Relative size can indicate relative importance

HUE (COLOR) — Used sparingly is the MOST STRATEGIC TOOL for directing our audience's attention

SPATIAL POSITION — Without other visual cues, we take in information starting at the top left and doing zig-zagging Z's across the page

Aim to work within this natural construct, placing important info at the top left — or making it clear what order to take it in otherwise

WHERE ARE YOUR EYES DRAWN?

A TEST to ASSESS whether YOU are using PREATTENTIVE ATTRIBUTES STRATEGICALLY

Close your eyes ...

... then look back at your slide / graph ...

take note of where your eyes go ...

this is where your audiences eyes will likely go

Evaluate & make changes as needed

PRACTICE with COLE

4.1
where
are your
eyes drawn?

4.2
focus
on...

4.3
direct
attention
many ways

4.4
visualize
all the
data

PRACTICE on your OWN

4.5
where are
your eyes
drawn?

4.6
focus within
your tabular
data

4.7
direct
attention
many ways

4.8
how can
we focus
attention
here?

PRACTICE at WORK

4.9
where are
your eyes
drawn?

4.10
practice
differentiating
in your
tool

4.11
figure out
where to
focus

4.12
let's
discuss

We'll start by looking at pictures to better understand what attracts our attention, then practice putting similar aspects into play to focus our audience, being clear on where we want them to look and taking intentional steps to make it happen.

Exercise 4.1: where are your eyes drawn?

I frequently employ a simple strategy to figure out whether I'm directing my audience's attention effectively—the "Where are your eyes drawn?" test. It's easy to do: create your graph or slide, then close your eyes or look away. Look back at it, taking note of the point your eyes go first. This is probably the place your audience's eyes will land as well. You can use this method to test whether you are directing attention in the right way and make adjustments as needed.

Let's practice this test with a few images and discuss the implications for when we are communicating with data.

For each of the following, close your eyes for a moment, then open them and look at the picture, paying attention to where your eyes go first. Why is this, do you think? What learnings from this exercise can you generalize and apply to your data visualizations? Write a couple of sentences or short paragraph for each.

FIGURE 4.1a Where are your eyes drawn?

PRACTICE with COLE

FIGURE 4.1b Where are your eyes drawn?

FIGURE 4.1c Where are your eyes drawn?

FIGURE 4.1d Where are your eyes drawn?

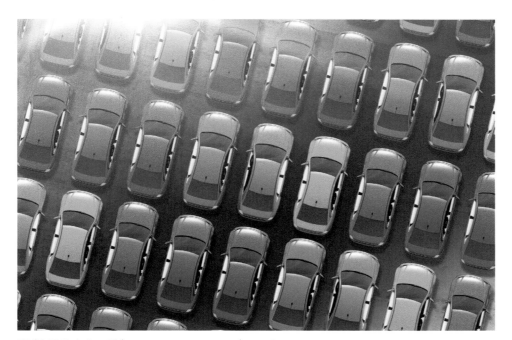

FIGURE 4.1e Where are your eyes drawn?

Solution 4.1: where are your eyes drawn?

I have a lot of fun with this test. It's interesting to see what things in our environment pull at our attention, and how we can generalize learnings from these observations. The following recounts where my eyes landed first in the preceding images and a few ideas for applying similar aspects when we communicate with data.

FIGURE 4.1a: My eyes immediately go to the speed limit sign on the right. This is for a number of reasons. The face of the sign is large compared to the rest of the elements in the picture. The big, bold, black number on white is striking. The red on the sign demands attention, both because it's very different from the background and because we are conditioned over time that red is often an alert to which we should pay attention. For someone who is red-green colorblind, however, red likely won't have the same effect. That's one of the reasons it can be useful to have some redundancy of signals to direct attention and make sure everyone in your audience can fully see what you are showing. Finally, there's a white outline at the edge of the sign that sets it apart from the background.

Let's consider how we can apply these elements to our data visualizations and the pages that contain them. Size, typeface, color, enclosure: these are all elements that, when used sparingly, indicate relative importance to our audience, signaling them where to look.

FIGURE 4.1b: My eyes go to the sun, then to the car, and then back to the sun again. When I focus on the sun, I can see the car in my peripheral vision. If I shift my focus to the car, I can still see the bright sun out of the corner of my eye. In applying learnings to data visualization, we should be aware of the tension that is introduced when we emphasize multiple things simultaneously in a graph or on a slide.

FIGURE 4.1c: My eyes landed first on the Queens Bronx sign. This happened due to a few reasons. It's crisp compared to some blurred elements in the photo. The sun is shining on this sign in a way that highlights it. It's larger than the other signs. Because of the large size and relatively fewer words, there is also more blank space, which really makes it stand out against the busy background. It appears first in the arrangement of the signs, so I find that my eyes go there initially, then continue rightward. Also take note of the various preattentive attributes to make things stand out in different ways on the signs themselves: bold, all caps, arrows, color (yellow). Speaking of color, the Exit Only portion of the Staten Island sign is also attention grabbing. There's a lot going on in this picture, which can complicate the process of getting everyone to look at the same thing first. Still, there are things to be learned from this.

How can we apply similar aspects when we visualize data? Keep key elements crisp and legible. Highlight strategically to make one thing in a row of similar things stand out. Make more important things bigger (and as a corollary: size things of similar importance consistently). Be conscious of how we organize elements on a page and try to do so in a way that draws our audience's eyes how we would like them to move.

FIGURE 4.1d: My eyes go immediately to the yellow car. Do me a favor and flip back to Figure 4.1d and do the exercise again. Notice both where your eyes go first and where they go *next*. Mine land on the car, then follow the road downward to the left. Other people may look at the car, then continue along the curvy road upward to the right. We didn't spend much time looking at the trees in the upper left or bottom right.

When we think about our graphs and slides, we want to be aware of how we are directing attention—either intentionally or inadvertently. Make sure you aren't accidentally directing your audience's attention away from something at which you want them to look.

FIGURE 4.1e: My eyes had trouble landing on anything in this colorful collection of cars. They bounced around from blue to yellow to red. Colorful is a good goal for a car dealership who wants to have the right color auto for everyone, but it's not a great goal when visualizing data. By making so many things different, we actually lose the potential strategic preattentive value of color. With so many shades, it's difficult to create sufficient contrast to focus our audience's eyes. Color used sparingly is one of the most effective ways to direct our audience's attention to where we want them to look. Check out Figure 4.1f for evidence.

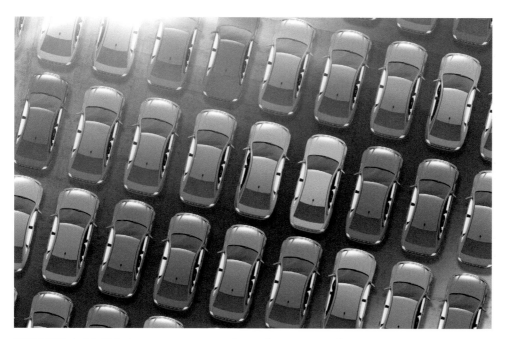

FIGURE 4.1f Where are your eyes drawn?

Exercise 4.2: focus on...

Let's continue to explore how we can focus attention and apply some of the learnings from Exercise 4.1 to graphs. When we visualize data, there are often various takeaways that we could highlight. It can sometimes be useful to show the same graph multiple times, each instance highlighting the point or points we want to focus on as we walk our audience through different nuances of the data. This allows them to know exactly where to look in the data as we are talking, or when they are reading corresponding text. Let's practice how we can achieve this with a specific example.

See the following visual, which shows year-over-year change ("YoY," measured as percent change in dollar sales volume) for cat food brands from a pet food manufacturer. Answer the following questions, download the data, and employ the strategies you outline in your tool.

FIGURE 4.2a Let's focus attention in this graph

QUESTION 1: Let's say you will be presenting this data live and want to begin by talking about the Lifestyle brand line: Lifestyle, Diet Lifestyle, and Lifestyle Plus. How would you visually indicate to your audience to look at those points of data?

QUESTION 2: Assume you next want to talk about the Feline brand group, which includes all of the brands with "Feline" in their name. The branding for this line of cat food has a purple logo. How would you indicate to your audience that they should focus here?

QUESTION 3: Next, you want to discuss the brands that had year-over-year declines. How could you draw your audience's attention there?

QUESTION 4: Let's imagine that within the declining brands, you want to talk specifically about the two brands that declined the most: Fran's Recipe and Wholesome Goodness. How might you achieve this?

QUESTION 5: Assume you want to talk about the brands that had year-over-year increases in sales. How would you draw your audience's attention there? What is similar to how you directed attention to the decreasing brands? Would you do anything different in comparison?

QUESTION 6: You want to create a final comprehensive view to be distributed that highlights each of the takeaways outlined previously: Lifestyle brands, Feline brands, decreasing brands (differentiating those decreasing most), and increasing brands (highlighting those that increased most). How would you achieve this? How would you pair this with explanatory text and make it clear how the text relates to the data?

PRACTICE *with* COLE

Solution 4.2: focus on...

We have a couple of elements at our disposal when it comes to drawing attention in this exercise: the data itself, and also the data labels that list the various brands. Color and bold type will be my primary tools for directing focus in this example. In my illustrations, I'm also going to use the title text to briefly describe the takeaway I'm highlighting, moving some of the original detail it contained into the subtitle.

QUESTION 1: When it comes to highlighting the Lifestyle brands, I decided to make those data points and the labels that go with them black, plus bold the label text. Other colors would work, too, but in the absence of much other context, I chose to stay neutral in this initial view. We'll look at more ways to use color and related considerations as we get further into this solution.

So that the specific data points really stand out, I made the other data and labels a slightly lighter shade of grey. I also used title text in matching black bold to briefly call out the takeaway.

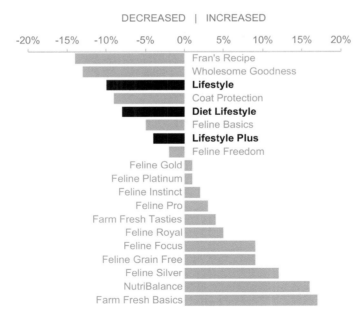

FIGURE 4.2b   Focus on Lifestyle brand line

QUESTION 2: Given the purple brand color, I could use this to emphasize the Feline line of brands, again pairing with bold brand labels and a matching graph title. We are using the preattentive attribute of hue, or color, to direct attention and the Gestalt principle of similarity (of color) to tie the spatially separated elements together. When it comes to other Gestalt principles, we might consider using position and put all of the Feline brands at the top of the graph; however, that would interfere with the thoughtful ordering and make the graph more difficult to understand.

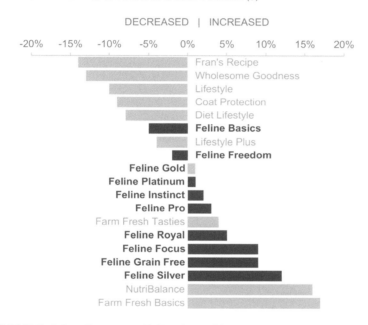

Cat food brands: **most in Feline line increased**
YEAR-OVER-YEAR % CHANGE IN SALES VOLUME ($)

FIGURE 4.2c Focus on Feline brand line

QUESTION 3: To draw attention to the brands that had decreases in year-over-year sales, I might choose a color that reinforces this negative point. I tend to avoid red and green for bad and good connotation, respectively, because of the inaccessibility for those who are colorblind (red/green colorblindness is the most prevalent, affecting nearly 10% of the population). I'll often use orange for negative and blue for positive, as I feel you still get the desired connotation. See Figure 4.2d, which uses orange to highlight the decreasing brands. In addition to the graph title, data points, and brand labels, I also made the Decreased title at the top orange. I chose not to bold the data labels, because I felt sufficient attention was already drawn by making them orange and the bold felt a little excessive.

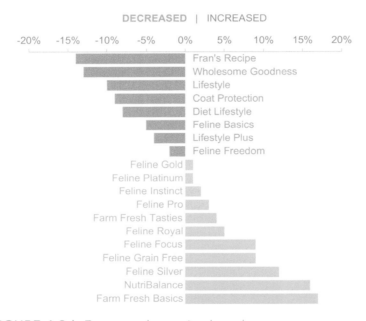

FIGURE 4.2d Focus on decreasing brands

QUESTION 4: To draw attention to the two brands that decreased the most, I could make those orange and everything else grey. If I'm progressing to this point from the view in Figure 4.2d, however, I could do this another way: keep all the decreasing brands orange, but vary intensity to draw attention to the two that decreased the most. See Figure 4.2e.

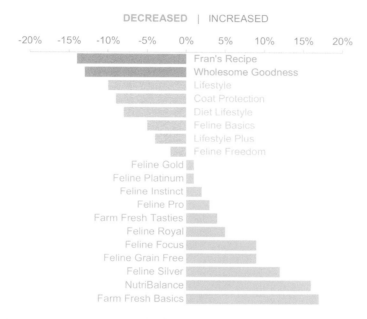

Cat food brands: 2 brands decreased the most
YEAR-OVER-YEAR % CHANGE IN SALES VOLUME ($)

FIGURE 4.2e Focus on the brands that most decreased

PRACTICE *with* COLE

QUESTION 5: To draw attention to brands having increasing sales, I could use blue, for the reasons described in my response to Question 3. See Figure 4.2f.

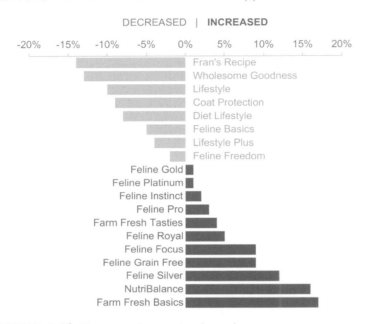

Cat food brands: **11 brands flat to increasing**
YEAR-OVER-YEAR % CHANGE IN SALES VOLUME ($)

FIGURE 4.2f   Focus on increasing brands

QUESTION 6: Finally, if I want to pull a number of these observations together, I might do so in two comprehensive slides. This would allow those processing the information on their own to get a similar progression to what I'd show in a live setting. Note that my text is mostly descriptive (or fabricated!)—ideally we'd have additional context on what drove the changes we're seeing, and perhaps related information to share, or a specific point to make or discussion to drive.

To me, this felt like too much to pack into a single slide, so I broke it into two views of the data in order to highlight everything that we did step by step previously. See Figures 4.2g and 4.2h.

PRACTICE with COLE

Cat food brands: **mixed results in sales year-over-year**
YEAR-OVER-YEAR % CHANGE IN SALES VOLUME ($)

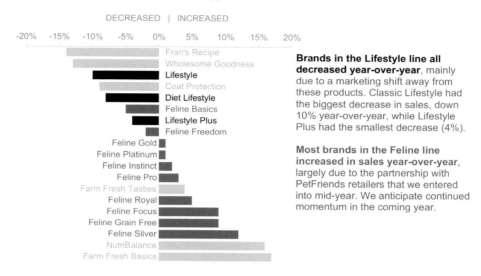

Brands in the Lifestyle line all decreased year-over-year, mainly due to a marketing shift away from these products. Classic Lifestyle had the biggest decrease in sales, down 10% year-over-year, while Lifestyle Plus had the smallest decrease (4%).

Most brands in the Feline line increased in sales year-over-year, largely due to the partnership with PetFriends retailers that we entered into mid-year. We anticipate continued momentum in the coming year.

FIGURE 4.2g   Comprehensive slide #1: Lifestyle and Feline brands

Cat food brands: **mixed results in sales year-over-year**
YEAR-OVER-YEAR % CHANGE IN SALES VOLUME ($)

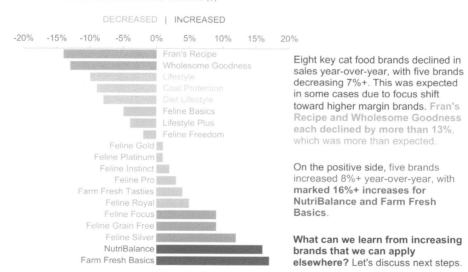

Eight key cat food brands declined in sales year-over-year, with five brands decreasing 7%+. This was expected in some cases due to focus shift toward higher margin brands. **Fran's Recipe and Wholesome Goodness each declined by more than 13%,** which was more than expected.

On the positive side, five brands increased 8%+ year-over-year, with **marked 16%+ increases for NutriBalance and Farm Fresh Basics.**

What can we learn from increasing brands that we can apply elsewhere? Let's discuss next steps.

FIGURE 4.2h   Comprehensive slide #2: decreasing and increasing brands

Exercise 4.3: direct attention many ways

As we saw in Exercise 4.2, color used sparingly can work well to direct our audience's attention to where we want them to look. But color is not the only visual element we can use to do this. More broadly, preattentive attributes are hugely important tools in our toolkit when it comes to creating effective visual designs. In addition to color (hue), these are things like size, position, and intensity that—when used thoughtfully and sparingly—help us to create contrast and direct our audience's attention. In other words, there are a lot of different attributes of our visual designs that we can play with to achieve this, and various circumstances or constraints may cause us to employ different strategies. Let's look at a specific example and explore the numerous ways we could indicate to our audience where we want them to look.

Check out the following graph, which shows conversion rate over time by acquisition channel. Assume you'd like to draw your audience's attention to the Referral line. How could you use preattentive attributes to do so? **How many different ways can you come up with to focus your audience's attention?** List them! To take it a step further, apply the strategies you've listed using your tool of choice.

Conversion rate over time

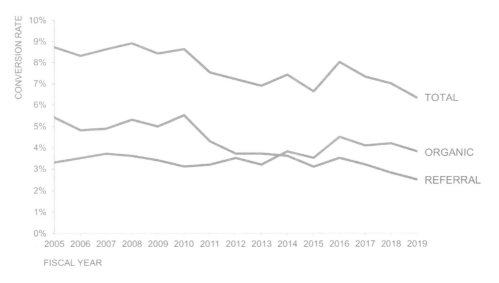

FIGURE 4.3a How could we focus attention on the Referral line in this graph?

Solution 4.3: direct attention many ways

I'm going to illustrate *15 ways* to indicate to my audience that I'd like them to focus on the Referral trend. Is your list shorter than this? If so, go back and see if you can generate a couple more ideas.

Ready? Let's check out the various ways we could direct attention. We'll start with a few brute force options, then get more nuanced from there.

1. Arrow. We could use an arrow to literally point to our audience what we'd like them to look at: the Referral line.

Conversion rate over time

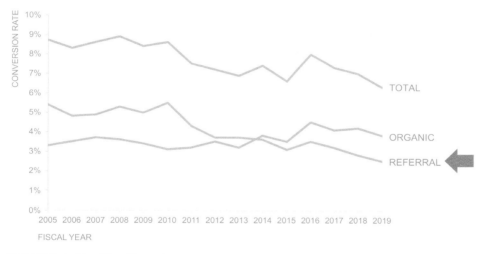

FIGURE 4.3b The "look here" arrow

2. Circle. We could circle the Referral line. Yes, this is another blunt tool. When it comes to the arrow and the circle—I love and hate these approaches with equal measure. I love the fact that it means someone looked at the data and said "I would like you to look *here*" and then did something to make that happen. The challenge is that the arrow, the circle—these are elements that we've added and, in and of themselves, carry no informative value. So from that standpoint, they add clutter. Still, they are better than nothing: I'd rather have a blunt tool that indicates to my audience where they should pay attention than nothing at all. But even better if I can find some aspect of the data to change to create this emphasis.

PRACTICE *with* COLE

PRACTICE with COLE

Conversion rate over time

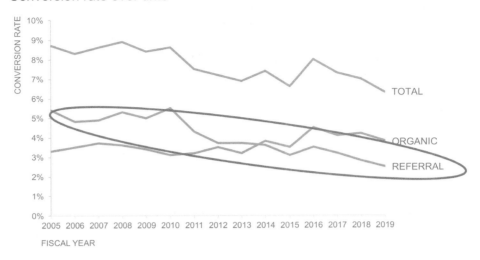

FIGURE 4.3c Circle the data

3. Transparent white boxes. Let's look at one more brute force method before we get more elegant: transparent white boxes. This method can be useful if you ever have to take a screenshot from a tool and don't have the ability to change the design of the data. Use transparent white boxes to cover up everything you want to push to the background. This has the effect of reducing the intensity of everything that is covered, while leaving what you want to draw attention to in full intensity. See Figure 4.3d.

Conversion rate over time

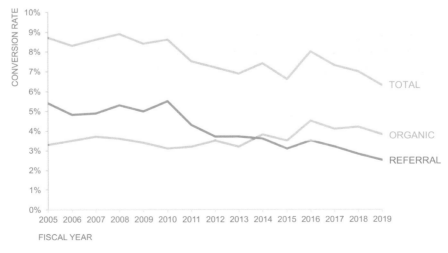

FIGURE 4.3d Cover everything else up with transparent white boxes

Depending on the shape of your data, you may have to use multiple boxes or other shapes to fully cover. If you look closely at Figure 4.3d, I didn't do a perfect job—near where the lines overlap in the middle of the graph, the Organic line didn't fully get covered. Figure 4.3e outlines my various transparent white boxes (some of them rotated to better fit the data) in black so you can see the monkeying that has to happen at times to make this work well.

Conversion rate over time

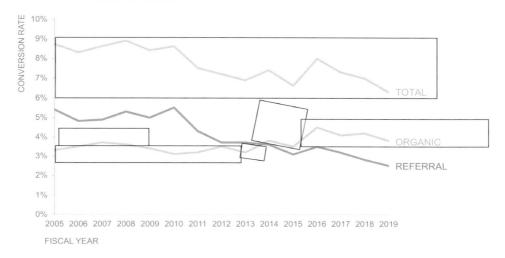

FIGURE 4.3e Highlighting the transparent white boxes

This is another brute force method, but depending on your constraints it can sometimes be useful. Next, let's look at some more elegant approaches for directing attention.

4. Thicken the line. We could make the Referral line thicker or the others thinner or a combination of these. We can also manipulate the word "Referral." In this case, I've also thickened it by making the text bold. See Figure 4.3f.

PRACTICE *with* COLE

Conversion rate over time

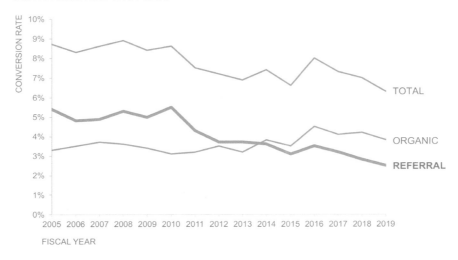

FIGURE 4.3f Thicken the line

5. Change the line style. Varying line style is another way to signal that something is different and direct attention. Dashed or dotted lines are super attention grabbing when they appear together with solid lines. The challenge is that from a cognitive burden standpoint, we've taken what could have been a single element (a line) and chopped it into many pieces. This adds some visual noise. Because of this, I recommend reserving the use of dotted lines for when there is uncertainty to depict: a forecast, a prediction, or a target or goal of some sort. In these cases, the visual sense of uncertainty that you get with the dotted line makes up for the additional visual clutter it introduces.

Conversion rate over time

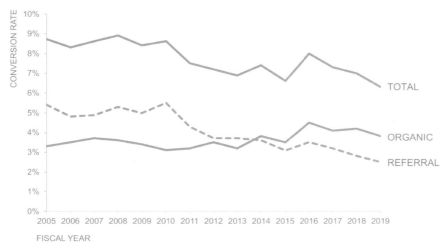

FIGURE 4.3g Change the line style

6. Leverage intensity. We can make the line we want to emphasize darker in color. See Figure 4.3h.

Conversion rate over time

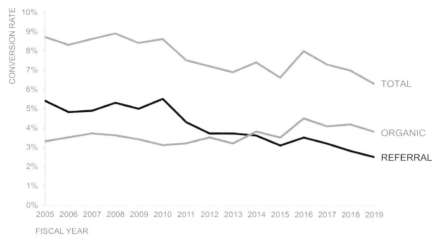

FIGURE 4.3h Make it darker

7. Position in front of other data. Position is another preattentive attribute. We can't change the order of the data when it comes to a line graph—it is where it is because of the data it plots. But we can take steps to ensure it doesn't fall behind other data. Take note of Figure 4.3h in the middle of the graph, where the grey Organic line crosses in front of Referral. We can pull the latter forward to correct this (this is typically dictated by the data series order, which you can modify in most tools). See Figure 4.3i.

Conversion rate over time

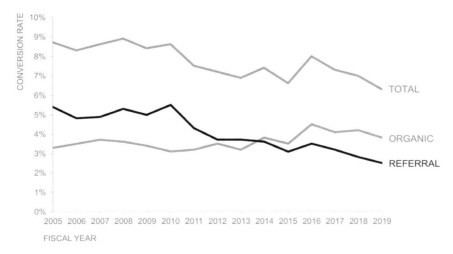

FIGURE 4.3i Position in front of other data

8. Change the hue. We can change the hue, or color, of the line we want our audience to focus on, leaving everything else grey. See Figure 4.3j.

Conversion rate over time

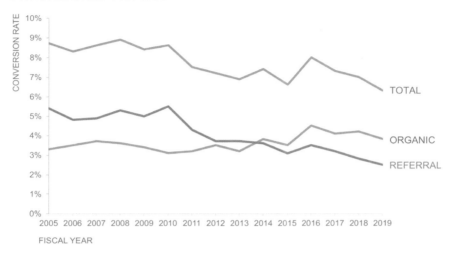

FIGURE 4.3j Change the hue

9. Use words to prime audience. In Figure 4.3k, I've added a takeaway to the title about the Referral data. Once my audience reads this, they know to look for the Referral line in the graph. We'll look at more examples of takeaway titles when we talk about words in the context of story in Chapter 6.

Conversion rate over time: Referral decreasing markedly since 2010

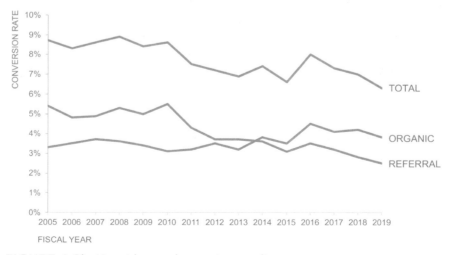

FIGURE 4.3k Use title words to prime audience

10. Eliminate the other data. One way to get the audience to focus on the data we want them to look at would be to eliminate all the other data, making it the only line at which they *can* look. You should always ask yourself whether you need all of the data you are showing. But also consider: any time you debate removing data, what context you lose when you do so and whether this tradeoff makes sense given what you need to communicate.

Conversion rate over time

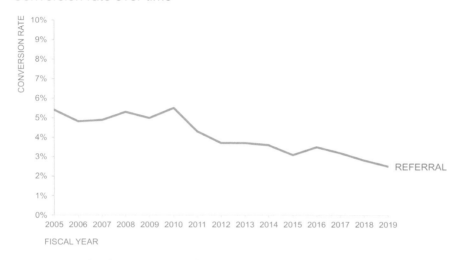

FIGURE 4.3l Eliminate the other data

11. Animate to appear. Though difficult to show in a static book, motion is the most attention-grabbing preattentive attribute and can work very well in a live setting (where you are presenting the graph and can flip through various views). Imagine we start with an empty graph that only has the x- and y-axes. Then we could add a line representing the Total conversion rate and discuss. Next, I could layer on the Organic conversion rate and talk about that. Finally, I could add the Referral line. The simple fact of it not being there and then appearing would garner attention.

The challenge with motion is that it's also easily annoying. The only animation I recommend is appear, disappear, and transparency. No flying, bouncing, or fading—these add glitz without value and are another form of visual clutter.

12. Add data markers. Reverting back to showing all the data, we can add data markers to draw attention. See Figure 4.3m.

Conversion rate over time

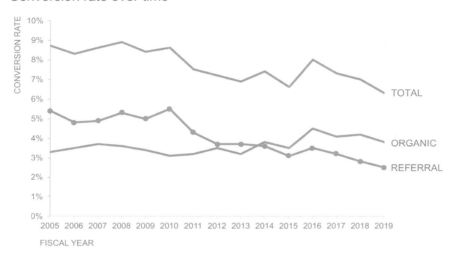

FIGURE 4.3m Add data markers

13. Add data labels. Taking it a step further, we could also add data labels to the various points on the line we want to emphasize. This is a way of saying to our audience, "Hey, this part of the data is so important, I even added some numbers there to help you interpret it." See Figure 4.3n. Text annotations that explain additional context or point out nuances in the data you want your audience to focus on can achieve a similar effect.

Conversion rate over time

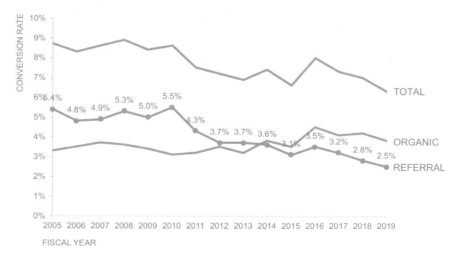

FIGURE 4.3n Add data labels

When we add data markers and data labels to every single data point, we can sometimes end up with a cluttered mess. That said, when we are sparing about which points we choose to put markers and labels on, we can direct our audience to make certain comparisons within the data. Let's check out an example of this next.

14. Employ end markers and labels. By putting end markers and labels on each line, as I've done in Figure 4.3o, one easy and obvious comparison for my audience to make is how the different conversion rates compare to each other as of the most recent point of data. This doesn't draw attention to the Referral line specifically, but we'll do that again in our next step.

Conversion rate over time

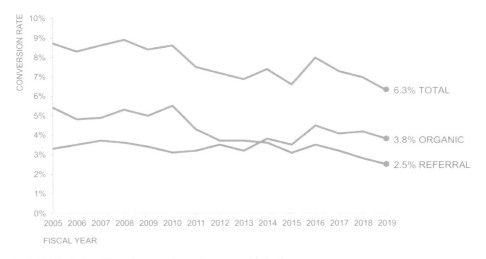

FIGURE 4.3o Employ end markers and labels

15. Combine multiple preattentive attributes. We can use multiple preattentive attributes to really make it clear where we want our audience to look. In Figure 4.3p, I've used words in the title to prime my audience (making them the same color as the data they describe, leveraging the Gestalt principle of similarity), and I can make the line I want my audience to pay attention to thicker, colored, add data markers and data labels. Annotations can also help explain additional context for the data of interest.

PRACTICE *with* COLE

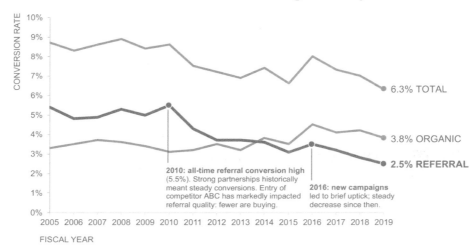

FIGURE 4.3p Combine multiple preattentive attributes

Practice the "Where are your eyes drawn?" test with Figure 4.3p. Where do your eyes go first? Where do they go next? What about after that?

When I close my eyes and then open them and look at Figure 4.3p, my eyes go first to the title text in red. Then they jump down to the red line in the graph. I move to the right and can easily compare the most recent data point (2019) between Referral conversion rate and Organic and Total. I can move my eyes leftwards to read additional detail via the annotations of what is driving some of what is being shown. In this way, I've used preattentive attributes to both direct attention and create visual hierarchy, making my overall visual easier for my audience to consume. Success!

Exercise 4.4: visualize *all* the data

Let's revisit an example we looked at in Chapter 2. You may recall the scenario where you work at Financial Savings and want to compare your bank's performance against your peers'. You have data on bank index (branch satisfaction) over time for your bank plus a number of your competitors. The original graph is shown in Figure 4.4a.

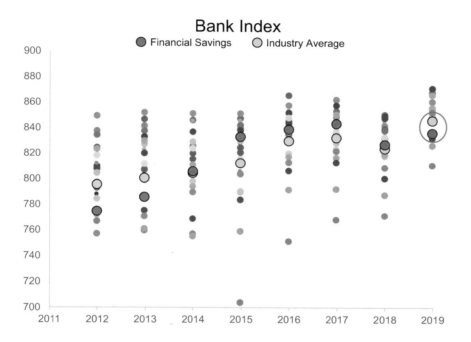

FIGURE 4.4a Bank index

We previously looked at an approach where we changed from this dot plot to a line graph and summarized all of the competitor data with a single average line (see Solution 2.7).

But what if we want to show all the data? How could we achieve this without it being overwhelming? Download the data and create your preferred view.

Solution 4.4: visualize *all* the data

We can get away with showing quite a lot of data if we push most of it to the background.

I've had people tell me at workshops before that they didn't realize the power of grey. This muted color works well for things that need to be present (axis labels, axis titles, non-message-impacting data) but don't need to draw a ton of attention. Check out how the strategic use of grey in Figure 4.4b helps us in this case.

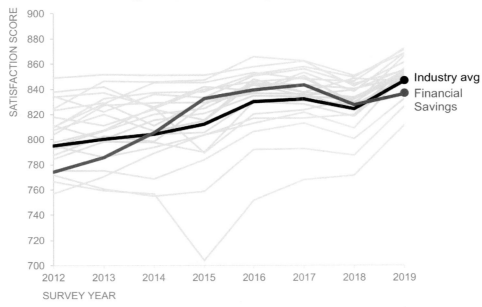

BRANCH SATISFACTION
Financial Savings below **industry** for first time in 5 years

FIGURE 4.4b   Can show all the data if we push most of it to the background

In addition to making the competitor banks grey, I also made the lines for that data thinner than both the Industry average and Financial Savings. This is another means for de-emphasizing them, so they are there for reference but not drawing attention. If there's an individual competitor bank we want to identify, that becomes difficult (we could cycle through various competitors through sparing emphasis in a live presentation, or label possibly one or two in a static view, though you can imagine how this will quickly get messy). If Financial Savings versus specific competitors is important, then this isn't the best way to look at this data. In that case, I could focus on just the latest data point across the various banks and plot as a single horizontal bar chart.

But sticking with this view, let's take things a step further. Say that within all of this and in addition to directing attention to the Industry average and Financial Savings, we want to make a point about the recent year. I can use an additional color to achieve this: see Figure 4.4c.

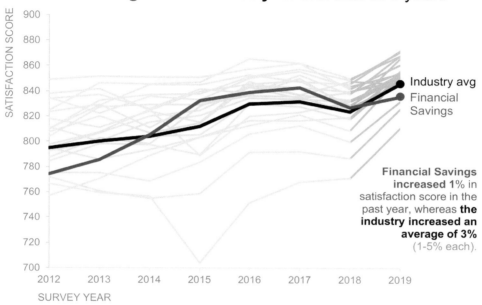

BRANCH SATISFACTION

Financial Savings below **industry** for first time in 5 years

FIGURE 4.4c Could focus on latest year-to-year period of time

Sparing emphasis allows us to direct attention even when showing a lot of data. Consider how you can employ this tactic in your own work.

Now that you've seen me solve some exercises related to focusing attention, let's shift to exercises for you to tackle on your own.

PRACTICE *with* COLE

Let's look at more pictures to understand the subtleties of what garners attention and how we can utilize those dimensions when communicating. There's not a single way to do this — there are many, which we'll continue to explore in the following exercises.

Exercise 4.5: where are your eyes drawn?

As we've seen, observing where our eyes land first in a graph or on a slide can help us determine whether we're using our preattentive attributes strategically to direct attention to the most important part and create clear visual hierarchy. Let's do some additional practice with this simple test.

Consider the following visuals. **For each, close your eyes or look away, then look back at it and take note of where your eyes go first.** Why is this? What can you learn from this activity that you can generalize to how to effectively communicate with data? Write a short paragraph answering these questions for each image.

FIGURE 4.5a   Where are your eyes drawn?

FIGURE 4.5b Where are your eyes drawn?

PRACTICE on your OWN

FIGURE 4.5c Where are your eyes drawn?

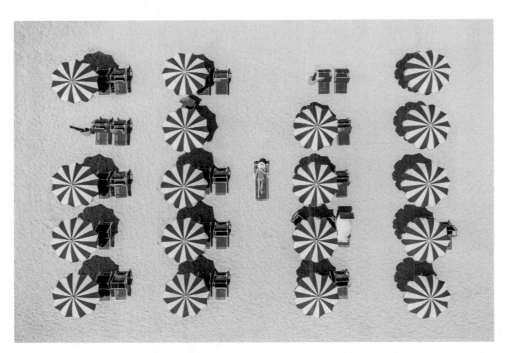

FIGURE 4.5d Where are your eyes drawn?

FIGURE 4.5e Where are your eyes drawn?

FIGURE 4.5f Where are your eyes drawn?

PRACTICE on your OWN

Exercise 4.6: focus within tabular data

While the examples that we've looked at in this chapter so far have all been images and graphs, we can use preattentive attributes to direct attention in tables, too.

Check out the following table, which shows data about the latest four weeks of sales for the top ten sales accounts for a popular brand of coffee. Answer the following questions.

WakeUp Coffee

Top 10 accounts: 4-week sales ending January 31st

Account	Sales Volume	% Change vs prior	Avg # of UPCs	% ACV Selling	Price per Pound
A	$15,753	3.60%	1.15	98	$10.43
B	$294,164	3.20%	1.75	83	$15.76
C	$21,856	-1.20%	1.00	84	$12.74
D	$547,265	5.60%	1.10	89	$9.45
E	$18,496	-4.70%	1.00	92	$14.85
F	$43,986	-2.40%	2.73	92	$12.86
G	$86,734	10.60%	1.00	100	$17.32
H	$11,645	37.90%	1.00	85	$11.43
I	$11,985	-0.70%	1.00	22	$20.82
J	$190,473	-8.70%	1.00	72	$11.24

UPC is the Universal Product Code, the barcode symbology.

ACV is All-Commodity Volume, measured as a percentage from 0 to 100.

FIGURE 4.6 Practice focusing attention within this table

QUESTION 1: Let's assume Sales Volume is the most important data in this table and that the rest of the data is there for additional context or because we know people in our audience will want to see it. We've already positioned it as the first column of data, but what else can we do to direct attention or make this data easier to process?

QUESTION 2: Account D is much bigger in terms of sales volume than any of the other accounts, yet it takes some time staring at this table to figure that out. How could we draw our audience's attention to Account D more quickly? List three specific strategies you could use to set this row apart from the rest. Which do you like best and why?

QUESTION 3: Let's continue with our focus on Account D. What if, within Account D, we wanted to highlight the low Price per Pound? How could you achieve this?

QUESTION 4: Let's reset and say you want to focus attention on the relative Price per Pound within this table. Does this change where you would position this column or how you might order the rows of data? What are three different ways you could indicate to your audience you want them to focus here?

QUESTION 5: Make the changes you've outlined. Download the data and tackle in the tool of your choice.

Exercise 4.7: direct attention many ways

As we've discussed, we have many options for indicating to our audience where they should pay attention in the data we show.

Take the following example, which shows market share over time for a given product. Let's assume we want to direct our audience's attention to Our Product. In what ways could you use preattentive attributes to do so? **How many different methods can you come up with to focus your audience's attention?** List them!

Market share over time

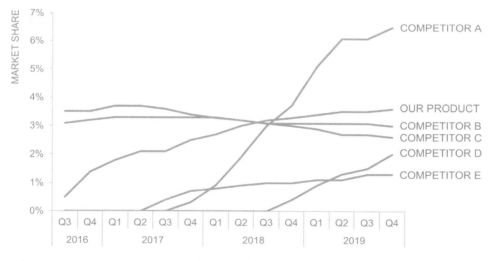

FIGURE 4.7 How could we direct attention to Our Product in this graph?

To take it a step further, download the data and apply the strategies you've listed using your tool of choice.

Exercise 4.8: how can we focus attention here?

You've practiced focusing attention with tables and lines; next let's take a stab at doing the same with bars.

Let's revisit an example from Chapter 2. Imagine you work for a regional health care center and want to assess the relative success of a recent flu vaccination education and administration program across your medical centers. Figure 4.8 is a slightly modified version of the original graph.

Let's assume we want to direct our audience's attention to those medical centers that are above average. In what ways could you use preattentive attributes to do so? **How many different methods can you come up with to focus your audience's attention?** List them!

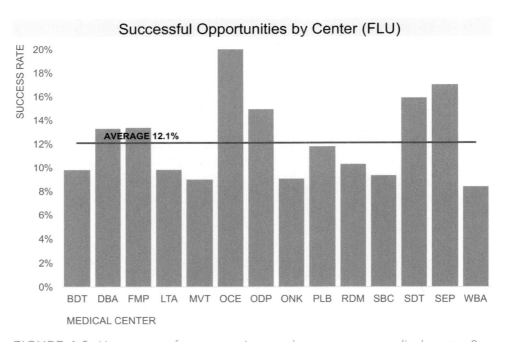

FIGURE 4.8 How can we focus attention on above average medical centers?

To take it a step further, download the data and practice applying the various ways you've listed for directing attention in your tool.

PRACTICE at WORK

To focus attention, we need to know how to modify various dimensions of our graphs in our tools— and figure out where to focus in the first place.

The following exercises will help you direct attention in your visual communications.

Exercise 4.9: where are your eyes drawn?

Your eyes and attention are a good initial proxy for your audience. After you create a graph or a slide, close your eyes or look away. Look back at it, taking note of where your eyes land first. Is this consistent with the place you want your audience to focus their attention first and foremost? If not, what changes can you make to achieve this? Consider how you are using preattentive attributes sparingly both to direct attention and create visual hierarchy.

Recognize, however, that since you are the one who designed the data, you already know things about it and are predisposed to focus on certain aspects in ways that your audience may not. Given this, after you've practiced the "Where are your eyes drawn?" test and iterated as needed to be happy with the result, solicit the assistance of someone else. Grab a friend or colleague and show them your graph or slide and ask *them* where their eyes go first. Is it to the place you want? Use this information to continue to iterate as needed.

Beyond where their eyes go first, have them talk you through how they process the information. What do they pay attention to first? After that? And then? What questions do they have? What observations do they make? Understanding this from someone who isn't as close to the data and information will give you important insight into what is working and whether and how you can make changes so that your audience knows where to look and how to process the information you put in front of them.

Exercise 4.10: practice differentiating in your tool

There are many different tools that can be used to visualize data. Each comes with its own set of abilities and constraints. To be effective in the way we visualize and communicate with data, we need to get to know our tools well enough to apply the various strategies that are covered here and in *SWD*. In some cases, this might mean writing code. The beauty of code is that once you've written it, there are likely lines or chunks of it that you can repurpose later (win!). Or it may mean finding the right combination of drop-down menus and selections in your tool (that you have to either template or apply each time: that's okay, it gets quicker with experience).

In any case, let's practice getting to know our tool—and what we can do with it—a bit better.

Take a graph you have created. This can be anything. If you don't have a work example handy to use for this, you can select data from any of the exercises in this book to download and create a graph with which to play. Create a line graph or bar chart. Figure out how to achieve the following in your tool of choice.

Bold/thick: Pick a text element within your graph and make it bold. Make a single line or bar thicker than those around it.

Color: Start by making everything grey. Pick a single line or series of bars and make them blue. Pick another and make it match your organization's primary brand color. Figure out how to take an individual data point—a point in a line graph or a single bar in a series—and change the color of just that point.

Position: Let's practice moving things around. If you are working with a bar chart, reorder the bars: make them ascending and then descending. If you are working with a line graph and have lines that cross each other, pick one and figure out how to move it in front of or behind the others.

Dotted or dashed line: Are there any lines in what you're showing that you can make dotted or dashed? I bet there are. If you are working with a line graph, figure out how to change the line style of one of the lines. If faced with a bar chart, determine how you could do this for the outline of one (or more) of the bars.

Intensity: Vary intensity by rendering some data in full intensity and the rest in a lesser intensity. You can do this by applying transparency, a pattern, or simply picking a less intense color. Consider both how you can do this by modifying the formatting of the data directly, as well as whether or how you could use transparent boxes or other shapes to achieve this effect in a brute force manner.

Label data points: Start by adding labels to an entire data series. Next, figure out how to move them around. On a line graph, position the labels above the data series, then below. In a bar chart, label them on top of bars, then pull the labels inside the ends of the bars. Next, determine how you'd approach it if you only wanted to label a single data point (or a couple of data points). If you're using a graphing application (not writing code) there are brute force solutions for adding one at a time or deleting individual labels. You might add another series of data (and make it invisible but use the positioning for labels, as one example) to streamline your process.

What else do you want to learn how to do in your tool? Make a list and determine what resources (colleagues, smart online searches, perhaps classes or tutorials) can help you achieve your goals. Learning any tool takes time. But it is nearly always time well spent. There is no better satisfaction than when you can use your tool to fully meet your needs!

PRACTICE *at* WORK

Exercise 4.11: figure out where to focus

SWD and this book generally make a big assumption: you've thoroughly analyzed your data and already have something specific that you want to communicate to your audience. I tend to draw a distinction between exploratory analysis and explanatory analysis, and assume that the former has been done and focus on teaching the latter. This sometimes leads to the question: how do you figure out where to focus in the first place?

This is a harder piece to teach and is as much art and science as what we focus on here with explanatory communication. While I characterize exploratory and explanatory as distinct phases, in reality there isn't a solid line between the two. Often, we cycle back and forth through each over the course of a project. When it comes to the "Where do I focus?" query, there are some questions you can ask yourself to help navigate. Consider the following (incomplete) list.

- When is it appropriate to aggregate the data?

- When and how should you disaggregate the data?

- What is the right time frame to consider? How far back should you go?

- How does it make sense to break the data down? Look at things by line of business, region, product, tenure, or other categories. Where are things similar? Where are they different? Why is that?

- Do things align with what you expect? In what instances are they different?

- How do different things relate to each other? Do some things drive others?

- What comparisons are meaningful or will lead to potential insight?

- What context may be useful that you don't have? Who can you ask about this?

- What questions could someone else looking at this data have?

- What assumptions are you making? How big of a deal is it if those assumptions are wrong?

- What is missing? Data doesn't typically tell the whole story. How can you address or understand the missing pieces?

- Is history likely to be the same or different as the future?

Exercise 4.12: let's discuss

Consider the following questions related to Chapter 4 lessons and exercises. Discuss with a partner or group.

1. What design elements do we have at our disposal for directing attention when visualizing and communicating with data? Which do you find most effective and why?

2. What is the "Where are your eyes drawn?" test? When and why would you use it?

3. There are numerous ways to direct attention in text, tables, points, lines, and bars. What are common ways to indicate to your audience where you want them to focus? How are the means by which you can achieve this across various graph types different?

4. What things are important to keep in mind when choosing the color(s) you use in your graphs? Are there any color combinations you will embrace or avoid going forward? Why is that?

5. How is sparing emphasis for explanatory communications different from how you would design a dashboard where the data is meant to be explored? How might you approach the use of color in a dashboard compared to when there is a specific takeaway you want to highlight?

6. What is visual hierarchy? Why is it useful to create visual hierarchy in your data visualizations and the pages that contain them?

7. Why does emphasis need to be sparing to be effective?

8. What is one specific goal you will set for yourself or your team related to the strategies outlined in this chapter? How can you hold yourself (or your team) accountable to this? Who will you turn to for feedback?

PRACTICE at WORK

think like
a designer

You know what great design looks like when you see it, but how do you actually achieve it—particularly if you don't consider yourself a designer? *SWD* covered four topics to help you think like a designer: affordances, aesthetics, accessibility, and acceptance. In this chapter, we'll practice applying these concepts and illustrate how minor changes can help take your visual from acceptable to exceptional. First, let's cover a quick reminder of what I mean by these terms.

In visual design, **affordances** are things we do to make it clear how to process what we show. This builds off of the lessons you've practiced in Chapters 3 and 4: tie related things visually together, push less important elements to the background, and bring the critical stuff forward. Direct your audience's attention intentionally to where you want them to look.

Spending time on the **aesthetics** of your visuals can translate into people taking more time with your work or having the patience to overlook issues. Attention to detail comes into play: often many seemingly minor components add up to create a great or poor experience. To achieve the former, we must edit ruthlessly.

People are each different, and **accessibility** means recognizing this and working to create designs that are usable by people of diverse skills and abilities. We've touched on colorblindness, but that only scratches the surface. We'll undertake exercises that will help you think about your designs more robustly. There is one simple thing that can help us improve the accessibility of our graphs broadly: using words wisely.

Finally, our visual designs only work if our audience **accepts** them and there are things we can do to make this more likely, which we'll explore.

Let's practice **thinking like a designer**!

First, we'll review the main lessons from *SWD* Chapter 5.

SWD BOOK CHAPTER 5

FIRST, LET'S RECAP
THINK *like* a DESIGNER

FORM *follows* FUNCTION

 1 FUNCTION

WHAT do you want to ENABLE your AUDIENCE to <u>DO</u> with your DATA?

 2 FORM

HOW can you BEST VISUALIZE to allow for this with EASE?

AFFORDANCES

ASPECTS of the DESIGN that make it OBVIOUS HOW to USE

GRATE HERE

HOLD HERE

Highlight the important stuff and eliminate distractions (at **most** 10% of the overall design)

FOCUS HERE

GRAPHIC DESIGN AFFORDANCES

Bold   CASE   Size
italics   typeface color
<u>underlining</u>   **inversing**

"You know you've achieved perfection, not when you have nothing left to add, but when you have nothing left to take away."

Antoine de Saint-Exupery

ACCESSIBILITY

DESIGN that is USABLE by PEOPLE of WIDELY VARYING TECHNICAL SKILLS

1. Make it LEGIBLE
2. Keep it CLEAN
3. Use PLAIN LANGUAGE
4. Remove UNNECCESSARY COMPLEXITY

AESTHETICS

More VISUALLY APPEALING DESIGNS are PERCEIVED as EASIER to USE and are MORE READILY ACCEPTED

Is it necessary to "make it pretty?" ...YES!

1. Be smart with color
2. Pay attention to alignment
3. Leverage white space

ACCEPTANCE

For your DESIGN to be EFFECTIVE, it must be ACCEPTED by the INTENDED AUDIENCE

What if they resist change?

1. Articulate the benefits
2. Show the side-by-side
3. Provide multiple options or seek input
4. Get a vocal audience member on board

PRACTICE with COLE

| 5.1 use words wisely | 5.2 do it better! | 5.3 pay attention to detail & design intuitively | 5.4 design in style |

PRACTICE on your OWN

| 5.5 examine and emulate | 5.6 make minor changes for major impact | 5.7 how could we improve this? | 5.8 brand this! |

PRACTICE at WORK

| 5.9 make data accessible with words | 5.10 create visual hierarchy | 5.11 pay attention to detail! | 5.12 design more accessibly |

| 5.13 garner acceptance for your designs | 5.14 let's discuss |

The words we pair with our graphs are important for making them comprehensible. We'll start with an exercise highlighting this, then practice using other aspects of design to improve our visuals, including paying attention to detail and incorporating branding.

Exercise 5.1: use words wisely

When we communicate with data, people sometimes have the false belief that words have no place or should be kept to a minimum. But words play a critical role in making the numbers and graphs that we use to communicate data understandable to our audience. The text we put on our graphs helps people comprehend what they are seeing and can assist in shaping their perceptions about the data.

Let's do a quick exercise to illustrate the importance of words on graphs.

Study Figure 5.1a, which shows sales over time for four brands of laundry detergent. There are already words on this graph: but are there enough? Could we use words more wisely? Consider these questions as you look at the data, then complete the following steps.

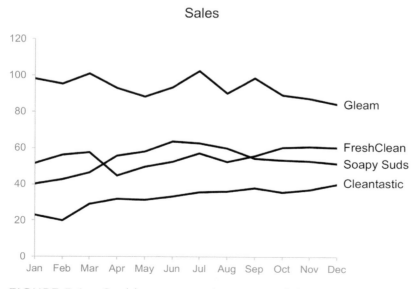

FIGURE 5.1a   Could we use words more wisely?

STEP 1: What questions do you have about the data shown in Figure 5.1a? List them! What assumptions would you have to make to interpret this data?

STEP 2: What words could you add to this graph to answer the questions you raised in Step 1? Freely make additions and changes to title and label so that what is being shown is perfectly clear.

STEP 3: How could putting *different* words on this graph change the interpretation of the data? How can you change axis titles and other text to cause an alternate understanding of what this visual shows? What implications does this have for what words should be present on every graph? Write a paragraph or two summarizing your learnings from this exercise.

STEP 4: For hands-on practice, write on Figure 5.1a or download the data or graph. Either add text to the existing graph or create a new one in the tool of your choice, practicing using words wisely to make the information accessible.

Solution 5.1: use words wisely

When you create a graph, the details are almost always clear to you. The challenge is that they aren't necessarily obvious to your audience, who may have different expectations or understanding of the context. In absence of text to make the data comprehendible, your audience is left to make assumptions, just as you had to do in this exercise. Not only does this make you use more brainpower than necessary, but worse—those assumptions might be wrong!

Let me take you through my approach to this exercise to illustrate how choice of words can lead us to completely different interpretations of the data.

STEP 1: I have four main questions about this data.

- **What is graphed on the y-axis?** We know from the titles that it represents sales, but that's not nearly descriptive enough. Are these actual number of units sold? Or hundreds of units sold? Or perhaps this represents monetary sales: for example, thousands of dollars, or millions of pounds.

- **What is graphed on the x-axis?** The month labels clearly indicate time, but this doesn't tell us enough. What time period is this? Are we looking back at historical data, projecting into the future, or possibly some combination of the two?

- **What broader context do the four brands fit into?** Do they represent all four brands carried on a particular website or at a specific store? Are they the four main brands of a given manufacturer? Or are they the top or bottom four brands of some greater population?

- **What realm does this data represent?** Without any frame of reference, I could assume this is a robust representation (e.g. worldwide sales or US Sales). But it could be for some subsegment: a certain city, state, or region; a specific product line; a particular manufacturer; or a given chain of stores.

Consider how different perspectives answering the questions raised above could lead us to totally different interpretations of this data. Let's look at that more specifically next.

STEP 2: Figure 5.1b shows one way I could add words to this graph to answer the questions I raised in Step 1.

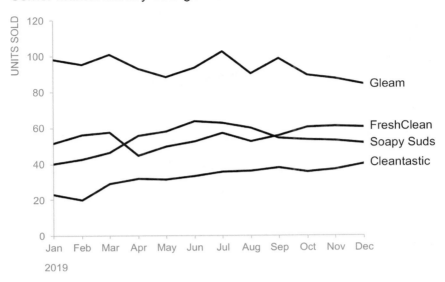

Corner Market laundry detergent sales

FIGURE 5.1b Clear title text aids understanding

In Figure 5.1b, I assumed these represent unit sales for the four brands of laundry detergent sold at a specific store. I made this clear through titling: substituting a more descriptive graph title and adding axis titles to both the y- and x-axes.

Let's review some specific design choices made with the text I added to this graph. I left-aligned the graph title. We've discussed the typical zigzagging "z" of information processing a couple of times already (in the solutions to exercises 2.1 and 3.4, as well as in *SWD*). As a reminder, without other visual cues, your audience will start at the top left of your graph and do zigzagging "z's" to take in the information. By orienting our graph title at the top left, our audience hits what they are looking at before they see the actual data. This is the same reason for orienting my axis titles at the top (y-axis) and left (x-axis).

I paid close attention to detail in the alignment of my axis titles, orienting the y-axis title to align with the top of the highest y-axis label, and the x-axis title is aligned at the left with the left-most axis label. I chose all caps for my y-axis titles (and will often do this for axis titles in general). Because capitalized letters are all the same height, this creates a neat rectangular shape (compared to what you'd get with mixed case: a jagged edge). I like the framing this lends to my graph. I also wrote the axis titles in grey text, so they are there to make it clear what we are looking at, but aren't drawing undue attention or distracting from the data.

STEP 3: Alternate words could lead to a totally different interpretation about what this data is and represents. See Figure 5.1c.

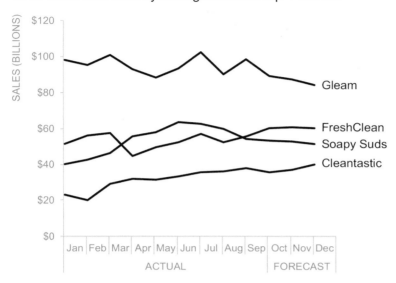

2019 worldwide laundry detergent sales: top 4 brands

SALES (BILLIONS)

Gleam

FreshClean
Soapy Suds
Cleantastic

Jan Feb Mar Apr May Jun Jul Aug Sep Oct Nov Dec

ACTUAL   FORECAST

FIGURE 5.1c Different text could lead to completely different interpretation

PRACTICE *with* COLE

This has implications for the words that should be present on every graph. I can generalize into a couple of guidelines. Every graph should have a title. When communicating with a slide deck, I use descriptive titles for my graphs and take-away titles for my slides (we'll talk more about the latter in Chapter 6). That's certainly not your only option, and we've looked at examples in this book where the graph title is both descriptive *and* highlights a takeaway. Be consistent in how you title with a given report or presentation.

Every axis should also have a title. Exceptions to this guideline are rare. Title explicitly so your audience doesn't have to spend their brainpower trying to figure out or make assumptions about what they are viewing.

Words make our visuals comprehensible for our audience. Use them!

Exercise 5.2: do it better!

The graphing applications we use to visualize data are built to meet the needs of many different scenarios. This means that it's rare that the default settings will meet the needs of any one of those scenarios exactly. That's where we come in—our understanding of the context and design sense can improve defaults tremendously, helping make information more easily digestible and simply more pleasant at which to look and with which to spend time.

Let's dissect a specific example, considering how we can use lessons in design to improve upon default output from a proprietary tool and create a more desirable experience for our audience. See Figure 5.2a, which shows the number of cars sold by dealership over time for a given region.

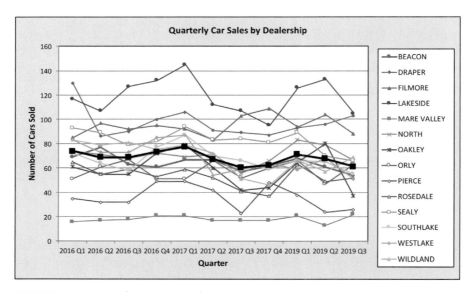

FIGURE 5.2a   Default output from tool

STEP 1: First, let's simply react to this graph. What words come to mind in terms of how this graph makes you *feel*? Make a short list of the feelings this graph evokes.

STEP 2: What changes would you make if you needed to communicate the data from this graph? Specifically, address:

- **Use of words:** As we've discussed, words make our data interpretable. We should consider not only what words we use to do this, but also where we put those words. How and why would you make changes to the titles or placement of titles in this visual? Are there other ways you can improve upon the way words are used in this example?

- **Visual hierarchy:** We've learned it can be helpful to highlight sparingly and push non-critical or non-message-impacting elements to the background. How might you do that here? Which pieces of information or aspects of the design would you focus on and which would you de-emphasize or eliminate?

- **Overall design:** Are there any elements of the design you find distracting currently? How could you more effectively use alignment and white space? What changes would you recommend making to the overall design of this information?

STEP 3: Download the data and graph. Remake the visual applying the changes you've outlined in the tool of your choice.

STEP 4: Imagine you have been asked to create a single slide focusing on this data that will fit into a broader deck to be shared with the management team who oversees these dealerships. How would that affect what you show or how you choose to show it? What additional words can you put around it to help it make sense? What other design considerations would you make? Create this slide in the tool of your choice.

PRACTICE with COLE

Solution 5.2: do it better!

STEP 1: My initial response to this graph brings to mind words like: confusing, chaotic, overwhelming, and complicated. These are reactions I'd like to avoid when I communicate with data!

STEP 2: The following describes how I would approach remaking this graph to both better get the information across and foster a more pleasant overall experience for my audience.

Use of words: I like the fact that everything is titled in the original, but I'm not a fan of the center alignment of the graph and axis titles. I would upper-left-most justify all of the titles so that when my audience starts at the top left, they encounter how to read the visual before they get to the data. I'll choose all caps for my y-axis title because of the nice rectangular framing that this, together with the graph title, creates for my graph. On the x-axis, we probably don't need the title of Quarter, as this is quite obvious from the individual labels. I'll omit this. There is currently a lot of redundancy with the x-axis labels given the repeated years, so I'll pull those out as super-category axis labels.

When it comes to creating **visual hierarchy**, I have to decide what to focus on in this graph. In the original, it's difficult to focus on anything because so much is competing for our attention. I see that Regional Avg is emphasized in the original via a thicker black line (though this doesn't stand out nearly as much as it could given all the other lines, colors, and shapes). I'm going to push everything else to the background. When it comes to eliminating distractions, I'll also remove the grey background, borders, and gridlines. Getting rid of these non-information-bearing elements will help my data stand out more and make for a less cluttered feeling visual overall.

In terms of additional changes I would make to the **overall design**, it currently takes work going back and forth between the alphabetical legend at the right and the data it describes. I'd like to eliminate this work for my audience. My typical method for resolving this is to label the lines directly. This is challenging here because many of the lines are close together, but I'm still going to try it and get a little creative in the process. This won't be the best view to show what is going on for a given dealership (unless I put them into different graphs or emphasize only one or a couple at a time), but I can still give a sense of the highest, the lowest, and which fall generally in the middle when it comes to the most recent data by labeling in groups on the right-hand side of the graph.

STEP 3: Figure 5.2b shows my visual with these changes incorporated.

Car sales over time

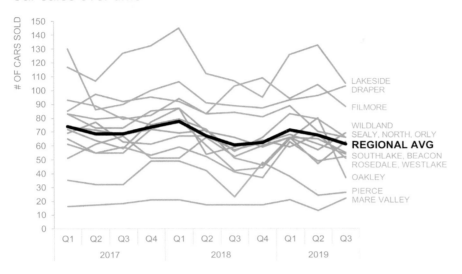

FIGURE 5.2b Remade visual

With Figure 5.2b, my audience can easily focus on the Regional Avg and also get a sense of the range and distribution over time across dealerships. If it's important to have a more specific understanding of what's happening for a given retailer, however, that's more difficult. If I need to solve for that as well, rather than try to do more with this graph, I might augment it with another view of the data. We'll look at that momentarily.

STEP 4: If I'm given a single slide to use as my communication vehicle, I'd want to put more words around everything to make sure it makes sense and attempt to answer the question of "So what?" I'd use titling and text together with my visuals—being conscious of white space and alignment—to create clear structure on the page. I'd also emphasize sparingly, both to create visual hierarchy and make the information scannable. This would help tie related elements together, easing the processing for my audience. See Figure 5.2c.

PRACTICE *with* COLE

Regional car sales: **mixed results**

OVERALL DECLINE IN REGIONAL AVERAGE

The total number of cars sold across all dealerships (not shown) has decreased over time from more than 1,000 in Q1 2017 to 857 in Q3 2019 (a 17% reduction). The average number of cars sold by dealership has also decreased over time.

Car sales over time

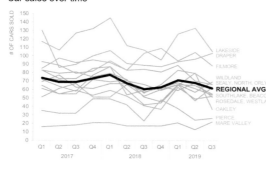

MARKED VARIANCE BY DEALERSHIP

In the latest quarter, **Lakeside, Draper, and Filmore had the most cars sold** (105, 103 and 88, respectively), while Oakley, Pierce, and Mare Valley had the fewest (less than 40 cars sold each).

Car sales by dealership: Q3 2019

Data source: Sales Database, includes cars sold onsite at regional dealerships through 9/30/19.

FIGURE 5.2c Presenting on a single slide

In Figure 5.2c, I added a second graph—horizontal bars showing how car sales across the various dealerships compare for the most recent time period. I'm making the assumption that this is the most relevant and that we don't necessarily need the full view over time for each (we can see the highs and lows with relative ease on the left, but if it's important to be able to distinguish the middle ones, that becomes impossible given the current design).

I've added more text around the graphs, both clear concise titling and descriptive text to help make what I'd like to highlight to my audience clear. I've used white space and alignment to create a two-sided layout. If we step back and consider how our audience is likely to process this information, they will probably start at the top left, read the slide title, then move downward and read "Overall decline in regional average" and see the black line below in the graph that depicts this. Then they'd typically move to the right-hand side, perhaps pausing on the "Marked variance by dealership" title or the blue and orange text. Finally, they'd look down to the right graph, see the black average tied to the graph on the left, as well as the blue and orange bars that are connected through similarity of color to the above words.

I did try out a second iteration of the left graph in Figure 5.2c that maintained consistent coloring of blue and orange for the top and bottom three dealerships as of Q3 2019 (those called out on the right). While I liked the consistency, I felt these competed too much for attention with the Regional Avg on the left, so I decided to use these colors sparingly on the right graph only.

The primary point here is to be thoughtful in the overall structure and design of your visuals and the pages that contain them. Don't simply rely on tool defaults; once you make a graph, there is still more work to be done. When we design thoughtfully, we can create a better experience for our audience, improving the odds of successful communication.

PRACTICE *with* COLE

Exercise 5.3: pay attention to detail & design intuitively

The following example employs a two-sided structure similar to where we ended in Exercise 5.2. However, clear structure is not the only thing we need for success. Attention to detail is a hugely important aspect of creating effective visual design. Let's look at another example and how attention to detail and thoughtful design choices can improve our visual communications.

Let's assume you work for an on-demand print company that targets small businesses. One of the metrics you track is customer touchpoints—how many times someone at your organization interacts directly with a customer—both in aggregate and on a per-customer basis. There are three primary modes of connection: phone, chat, and email.

Your colleague has put together the following slide summarizing touchpoints over time and asked for your feedback. Spend a moment examining Figure 5.3a, then tackle the following.

Total touchpoints and touchpoint per customer remains flat

Total touchpoints have increased slightly to ~500K (+3.8% y/y)

Touchpoints per customer remain flat over the past 3 years

	Phone	Chat	Email	Total
January '18	0.43	0.13	0.55	1.11
January '19	0.45	0.16	0.58	1.19
January-20	0.29	0.26	0.5	1.10

FIGURE 5.3a Your colleague's original slide

STEP 1: What feedback would you give your colleague about the design of their slide related to attention to detail? Write down your thoughts. Focus on not only *what* you would recommend changing, but also *why*. Ground your feedback using design principles we have discussed.

STEP 2: Take a step back and think about how the data is designed: stacked bars on the left, table on the right, and additional numbers in the text. Are there changes you would make to the way this data is shown? How might you design the data in a way that is more intuitive for our audience? Write down your ideas.

STEP 3: Download the data and original visuals. Remake the slide, incorporating your feedback and ideas in the tool of your choice.

PRACTICE *with* COLE

Solution 5.3: pay attention to detail & design intuitively

STEP 1: First, let me say that attention to detail is hugely important in our visual designs. Typically, the graph or the slide is the only part of the analytical process that our audience actually *sees*. Whether they should or not, people tend to assume things about the overall level of detail that was paid based on this piece that they can directly observe. So make your visuals and the pages that contain them imply good things about your overall work!

Related to attention to detail, I would concentrate my feedback on three areas: consistency, alignment, and intuitive axis labels. Let's review each of these.

Consistency is an important aspect when it comes to attention to detail: be consistent in your approach *unless* it makes sense for some reason not to be. Changing design elements up randomly or otherwise introducing unnecessary inconsistency can be attention grabbing, distracting and looks sloppy. Specific things that catch my eye in this case are: inconsistent decimal points on y-axis labels of graph and in the bottom Email cell of the table. Also the way the dates are shown is inconsistent between the graph and the table, and not even consistent *within* the table!

When it comes to **alignment**, as we've discussed, centered text often looks messy. When it flows onto multiple lines, it creates jagged edges, as we see in the center-aligned statements above the graph and table. While I might preserve the centering of numbers in the table (*if* I were to keep the table; more on that shortly), I would be consistent in the vertical alignment. I would center consistently in that direction as well (currently the dates in the table are top aligned, while the numbers are center aligned vertically). Also, the overall elements on the page could be aligned a little better—the table isn't directly under the line above it and the orange box on the far right could be sized to better fit the cells it's meant to highlight.

My final main point of feedback on the current design would be in regards to **intuitive axis labels** in the graph. Currently, every fifth month is labeled on the x-axis. We can see why this was done: there isn't sufficient space to label every point, particularly given the long format of the dates. One method is to label only some, though we should be thoughtful with what frequency we choose to label. Choose a frequency that will be intuitive based on the data being shown. For example, every seventh point labeled would make sense for daily data (since there are seven days in a week) or it could make sense to label by weeks instead of days. For monthly data, every third or sixth month would be more intuitive. If you have limited space with time on the x-axis, you could label by quarters or years. We could pull the years out as a supercategory and either abbreviate the months and arrange the text vertically, or just use the first letter of each month to maintain horizontal text. I'll employ this latter method in my solution. There isn't a single or preferred approach: choose axis labels that will be intuitive, helpful, and legible for your audience.

As additional points of feedback, I'd reduce redundancy by removing "Touch-points" from each category label in the graph and also label the data directly so my audience doesn't have to go back and forth between the legend and the graph to decipher the data. Color is also clearly something we can play with here, but I'll reserve that for when I consider the overall design momentarily.

Figure 5.3b illustrates what my remake of the graph would look like incorporating the changes I've outlined.

Touchpoints per customer over time

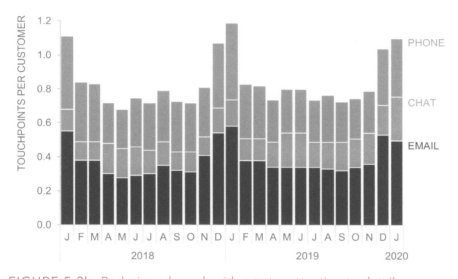

FIGURE 5.3b Redesigned graph with greater attention to detail

STEP 2: When it comes to stepping back and designing the data in a way that makes sense, there are more sweeping changes I would recommend. Let's shift next to how we might **design the data to make sense**.

Going back to Figure 5.3a, there are a lot of numbers between those called out in the titles, those added to the graph, and those in the table. We don't need all of these. Let's talk first about total number of touchpoints. This is referred to in the title and through text and numbers that have been added to the graph. If this information is critical, I could break it out on a separate slide and graph it (and would probably include more data than simply the two yearly numbers that are mentioned currently). Otherwise, I'd be apt to include the additional context as a sentence rather than clutter my graph with it.

Turning our attention to the table: this doesn't add any new information. The data shown there is already graphed in the January points in the graph on the left. So rather than break it out separately, if these specific numbers are of interest, I'd recommend putting them on the graph directly with the data. In this case, I don't think these numbers are critical. If we step back and think about the *story*, that will lead us to look at different views of the data, both to get a better understanding of where we want to focus and the story we can tell, as well as to figure out how to make that clear and easy for our audience.

Let's focus on other ways we could visualize the data. One challenge with stacked bars is that we can really only compare the first data series at the bottom of the stack and the total (overall height of bars) with ease. If anything interesting is happening in a data series up the stack, it becomes quite difficult to see because those pieces are stacked on top of other pieces that are also changing. To allow for both of these comparisons with greater ease, I could unstack the bars and turn them into lines: see Figure 5.3c.

Touchpoints per customer over time

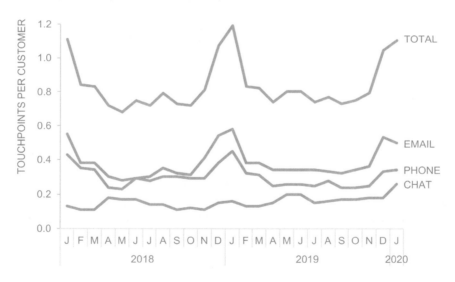

FIGURE 5.3c Graph the data as lines

In Figure 5.3c, I unstacked the categories and graphed each type of touchpoint—Email, Phone, Chat—as lines. I added an additional line representing the Total. I also stripped color out of the graph entirely, so we can look at all of the data critically and determine where it might make sense to focus. We'll add some color back in a later step.

When I look at this data, what jumps out at me—even more than with the stacked bars—is the apparent seasonality. When we want to clearly see seasonality (or in some cases, a lack of seasonality), it can work well to use a single year of months—for example, from January to December—for our x-axis, with a different line for each year. This change will result in a lot of lines if we do it for every category. With different data, we may need to split it into multiple graphs. However, here, given the spread of the data, we can make it work in a single graph. See Figure 5.4d.

Touchpoints per customer over time

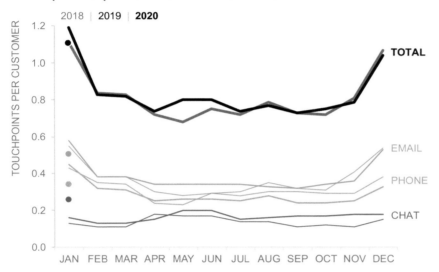

FIGURE 5.3d Change x-axis to monthly calendar year to better see seasonality

In Figure 5.3d, I've changed the x-axis to January through December, plotting each year as its own line. Within each color grouping, the thin line represents 2018, the thick line represents 2019, and the circle points at the left represent our single month of data—January—for 2020. Notice that we see pretty consistent seasonality in Total touchpoints, with higher touchpoints per customer in January and December and relatively lower through the rest of the year. Don't worry if you aren't loving this graph—it's an interim step to help get us to where we're going next.

I'm going to assume that we're standing in February 2020, since the most recent data point is January 2020. Given this, plus the shape of the data over the course of the year (higher at beginning and end, as mentioned, and lower in the middle), I am going to adjust my x-axis. Rather than the typical calendar year (January to December), I will change it to go from July to June to make it easier to see how recent months have compared year-over-year. In doing this, I'll also eliminate some data, solve for the awkward single data points in 2020, and simplify my lines to "This Year" and "Last Year." See Figure 5.3e.

PRACTICE *with* COLE

Touchpoints per customer over time

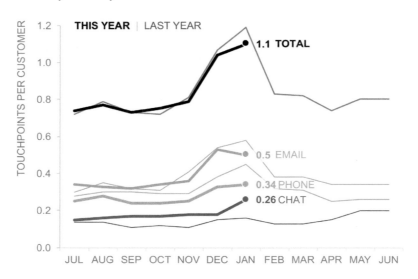

FIGURE 5.3e Change x-axis to run from July to June

With this view, I can make a couple of observations that didn't jump out at me before. First, let's pause on the Total: we see this year's trend has followed last year's closely. However, January touchpoints per customer are lower than last year. Moving downward, we see both Email and Phone touchpoints are trending lower this year compared to last year. Chat touchpoints, on the other hand, illustrate something different: Chat touchpoints have been consistently higher this year compared to last, with that difference increasing in January.

You may notice the varying decimal places on the labels in Figure 5.3e. I chose to round to one point past the decimal for Total and Email given the magnitude of the numbers. I took it out to an additional place past the decimal for Phone and Chat, both so that we can evaluate the small but potentially meaningful difference and so two points of varying heights wouldn't be labeled with the same number (in this case 0.3), which could cause confusion.

STEP 3: Pulling this all together and putting words back around it, my final slide might look something like Figure 5.3f.

Total touchpoints flat, shift toward **chat**

There is clear seasonality to customer touchpoints, which **peak in January**.
While email and phone are down year-over-year, **chat touchpoints have increased**.

LET'S DISCUSS: **How should this inform go-forward strategy and goals?**

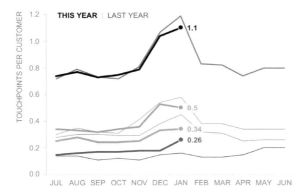

Touchpoints per customer over time

TOUCHPOINTS PER CUSTOMER

THIS YEAR | LAST YEAR

1.1

0.5

0.34

0.26

JUL AUG SEP OCT NOV DEC JAN FEB MAR APR MAY JUN

OVERALL recent months have followed last year's trend closely, with slightly lower touchpoints per customer as of Jan.

EMAIL continues to make up the highest volume of touchpoints, though as of Jan is slightly lower than last year (0.50 vs. 0.58).

PHONE at 0.34 touchpoints per customer also decreased year-over-year (0.45 at same time last year).

CHAT touchpoints have increased steadily in recent months. While only 0.26, this accounts for an increasing proportion of total and reflects nearly doubling year-over-year. Add more context here: whether this is desired, expected to continue, etc.

FIGURE 5.3f My redesigned slide

If I were talking through this information in a live setting, my slides would focus on the graph and I would build it piece by piece (we'll look at examples of this in Chapters 6 and 7). However, if I have a single slide to get the information across—perhaps this is a slide that's being incorporated into a broader deck that will be sent around—then I want to put all of the words around it so it makes sense. The words I've added are mostly descriptive; ideally we'd use this annotation to lend additional context, provide framing of whether what we are seeing is good, expected, and so on. I tied words to the data they describe through similarity of color. The result: when my audience reads the words, they know where to look for evidence in the data and vice versa. I used sparing color, relative size, and position on the page to create visual hierarchy and help make the information scannable.

By being thoughtful in all aspects of our design, we can make our data more easily consumable for our audience, helping ensure that our message comes across clearly.

Exercise 5.4: design in style

Something we haven't touched upon yet that can influence our design style when communicating with data is *brand*. Companies often go through great amounts of time and expense to create their branding: logos, colors, fonts, templates, and related style guidelines. Beyond being required to use this, there can be value in rolling branding into how you visualize data: it helps create a cohesive look and feel and can even add some personality into your data communications. Let's practice applying branding to a graph!

We originally looked at the following graph in Exercise 3.1. Figure 5.4a shows market size over time for a given product. The *storytelling with data* typical look and feel has been applied. The font is Arial. Titles have been justified at upper left. Axis titles are in all caps. Most elements are in grey except sparing use of color to direct attention (orange for a negative callout and associated data point, brand blue for positive data point and corresponding comment).

Market size over time

FIGURE 5.4a Graph with *storytelling with data* branding

Download the data and graph then complete the following.

STEP 1: Imagine you work for a brand similar to United Airlines and need to pull together an annual report that involves looking at market size. Start by doing some research: visit United's website, search Google images, and browse related pics. Write down 10 adjectives that describe the brand. Recreate Figure 5.4a, rebranding with a style similar to United Airlines. Reflect on how this affects your choice of colors and font. How else might this brand influence changes in the design of this graph?

STEP 2: Let's do this a second time. In this instance, you are an analyst at Coca Cola. Repeat the exercise, first by doing some research and making a list of words or feelings you'd associate with the brand. Then recreate this graph again, re-branding based on your research. What changes did you make to achieve this? How does red as a brand color play into your design?

Solution 5.4: design in style

STEP 1: Words that come to mind when I look at the United Airlines website and search Google for related images include: clean, classic, bold, blue, navigable, open, minimal, simple, serious, and structured. The logo has an intense dark blue background, with center-aligned, bold, white, capital letter text and sparing use of a lighter, more muted shade of blue. I can incorporate these feelings and elements into my design of the graph. See Figure 5.4b.

FIGURE 5.4b Branding inspired by United Airlines

My main initial changes were to color and font. I used the dark and light blues throughout, with the exception of the graph axes: choosing black for axis titles and labels and grey for axis lines. The font I chose (Gill Sans) takes up a bit more space than Arial. This looked overly crowded with the text boxes above the data line. To remedy this, I moved the text boxes below the data and also reduced the y-axis maximum to shift the line upward, creating room below it to reposition the text boxes. I positioned the footnote below the graph.

I center-aligned most of the text (I played with left and right alignment of the large text boxes, and while I liked the structure of the clean edge that created, something about it didn't feel fitting with the rest of the graph). The United logo and brand connote a feeling of clear organization to me, so I manifested that here by adding blue rectangles behind the title and footnote and also a blue border around the graph. I thickened the data line because I like how this balances out the bold title text. Even though the primary brand color is blue (similar to SWD), this rebranded graph feels quite different than the original Figure 5.4a as a result of these changes.

STEP 2: Next, let's be inspired by the Coca Cola brand. I reviewed can and bottle labels, logos, and advertisements. Words I would associate with this brand include: red, silver, round, classic, bold, sweet, playful, international, diverse, and wet (there's often condensation shown on the cans!). I observe a heavy use of red backgrounds, contrasting white text and sparing use of black. Text is typically center-aligned and frequently features a combination of bold all caps surrounded by slightly smaller non-bold all cap text. Words are used minimally. I'll fold these components into my redesign. See Figure 5.4c.

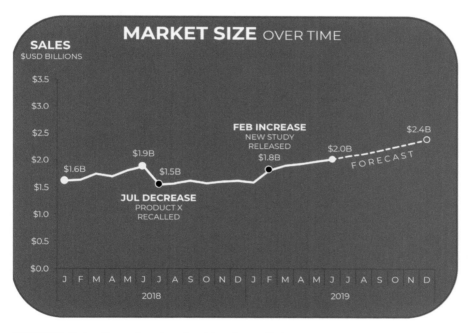

FIGURE 5.4c Branding inspired by Coca Cola

One aspect of the Coca Cola brand that I chose *not* to incorporate is the cursive-like text in the Coca Cola logo. While this is fine for a logo, my priority for text related to the graph is legibility.

Text should be large enough to read and in a font that is easy to read. I opted for a sans serif font similar to the supporting text I saw on can and bottle labels (Montserrat, a free font that I downloaded). To incorporate some of the round feel that you get from the logo, I opted for a rounded (rather than rectangular) background shape.

PRACTICE *with* COLE

Speaking of the background, the red background in Figure 5.4c is quite bold. This might be fine if it is the only graph we are looking at, or if graphs will be projected one by one on slides. If there will be multiple graphs on a single page or if I anticipate that my audience will want to print it, I may opt for a lighter "Diet Coke" version. See Figure 5.4d.

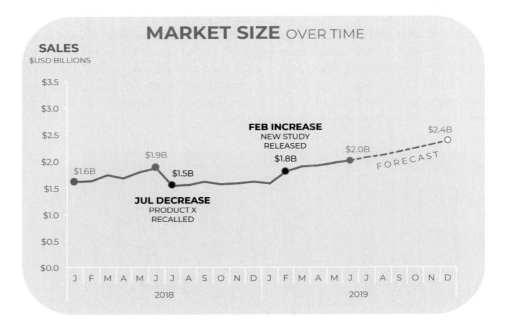

FIGURE 5.4d Less ink-heavy background

In Figure 5.4d, I opted for a light grey background, similar to the silver I saw incorporated into some of Coca Cola's designs. With this lighter background, black stands out more, so I opted for a few more black elements compared to the original remake. I can use white, which fades to the background on grey (whereas it stood out a lot against red) for elements such as axis lines. I limited my use of brand red to the graph title and data.

Red as a brand color works well with grey and sparing use of black, and looks quite slick as we see in Figure 5.4d. When it comes to colors, there is a tendency to use red and green to denote bad and good or negative and positive, respectively. While I recommend against this due to considerations for colorblindness, I especially discourage it for organizations having red as a brand color. You want positive things associated with your brand, so if your brand color is red, don't associate red with negative or bad things. One alternative in this circumstance can be to use red for good and black for bad. In the preceding graph, I've used red for general data and black for call outs (without connotation of bad or good), which is another option.

Stepping back and summing up: there can be value from rolling branding into how you communicate with data. If you work with client organizations, consider how you can undertake research similar to what we've done here and integrate your learnings into your designs. When it comes to you own organization's brand, many companies have style guides that you can use to better understand the brand and what options you may have. Regard these not as annoying constraints, but rather as a lodestar that can inspire creativity and cohesiveness across your data communications.

PRACTICE *with* COLE

PRACTICE on your OWN

We can learn a great deal by emulating effective data visualizations, so we'll begin with an exercise focused on that, then continue our practice designing intuitively to improve less-than-ideal visuals.

Exercise 5.5: examine & emulate

One piece of advice I often give is to simply observe the examples of data visualization you encounter in the world around you. Pause to reflect: for the good ones, what works well that you can emulate in your own work? For the not-so-good ones, identify what pitfalls the creator fell into that you can avoid. Let's do an exercise when it comes to the effective side of things.

Rather than simply pause and figure out what works well, we can go a step further and take the time to emulate the effective examples we identify, recreating them and learning how to achieve the aspects of effective designs in our tools. The level of attention to detail this process forces can help us be more thoughtful in our own work and sharpen our visual design skills and style. Let's practice all of this!

First, identify a visual (graph or slide) someone else created that you believe is effective. This could be an example from a colleague at work, the media, storytelling-withdata.com, or elsewhere. After you've chosen an example, tackle the following.

STEP 1: Consider the four aspects of design we've discussed: (1) affordances, (2) aesthetics, (3) accessibility, and (4) acceptance. Judging from the visual you've chosen and making assumptions as needed for the purpose of the exercise—how did the creator account for each of these areas through the choices they made in their design? Write a few sentences describing how each of these four aspects of design were achieved.

STEP 2: Stepping back, *why* is it that the example you've chosen is effective? Are there specific elements of thoughtful design that make it work that you haven't already described? How might you generally apply these learnings to your own work?

STEP 3: Is there anything about the example you've chosen that you believe is not ideal or that you would have done differently? Write a couple of sentences outlining your thoughts.

STEP 4: Recreate the visual you've identified in the tool of your choice. First, work to emulate it as closely as you can when it comes to the specifics (typography, color, and overall style).

STEP 5: Make another version that incorporates any of the aspects you outlined in Step 3 that you would have approached differently. Look at your visuals from Step 4 and Step 5 side by side. Which do you prefer and why?

Exercise 5.6: make minor changes for major impact

It's frequently a lot of little things that work together to create a great or not-so-great experience for our audience in the data communications we design. This means that small changes can have big impact in improving our visual designs. Let's look at an example and also practice how these modifications can add up to help us take work from acceptable to exceptional.

Let's say you work at an advertising agency and have been asked to assess a recent six-week ad campaign for a client. The data you are focusing on is incremental reach, which you measure "per 1,000 impressions." You have a colleague who did a similar analysis for a different client recently, so rather than start from scratch, you've updated her visuals with your data as a starting point. Next, you want to edit and refine.

Figure 5.6 shows the visual you've created. Spend a couple of minutes to familiarize yourself with the details, then complete the following.

Incremental Reach per 1,000 Impressions

Digital platforms proved successful at reaching new viewers later in the campaign that were not exposed to TV ads.

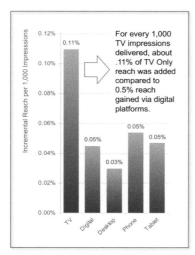
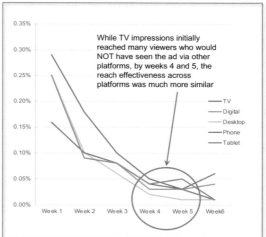

FIGURE 5.6 Your original slide

STEP 1: Pause first to consider what is working well. What do you like about the current view of the data?

STEP 2: A number of steps have been taken in Figure 5.6 to direct attention and help explain. Which are working well? Where and how might you adjust?

STEP 3: What clutter would you eliminate? What elements would you push to the background?

STEP 4: What other design choices made here do you question given the lessons in this chapter? What additional changes would you make?

STEP 5: Download the data and current graphs. Refine the visual by making the changes you've outlined in the steps above using the tool of your choice.

Exercise 5.7: how could we improve this?

Imagine you work for the same on-demand printing company that we assumed in Exercise 5.3 when we looked at customer touchpoints data. How your company interacts with customers is one possibly interesting topic, as we saw. Another might be the competitive landscape for your products. As part of this latter area of focus, your colleague has been asked to pull together some data on your main competitors' market share over time.

He comes to you with his slide—Figure 5.7—and asks for feedback.

Study Figure 5.7, then complete the following.

PRACTICE on your OWN

Top competitors remain present, with an increase in use of XBX Business

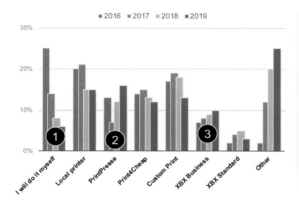

- **Reduction in in-house solutions continues:** likely because of the shifting mix of our customer base

- **PrintPresse gains importance—** it's becoming a bigger threat due to the nature of its offering (integrated, high quality)

- **XBX's business-centric offering is gaining ground,** while Pring4Cheap and CustomPrint show a decrease. At the same time, XBX has seen slippage in their standard offering.

FIGURE 5.7 How could we improve this?

STEP 1: List 5 design improvements you would recommend making to this slide. Articulate not only what, but also why. How specifically will your ideas improve the design?

STEP 2: Download the data and execute the changes you've outlined in the tool of your choice.

STEP 3: Consider how you would present this material in a live meeting compared to something that has to be sent around as a stand-alone document. How would your approach change between these two instances? Write a few sentences to explain.

Exercise 5.8: brand this!

As we explored in exercise 5.4, there are ways that we can incorporate company or personal brand into how we communicate with data. This can be facilitated through choice of font, color, and other elements. In some cases, it may mean incorporating a logo or using a customized slide or graph template. Let's practice how you can incorporate branding in a graph.

Suppose you work for a pet food manufacturing company. Look at the following graph, Figure 5.8, which depicts relative cat food sales over time (expressed in terms of % of total) for a given brand line, Lifestyle. Complete the following.

PRACTICE on your OWN

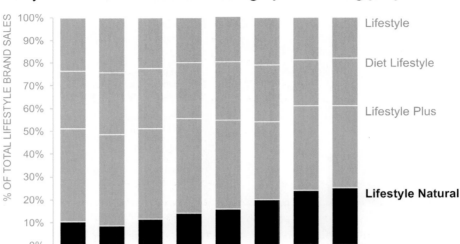

FIGURE 5.8 Brand this!

STEP 1: Identify two recognizable brands. They don't have to be at all relevant to this example—these could be company brands or sports teams, for instance. It will be more fun and a better exercise if you pick two that are quite different from each other in terms of style. Research images related to the brand and list 10 adjectives that describe the look and feel of each. Remake this visual two times, incorporating branding components of each of these, respectively.

STEP 2: Take a step back and compare the two visuals you've created. How does each *feel*? Were you successful bringing to life the adjectives you outlined in Step 1? How can branding affect how we communicate with data generally? What are some pros and cons of this? Write a few sentences with your thoughts.

STEP 3: Consider your company or school's brand. What descriptors would you associate with it? Remake the graph again, styling it accordingly. To take it a step further, integrate your branded graph into a slide, applying consistent branding to any elements you add (title, text, logos, and colors).

STEP 4: How would you generalize the components of brand we should think about when we visualize and communicate with data? What are the benefits of doing so? Are there scenarios where we may *not* want to be consistent with brand in our data communications? Write a few sentences outlining your thoughts.

PRACTICE on your OWN

PRACTICE at WORK

Accessibility, attention to detail, building acceptance — when done well, people are likely to spend more time with our creations, improving our ability to drive action. Pick a work project and practice thinking like a designer via the following exercises.

Exercise 5.9: make data accessible with words

When you look at a graph you made, it's likely you know what you're looking at: what to pay attention to, how to interpret it, and what to take away. But as we've discussed, this isn't necessarily clear to our audience in the same way. Words used well can be a strategic tool for making our data comprehensible for our audience, answering questions before they arise, and helping them to draw the same conclusion that you have.

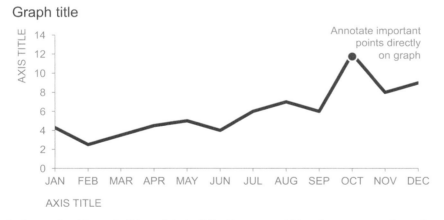

FIGURE 5.9 Use words wisely

There are some words that have to be present: every graph needs a title and every axis needs a title. Exceptions to this will be rare (for example, if your x-axis reflects months, you probably don't need to title it "months of the year"—you do, however, need to make it clear what year it is!). Make it your default to title axes

PRACTICE at WORK

directly so your audience doesn't have to guess or make assumptions about that at which they are looking. Also don't assume that people looking at the same data are going to walk away with the same conclusion. If there is a conclusion you want your audience to draw—which there should be when using data for explanatory purposes—state that in words. Use what we know about preattentive attributes to make those words stand out: make them big, make them bold, and put them in high priority places such as the top of the page.

Speaking of which—the top of the page (in Figure 5.9, "Words make data accessible!") is precious real estate. It's the first thing your audience encounters when they see your page or screen. Too often, we use this precious real estate for descriptive titles. Instead, use this for an active title; put your key takeaway there so your audience doesn't miss it. This also works to set up what will follow on the rest of the page. (We'll further explore and practice takeaway titling in Chapter 6.)

Also consider what is helpful to have present but doesn't necessarily need to draw attention. For example, when showing data, it is often useful to have a footnote that lists details such as the data source, the time period represented (or time at which the data was extracted), assumptions, or methodology details. These are things that can help your audience interpret the data and lend credibility, as well as give you a reference in the event you need to replicate and create something similar in the future. It's important, but doesn't need to compete with other things for attention. This text can be smaller, grey, and in lower-priority places on the page, like the bottom.

After you've created your graph or slide, run through the following questions to help ensure you are using words wisely:

- What is the key takeaway? Have you stated it in words prominently so your audience doesn't miss it?

- Does your graph have a title? Is it descriptive enough to set the right expectation for your audience when looking at the data?

- Are all axes labeled and titled directly? If not, what steps have you taken to make it clear to your audience?

- Do you have a footnote listing details that are important, but don't need to take main stage? If not, should you?

- Stepping back: does this seem like an appropriate amount of words given how you'll be communicating to your audience? Typically, you'll have fewer words on a slide for something you'll be presenting live and more words for something that is being sent around and has to stand on its own. Does your level of words in the given case match how the data will be communicated?

PRACTICE at WORK

Exercise 5.10: create visual hierarchy

Affordances are aspects of our visual design that help our audience understand how to interact with the data we are communicating. We can draw attention to some components and push others to the background to create visual hierarchy and make our communications scannable. Want a quick test to see if you've done this well? Squint your eyes to see the overall impression of the chart. This changes your perception enough to get fresh eyes on a design. The most important elements should be the first things you see and the most prominent.

For more specific tips on how to achieve visual hierarchy, read through the following from *SWD* (paraphrased from Lidwell, Holden, and Butler's *Universal Principles of Design*) for highlighting the important stuff and eliminating distractions. Determine how you can apply these to your next project!

Highlight the important stuff

- **Bold**, *italics*, and underlining: Use for titles, labels, captions, and short word sequences to differentiate elements. Bold is generally preferred over italics and underlining because it adds minimal noise to the design while clearly highlighting chosen elements. Italics add minimal noise, but also don't stand out as much and are less legible. Underlining adds noise and compromises legibility, so should be used sparingly (if at all).

- CASE and typeface: Uppercase text in short word sequences is easily scanned, which can work well when applied to titles, labels, and keywords. Avoid using different fonts as a highlighting technique, as it's difficult to attain a noticeable difference without disrupting aesthetics.

- Color is an effective highlighting technique when used sparingly and generally in concert with other highlighting techniques (for example, bold).

- Inversing elements is effective at attracting attention, but can add considerable noise to a design so should be used sparingly.

- Size is another way to attract attention and signal importance.

Eliminate distractions

- **Not all data are equally important.** Use your space and audience's attention wisely by getting rid of noncritical data or components.

- **When detail isn't needed, summarize.** You should be familiar with all the details, but that doesn't mean your audience needs to be. Consider whether summarizing makes sense.

PRACTICE at WORK

- **Ask yourself:** would eliminating this change anything? No? Take it out! Resist the temptation to keep things because you worked hard to create them; if they don't support the message, they don't serve the purpose of the communication.

- **Push necessary, but non-message-impacting items to the background.** Use your knowledge of preattentive attributes to de-emphasize supporting details. Grey works well for this.

Exercise 5.11: pay attention to detail!

Many elements add up to create the overall experience our audience feels when faced with the visuals we create. Have you ever noticed how some designs feel easy and elegant, while others feel clunky and complicated? Paying close attention to details can help ensure the visuals we create are met with happiness by our audience. Here are some specific aspects of your visual design to consider to achieve this—the next time you create a graph or slide, read through and apply the following.

- **Use correct spelling, grammar, punctuation, and math.** This should go without saying, but I encounter examples regularly where there are issues of this sort. When it comes to misspellings, this is an excellent reason to get a second set of eyes on your work, soliciting feedback from someone else. Our brains actually fix errors in our work so that you might not even catch a mistake you've made! (Unfortunately, that innocent oversight may end up being the unintended focus of your audience's attention.) A trick I once heard for spell-checking your own work is to read it backwards: you can't skim when you do this and so it's easier to identify mistakes. Or you can put it in a really ugly font, which has a similar effect. Also if you show math, make sure it is correct— there's no bigger credibility-killer than math that doesn't add up!

- **Precisely align elements.** As much as possible, aim to create clean vertical and horizontal structure across all elements (avoid diagonal, which looks messy, is attention grabbing, and slower to read in the case of text). Use table structure or turn on gridlines or rulers in your tool to precisely line things up. As I've mentioned, I'm a fan of upper-left-most justifying graph titles and axis titles. This creates nice framing for the graph (particularly with all cap axis titles, which form clean rectangles compared to mixed case). Also, given the typical zigzagging "z" of processing, this positioning means your audience hits how to read the data before they get to the actual data. Bonus!

- **Use white space strategically.** Don't fear white space or fill it just because it's there. White space helps make the things that aren't white space stand out. Use white space to set things apart. Paired with good alignment, this can help you create organized structure in your graph or on your page.

- **Visually tie related things together.** When someone looks at the data, make it clear where to look in accompanying text for related info. When they read text, make it clear where they should look in the data for evidence of what's being said. Think back to the Gestalt principles that we covered in Chapter 3 for methods to visually tie elements together; specifically, turn back to Exercise and Solution 3.2 for an illustration.

- **Maintain consistency when it makes sense.** When things are different, people wonder why. Don't make your audience use their brainpower for this unnecessarily. If it makes sense to graph things in a similar manner, do so. If you use a specific color to direct attention in one place, keep this consistent elsewhere unless you have a good reason to change it.

- **Observe the overall "feel" of your visual.** Step back and consider: how does the visual you've created feel to look at? Is it heavy or complicated? How can you ease this? If unsure, get feedback from someone else—ask them for adjectives they would use to describe your work and refine as needed.

Exercise 5.12: design more accessibly

The following is adapted from Amy Cesal's guest post on the SWD blog; you can read her full article, which includes a number of examples and links to additional resources, at storytellingwithdata.com under the title "accessible data viz is better data viz."

Often, when we are creating charts and graphs, we think of ourselves as the ideal user. This is not only a problem because we know more about the data than the target user but also because other users might have a different set of constraints than we do.

Inclusive design principles and accessibility are important to take into consideration when designing data visualization because they help a broader audience understand your graphic. Designing with accessibility in mind can even help make your visualizations easier to understand for people without disabilities.

Being clear with text, distinctive labeling, and adding multiple ways to identify the point to your visuals will make it easier for people with impairments and those without to interpret your graphs. There are easy ways to add the principles of accessibility into your visual communications. Here are five simple ones:

1. **Add alt text.** Alternative text (referred to as alt text) is displayed when the image cannot be. Screen readers, the assistive technology used by people who are visually impaired, read alt text out loud in place of people seeing the image. It's important to have valuable alt text instead of "figure-13.jpg,"

which doesn't help a user understand the content they are missing. Screen readers speak alt text without allowing users to speed up or skip, so make sure the information is descriptive but succinct. Good alt text includes one sentence of what the chart is, including the chart type for users with limited vision who may only see part of it. It should also include a link to a CSV or other machine-readable data format so people with impaired vision can tab through the chart data with a screen reader.

2. **Employ a takeaway title.** Research suggests that users read the title of the graph first. People also tend to just rephrase the title of the graph when asked to interpret the meaning of the visualization. When the graph title includes the point, the cognitive load of understanding the chart decreases. People know what to look for in the data when they read the graph takeaway first as part of the title.

3. **Label data directly.** Another way to reduce cognitive burden on users is to directly label your data rather than using legends. This is especially useful for colorblind or visually impaired users who may have difficulty matching colors within the plot to those in the legend. It also decreases the work of scanning back and forth trying to match the legend with the data.

4. **Check type and color contrast.** Colorblindness is an issue for 8% of men and 0.5% of women with Northern European ancestry. However, we should also consider users with low vision and a variety of other conditions that affect vision. The Web Content Accessibility Guidelines (www.w3.org) specify necessary contrast and text sizes for readability on screen. There are a number of tools to help you abide by these contrast and size standards, for example, the Color Palette Accessibility Evaluator.

5. **Use white space.** White space is your friend. When information is too densely packed, the graphic can feel overwhelming and unreadable. It can be helpful to leave a gap between sections of a chart (for example, outlining the sections of a stacked bar in white). Judicious use of white space increases the legibility by helping to demarcate and distinguish between different sections without relying only on color. This can also supplement accessible color choices by helping users distinguish the difference between colors that identify separate sections.

These are just a few things you can do to help everyone easily comprehend the graphs that you create. You should strive to make sure that everyone—not just you or your ideal user—understands the point of the visualization. When you consider accessibility, you create a better product for all.

The next time you need to communicate with data, refer to and apply these tips!

PRACTICE at WORK

Exercise 5.13: garner acceptance for your designs

People dislike change. This is a simple fact of human nature. In the scenario where we've always shown data in a certain way and people are attached to it—how do we convince them to do things differently? What should we do in general when met with resistance from our audience?

This is a change management process. In the same way that we considered our audience in the exercises in Chapter 1 and tried to understand what motivates them, we can do that here as well: in this situation our audience becomes those whose behavior we want to influence. First and foremost, when we want to convince our audience to be open to our designs, we need to do it in a way that works for *them*.

The *wrong* way to go about changing their minds sounds something like this, "I just read this book, and I learned that we've been doing it wrong; we should really be looking at it like *this*." That might be easy, but it's not so compelling or inspiring. So unless you're the boss and people have to do what you say (even if that is the case, you should probably be more subtle in your approach!), you have to work to influence your stakeholders or colleagues to change.

Here are a few strategies from *SWD*—plus a couple of new ideas—that you can leverage for gaining acceptance in the design of your data visualization.

- **Articulate the benefits of the new or different design.** Sometimes simply giving people transparency into why things will look different going forward can help them feel more comfortable. Are there new or improved observations you can make by looking at the data in a different way? Or other benefits you can articulate to help convince your audience to be open to the change?

- **Show the side-by-side.** If a different approach is clearly superior to the way things have been done, showing them next to each other will demonstrate this. Couple this with the prior suggestion by showing the before-and-after *and* explaining why you want to shift the way you are looking at things.

- **Provide multiple options and seek input.** Rather than prescribing the design, create several options and get feedback from colleagues or your audience (if appropriate) to determine which design will best meet the given needs. Involve stakeholders in the process—they'll be more bought into the solution as a result.

- **Get a vocal member of your audience on board.** Identify influential members of your audience and talk to them one-on-one in an effort to gain acceptance of your design. Ask for their feedback and incorporate it. Identify champions—people outside of your team who support what you want to do and can help influence others. If you can get one or a couple of vocal members of your audience or their peers bought in, others may follow.

- **Start with the familiar and transition from there.** This can be a particularly effective strategy in a live setting. Begin with the view that your audience is used to seeing, then pivot to a different one, making it clear how this ties back to the original and highlighting what the new visual allows you to see, or how it can help frame the conversation in a new way. When a graph is done well, you'll often find that you don't have to spend a lot of time talking about the graph but rather can spend it discussing what the data shows. This can shift the overall conversation in a really helpful way.

- **Don't replace—augment.** As an interim step, rather than change *anything*, leave it all as it is. Add to this with your new view(s). For example, rather than redesign your regular report, keep it the same. Integrate a couple of slides up front or add content to the email that distributes it, applying best practices in these places. If done well, this is like saying to your audience, "We haven't changed anything—the data is all there and we are happy to go through it with you, but we've already taken the time to do that and here (up front, applying the lessons covered throughout *SWD* and this book) are the things you should focus on this time." As your audience gains confidence in your ability to hone in on the right things in effective ways, you can wean dependence on all the data and potentially reduce what you share with your audience over time.

Reflect on whether any of the above can be employed in your situation to help you drive the change that you seek and the acceptance of your visual designs. In general, think about how you can set yourself up for success. Getting to know your audience—those you want to influence to accept your design—and what drives their behaviors can help. Think about not why you think they should change, but why they should want to. Make your approach work first and foremost for them. Refer back to Chapter 1 for exercises that will help you get to know your audience.

Also consider whether it's a fight worth fighting. Don't start with big battles. Start with low-hanging fruit and achieve small victories. Over time, you'll build credibility so if and when you do want to make more sweeping changes, you'll have earned your colleagues' and audience's respect and hopefully have an easier time making it happen!

PRACTICE at WORK

Exercise 5.14: let's discuss

Consider the following questions related to Chapter 5 lessons and exercises. Discuss with a partner or group.

1. What role do words play in making our data visualizations comprehendible? What kind of text should be present in every graph? Are there any exceptions to this?

2. When creating visual hierarchy in our designs, it's important both to highlight the important stuff *and* to de-emphasize some aspects. Which elements of our graphs and slides are good candidates for de-emphasizing? How can we visually push things to the background?

3. How would you describe thoughtful design when it comes to data visualization?

4. What does *accessibility* mean when it comes to communicating with data? What steps can we take to make our designs more accessible?

5. Is it worthwhile to take the time to make our graphs pretty? Why or why not?

6. How does personal or company brand come into play when communicating with data? What are some advantages of this? Are there any disadvantages?

7. Have you ever wanted to make a change to a graph or the way that you visualize data and been met with resistance? What did you do? Were you successful? What strategies can we use to influence our audience in general when this happens? What will you do the next time you face this situation?

8. What is one specific goal you will set for yourself or your team related to the strategies outlined in this chapter? How can you hold yourself (or your team) accountable to this? Who will you turn to for feedback?

PRACTICE *at* WORK

tell a story

Data in a spreadsheet or facts on a slide aren't things that naturally stick with us—they are easily forgotten. Stories, on the other hand, are memorable. Pairing the potency of story with effective visuals means that our audience can recall what they heard or read in addition to what they saw. This is powerful, and we'll explore using story to communicate data in concrete ways in this chapter.

As an aside, my order of lessons sometimes surprises people. Some elements of story relate to things that came up when we explored context in Chapter 1—why didn't we discuss story then? For me, this is the natural progression. Start with context, audience, and message. Time spent there will serve you well even if you don't take things full course and employ story. There's value in doing these things up front before you spend much time with your data: they can help you target your data visualization process and make it more efficient. But then *after* you've spent time with your data, know it well, and have identified what you can use it to help others see, it's time to look at the big picture again and figure out how to best communicate it to your audience. This is the precise moment story comes into play.

Words, tension, and the narrative arc—these are components of story that we can use to get our audience's attention, build credibility, and inspire action. Not only are well told data stories memorable, but they can also be retold, empowering our audience to help spread our message. In this chapter, we'll undertake exercises that help highlight the importance of not just showing data, but making data a pivotal point in an overarching story.

Let's practice **telling a story**!

First, we'll review the main lessons from the relevant chapter in *SWD* Chapter 6.

FIRST, LET'S RECAP
LESSONS in STORYTELLING

RED RIDING HOOD

EVIDENCE of the KEY ELEMENTS of STORY in PRACTICE

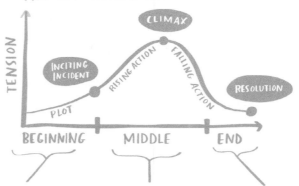

conflict & tension are an integral part

THE NARRATIVE ARC

TENSION

INCITING INCIDENT

RISING ACTION

CLIMAX

FALLING ACTION

RESOLUTION

PLOT

BEGINNING   MIDDLE   END

- Introduce the plot
- Build context for the audience
- Answer "why should I pay attention?"

- Develop "what could be"
  – illustrate with examples
  – include data that demonstrates problem
  – articulate what could happen if no action is taken

- Call to action
- Make it clear what you want your audience to do with the new understanding

NARRATIVE STRUCTURE

SPOKEN or WRITTEN WORDS (or both) that TELL the STORY in an ORDER that MAKES SENSE and GETS PEOPLE to PAY ATTENTION

NARRATIVE FLOW

The ORDER of YOUR STORY...
the PATH on which YOU TAKE YOUR AUDIENCE

CHRONOLOGICAL

PROBLEM → GATHER DATA
↓
ANALYZE DATA → FINDING EMERGES
↓
RECOMMEND ACTION

LEAD with the ENDING

CALL to ACTION
↓
SUPPORTING POINT #1 → SUPPORTING POINT #2
↓
... ETC.

SPOKEN vs. WRITTEN NARRATIVE

ARTICULATE CLEARLY the ROLE you WANT your AUDIENCE to PLAY

WRITTEN REPORT

Audience is on their own to make the content relevant... use written narrative to make the "So What?" clear

LIVE PRESENTATION

Make the "So What?" clear through the words you say, use visuals to reinforce

REPETITION

HELPS MOVE THINGS from SHORT-TERM to LONG-TERM MEMORY

BING → **BANG** → **BONGO**

What you are going to cover

Detail & main content

Summary & review

PRACTICE with COLE

6.1
use takeaway titles

6.2
put it into words

6.3
identify the tension

6.4
utilize the components of story

6.5
arrange along the narrative arc

6.6
differentiate between live and stand-alone stories

6.7
transition from dashboard to story

PRACTICE on your OWN

6.8
identify the tension

6.9
move from linear path to narrative arc

6.10
build a narrative arc

6.11
evolve from report to story

PRACTICE at WORK

6.12
form a pithy, repeatable phrase

6.13
what's the story?

6.14
employ the narrative arc

6.15
let's discuss

We'll begin by exploring two specific strategies with words to get clear on our message and how to tell it.

Then we'll talk about tension and introduce the narrative arc as a powerful tool for building and communicating our data stories.

Exercise 6.1: use takeaway titles

As we illustrated through exercises in Chapter 5 (5.1 and 5.9), text plays an important role when we communicate with data because words help make data understandable to our audience. Slide titles represent one important—and often underutilized—place to use words well.

Picture a slide. Typically, there is a title at the top. This title space is precious real estate. It is the first thing our audience encounters when they see the page: whether projected on a a big screen or their computer monitor or printed on a piece of paper. Too often, we use this precious real estate for descriptive titles. Instead, I'm a fan of using action titles. If there is a key takeaway—which there should be—put it there, so your audience doesn't miss it!

Studies have shown that effective titles can help improve both the memorability and recall of what is shown in a graph. Titling with the key takeaway also creates the right expectation for our audience: when we've done it well, it sets up what is to follow on the rest of the page.

Let's practice forming takeaway titles and understanding how changing titles can direct our audience to focus on different aspects of our data. See Figure 6.1, which shows Net Promoter Score (NPS) for our business and our top competitors. NPS is a common metric used in voice of customer analytics. The higher the number, the better.

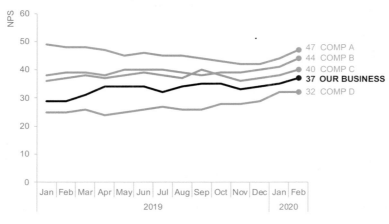

What's the story?

FIGURE 6.1 What's the story?

STEP 1: Create a takeaway title to answer the question posed at the top: "What's the story?" Write it down. What does the title encourage your audience to focus on in the graph? Write a sentence or two.

STEP 2: Create a *different* takeaway title for this slide and repeat the other actions from Step 1.

STEP 3: Consider whether the takeaway titles you've created provide any sentiment for your audience: do they tell your audience how to *feel* about this data? If so, how? If not, how might you retitle to convey a positive or negative message?

PRACTICE *with* COLE

Solution 6.1: use takeaway titles

What's the story? This is a question we sometimes ask when we don't mean *story* at all. Rather, we mean What's the point?, What's the takeaway?, or So what? For me, this is the minimum level of "story" that should exist any time we show data for explanatory purposes. We can use our title space to make our primary point clear.

STEP 1: I could title this slide, "**NPS is increasing over time**." If I were to do so, my audience would simply read those words and then be primed to be looking for a line increasing upwards to the right. Upon seeing the graph, with attention drawn to Our Business, the words read in the title would be confirmed in the picture.

STEP 2: As an alternative title, I might go with "**NPS: we rank 4th among competitors**." This prompts my reader to turn to the graph and start counting down the right-hand side... 1, 2, 3, yep—4th indeed. The words set a notion for what is to come in the graph and the graph reinforces the words in the title.

STEP 3: I can also use this title space to set an expectation with my audience: Is this a good thing? Is it a bad thing? My previous suggested titles did not do this. But imagine that I title the slide, "**Great work! NPS is increasing over time**." Doing so would cause you to feel very differently about the data than if I were to title it "**More work ahead: we still haven't hit top 3**." The words we put around our data visualizations are critically important. Use this power carefully!

As a related aside, I'm often asked about my choice of case (capital and lower-case letters). For slide titles, I am in the habit of using sentence case (where the first word is capitalized and the rest is lowercase). I do this because I think sentence case lends itself more easily to action or takeaway titles (rather than title case, where every word is capitalized and is more likely to end up being a descriptive title, e.g. "NPS Over Time"). Be thoughtful and consistent in your use of letter case.

And beyond all else, as we've seen before and will continue to explore—use words wisely! Employing takeaway titles is one way to use your words well.

PRACTICE with COLE

PRACTICE with COLE

Exercise 6.2: put it into words

After creating a graph, I find it can be useful to come up with a sentence that describes the graph. This practice forces me to articulate a takeaway (or in some instances, a number of potential takeaways), which can sometimes even lead to different ways to show the data to better highlight the main point I want to make.

Let's practice doing this with a specific graph. Imagine you work at a bank and you are analyzing collections data. Collections departments often use dialers, machines that automatically place calls. Many calls go unanswered. When someone does answer, the collections agent is connected so they can talk to the individual to work out a payment plan and the account has been "worked." Numerous metrics are tracked related to this—we'll look at penetration rate, which is the proportion of accounts worked relative to the total number of accounts dialed.

Consider Figure 6.2a, which shows Accounts Worked, Dials Made, and the Penetration Rate.

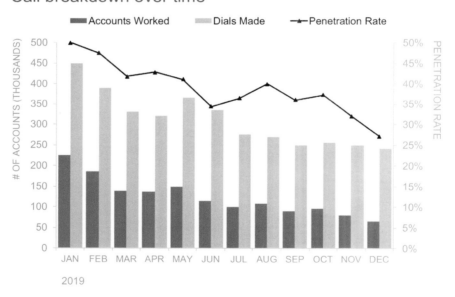

FIGURE 6.2a Put it into words

STEP 1: Write three distinct sentences articulating three different observations from this data. You may think of these as three potential takeaways that you could highlight in this data.

STEP 2: Which of the three sentences you've written would you focus on if you were communicating this data? Why? Are there any aspects of the others you'd also want to include? How can you achieve this?

STEP 3: Are there any changes you'd make to the visual to better focus the audience on the takeaway you've chosen to highlight? Outline those changes.

STEP 4: Download the data and make the changes you've outlined in the tool of your choice.

PRACTICE *with* COLE

Solution 6.2: put it into words

Describing my graph in words forces me to really look at the data and think about what is important and which aspects I may want to point out to my audience.

STEP 1: When I look at the data, I see things generally decreasing over the course of the year. But we can get more specific than that, which is one benefit from writing multiple sentences about a single graph (rather than just the first one that comes to mind). There are three data series depicted, so I'll write one observation about each:

1. The number of accounts worked varies over time and has generally decreased over the course of the year.

2. Dials made decreased 47% between January and December, with roughly 250,000 dials made in December.

3. Penetration rate has decreased markedly over time.

STEP 2: I'm inclined to want to focus on the decrease in Penetration Rate, since this reflects pieces of both of the other data series. That said, I wouldn't want to let go of all the other content, because this lends important context. It's interesting, for example, that Penetration Rate has decreased *in spite* of decreasing Dials Made. One might think that as fewer dials are made, the relative number of accounts worked would go up, but that clearly isn't what is happening. Maybe the easy accounts (those reachable or more likely to pay) have all been worked, so now there are fewer accounts to dial and work, but they are the more difficult ones? I'm guessing, but this would be the sort of context I'd be eager to learn more about in order to better understand what's driving what we are seeing in the data.

Coming back to the question of how I'd incorporate aspects of the data—and playing off this exercise title—I could plan to put some of it into words. For example, my second sentence outlined above, "Dials made decreased 47% between January and December, with roughly 250,000 dials made in December," could be context I incorporate by simply saying or writing it. Doing so opens up some additional potential ways to show the data, which we'll look at momentarily.

STEP 3: Yes, there are changes I would make to how this data is shown. I like the general clean design of the graph. But currently both the legend at the top and secondary y-axis at the right mean my audience has to do work—some back and forth—to figure out how to read this data. I'd like to make this easier. Also, as mentioned, I think there is an opportunity to articulate some of the context in words so that we can focus on the Penetration Rate in the graph.

STEP 4: Let's progress through a few views of this data so I can show you my thought process. First, I'll get rid of the secondary y-axis and Penetration Rate

data series that went with it (we'll reincorporate the latter momentarily). Notice also that the Accounts Worked in the original graph is a proportion of Dials Made, so if I change the data a bit, I can show these together. Rather than Dials Made and Accounts Worked, we can show those Worked and those Not Reached. See Figure 6.2b.

Call breakdown over time

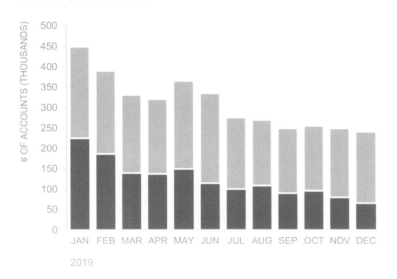

2019

FIGURE 6.2b Modify the data so we can stack it

In Figure 6.2b, the overall height of the bars (Worked plus those Not Reached) represents the total number of accounts that are dialed. We've already said we'll articulate the decrease in accounts dialed in words, which means we don't necessarily have to show it directly. In that case, one option could be to turn these into 100% stacked bars. We'll lose sight to the decrease in accounts dialed, but gain a clearer picture of the ratio of accounts Worked versus those Not Reached—the Penetration Rate. See Figure 6.2c.

PRACTICE with COLE

Call breakdown over time
WORKED | NOT REACHED

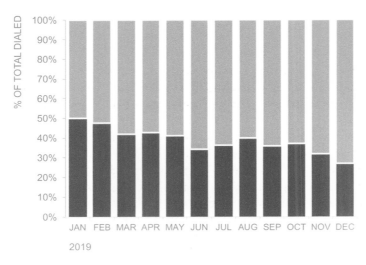

FIGURE 6.2c Change to stacked 100% bars

The benefit to moving from absolute bars to 100% bars is to be able to more easily see the proportion of accounts dialed that are worked. We can take this a step further, eliminating the space between the bars and modifying to an area graph. See Figure 6.2d.

Call breakdown over time
WORKED | NOT REACHED

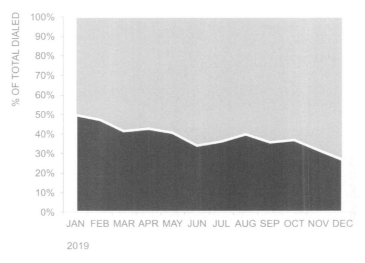

FIGURE 6.2d Let's change to stacked area

I don't often use area graphs, but there are situations where they can work well and I think this is one of those. One sometimes-con of area graphs is that it isn't always clear whether the individual series are stacked on top of each other or meant to be read from the x-axis up in cumulative fashion. Here, given the 100% stack, this is likely intuitive.

We get a couple of benefits from this view. We can clearly focus on the proportion of accounts that are Worked, given the emphasis via color. In this picture, the line that separates the green from the grey now represents the Penetration Rate.

One of the things I was originally hoping to solve for was any back and forth between the legend and the data. As we've seen in other examples, one method I'll often employ is to place the legend at the upper left (often just under the graph title, as I've done in this case). Given the zigzagging "z" of processing, this helps ensure my audience sees how to read the data before they get to the actual data. Another alternative is to label the data directly. I tried that, placing the Not Reached and Worked labels in the area graph as white text at the left and another option with them aligned to the right. These both looked messy to me, so I kept the legend separate at the top and chose to label just the Penetration Rate directly.

Let's do that plus put a few additional words around the data and highlight the final data point. Without additional context to know what's driving what we're seeing, Figure 6.2e is where I'd end on this one.

Total accounts dialed decreased 47% from January to December to 250K. During the same time period, **penetration rate has declined markedly**.

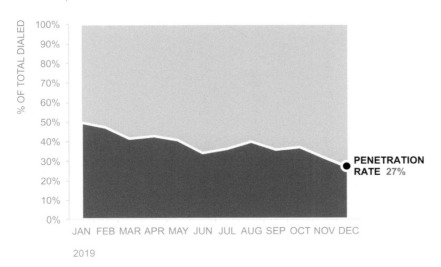

Call breakdown over time
WORKED | NOT REACHED

FIGURE 6.2e Put it into words!

I should probably mention that this particular makeover has been met with mixed responses. Some found the 100% aspect confusing or preferred the simple stacked bar view that also gave insight into absolute numbers. It's possible I've become overly attached to the solution I created. In spite of this feedback, I've chosen to include it here because it highlights a different approach than we typically take, reinforcing the idea that it is okay to try things that are outside of the norm. If I were planning to use this in a business setting, I'd get additional feedback to determine whether to push forward with this solution or modify it to best meet my audience's needs.

The primary point is: putting our graphs into words can help us get clear on what we want to show and effective ways to show it. It can be helpful to put those words directly with the graph to help ensure it makes sense to our audience!

Exercise 6.3: identify the tension

Let's step away from data and graphs for the next few exercises and dive deeper into elements of story.

Tension is a critical—and often overlooked—component when we communicate with data. When I teach the lesson on story in my workshops, I often get quite dramatic in my delivery, particularly in the discussion about tension. This is to emphasize the point, but shouldn't be taken as if we have to create drama for our stories to be effective. It's not about making up tension—if there weren't tension present, we'd have nothing to communicate about in the first place. Rather, it's about figuring out what tension exists and how we can illuminate it for our audience. When we do this well, we get their attention and are in a better position to motivate them to act.

Thinking back to some of the lessons we practiced in Chapter 1, getting to know our audience and what matters to them cannot be emphasized enough. It's easy to focus on what matters to us, but that's not a good way to influence. Rather, we need to step outside of ourselves and think about what tension exists *for our audience*. This relates back to one of the components of the Big Idea that we discussed: what is at stake? When we've effectively identified the tension in a situation, then the action we want our audience to take becomes how they can resolve the tension in the data story (we'll talk about this idea further in a number of the forthcoming exercises in this chapter).

Let's look at a few different scenarios—some may sound familiar that we've discussed before and some are new—and practice identifying the tension. Consider each of the following. **First, identify the tension. Next, identify an action the given audience can take to resolve the tension you've identified.**

SCENARIO 1: You are an analyst working at a national retailer. You've just conducted a survey from the recent back-to-school shopping season, asking both your store's customers and your main competitors' customers about various dimensions of the shopping experience. On the positive side, you've found the data confirms some things you thought to be true: people enjoy the overall experience of shopping in your store and they have positive brand association. When it comes to opportunities, you've found there are inconsistencies in the service levels that customers are reporting across your stores. Your team has brainstormed solutions to this and wants to put forth a specific recommendation to the Head of Retail: sales associate training should be developed and rolled out to create shared understanding of what good service looks like to provide consistent exemplary customer service.

SCENARIO 2: You run HR at a company that has historically intentionally filled leadership at the director level through internal promotions (not hiring externally).

Attrition—people leaving the company—at the director level has increased recently. In light of this, you asked your team to build a forecast projecting the next five years based on recent trends for promotions, acquisitions, and attrition. You believe, based on the expected continued growth of the company, that unless something changes, you will face a gap in future leadership talent needed compared to what you'll have. You'd like to use this data to drive a conversation among the executive team about what to do. The options, as you see them, are to better understand what's driving attrition at the director level and work to curb it, invest in manager development so you can promote at a faster rate, make strategic acquisitions to bring leadership talent into the organization, or change your hiring strategy and start to fill director-level positions through external hires.

SCENARIO 3: You work as a data analyst at a regional health care center. As part of ongoing initiatives to improve overall efficiency, cost, and quality of care, there has been a push in recent years for greater use of virtual communications by physicians (via email, phone, and video) when possible in place of in-person visits. You've been asked to pull together data for inclusion in the annual review to assess whether the desired shift towards virtual is happening and make recommendations for targets for the coming year. The main audience is leadership across the health care centers. Your analysis indicates there has indeed been a relative increase in virtual encounters across both primary and specialty care. You've forecast the coming year and expect these trends to continue. You can use recent data and your forecast to inform targets. You believe seeking physician input is also necessary to avoid being over-aggressive and setting targets that may inadvertently lead to negative impact on quality of care.

Solution 6.3: identify the tension

There isn't a single right answer, but the following outlines how I would frame the tension and resolution in each of these cases.

SCENARIO 1:

- **Tension:** There is inconsistency in service levels across stores.

- **Resolution:** Devote resources to developing and conducting sales associate training.

SCENARIO 2:

- **Tension:** Looking forward, we expect a shortage of directors given recent trends.

- **Resolution:** Discuss and make a decision about what strategic change(s) we should make to fill roles at the leadership level.

SCENARIO 3:

- **Tension:** What's more important: efficiency or quality of care? The desired shift towards virtual encounters is happening, but how much more do we want to push?

- **Resolution:** Use data together with physician input to set reasonable targets for the coming year to appropriately balance efficiency with quality of care.

PRACTICE *with* COLE

Exercise 6.4: utilize the components of story

The way I approach story has changed perhaps the most since writing *SWD*. In *SWD*, story was examined through plays, books, and movies. The general structure of story I put forth was that a story is comprised of a beginning, middle, and end. While this is useful, I believe we can take things a step further by considering the narrative arc.

Stories have a shape. They start off with a plot. Tension is introduced. This tension builds in the form of a rising action. It reaches a point of climax. There is a falling action. The story concludes with a resolution. We are hardwired to engage with and remember information that comes to us in this general structure.

The challenge is that the typical business presentation doesn't look anything like this! The typical business presentation follows a linear path. There is no up or down; we move straight through it. We start with the question we set out to answer, then discuss the data, followed by our analysis, and finally our findings or recommendation. This linear path—by the way—is what our storyboards mainly looked like back in Chapter 1. Big advantage can be gained by rethinking the components of our storyboards along the narrative arc. Figure 6.4a shows the narrative arc.

FIGURE 6.4a The narrative arc

Let's revisit a storyboard we've already completed. Refer back to Exercise 1.7, where we storyboarded about back-to-school shopping. Look to either your storyboard or mine (Solution 1.7). **How could you arrange these components along the narrative arc? Does this mean you reorder, add, or eliminate pieces?**

One way to accomplish this is to get a pile of sticky notes and write out the components of the storyboard from Solution 1.7. Then arrange them along the arc, augmenting with additional ideas and removing and rearranging as makes sense.

Solution 6.4: utilize the components of story

Figure 6.4b shows how I might arrange components of the back-to-school shopping scenario along the narrative arc.

FIGURE 6.4b Back-to-school shopping narrative arc

I could start by setting the **plot**. This is the basic information—the framing—that my audience needs to know to have consistent context to use as a jumping off point: "The back-to-school shopping season is a critical part of our business and we haven't historically been data-driven in how we've approached it."

Next, I introduce tension and start to build the **rising action**. "We've conducted a survey, and, for the first time ever, we have data. The data shows that we are doing well in some areas, but underperform in several key areas!" This is the **climax**, where tension peaks. I can talk specifically about the areas that underperform and what is at stake for my audience as a result of this: we are losing to the competition and will continue to do so unless we make a change.

I can then soften things with the **falling action**. "Not all areas are equally important, and we've identified a small handful on which to focus. Plus, we've already looked into several ideas for solving the issue and have narrowed in on one we think will have a big impact." **Ending**: "Let's invest in employee training to improve the in-store customer experience and make the upcoming back-to-school shopping season the best one yet." Here is what you—the audience—can do to resolve the tension I've brought to light.

PRACTICE with COLE

Exercise 6.5: arrange along the narrative arc

Let's look at another example of arranging the components of a story along the narrative arc. We'll revisit a situation we looked at a couple of times in Chapter 1.

Refer back to Exercise 1.8. Reread the pet adoption scenario. Did you complete this exercise and create a storyboard? If not, you can take some time to do so now, or review my example storyboard from Solution 1.8. How can you rethink the components making use of the narrative arc?

For reference, a blank narrative arc follows (it will look familiar if you've already completed the preceding exercise; if not, you may want to read through it for additional general context). One way to complete this exercise is to write the components of your story on small sticky notes and arrange them over or under Figure 6.5a. Your stickies need not match those in the original storyboard: feel free to depart from this as you make use of this shape and its components. Be creative in your approach!

FIGURE 6.5a The narrative arc

Solution 6.5: arrange along the narrative arc

This scenario seems like it may call for less rigidity than a typical business presentation. On the other hand, lives are actually at stake (the animals who are potentially being adopted), so considering our audience and how best to convince them to get what we need is definitely important. Thinking back to exercises we tackled in Chapter 1: what motivates our audience? Is it meeting our adoption goal, or might we go beyond that? Different context and assumptions here will change how you approach.

The narrative arc I created is shown in Figure 6.5b.

FIGURE 6.5b   Pet adoptions narrative arc

I took a bit of a risk in this example, starting by painting a picture (the **plot**) of a beautiful day at the park, where we are running a normal adoption event. **Tension** is introduced when we only have a few successful adoptions. This tension builds in the form of a **rising action** as I run my audience through the normal course of events for animals that end up in our shelter. This tension reaches a point of climax when innocent animals face euthanization. I can soften that climax (**falling action**) by describing the recent event that was unexpectedly moved to a local pet retailer due to inclement weather and the success of the event. I can summarize the limited resources we'd need to do it again. My audience can resolve the tension (**ending**) by approving resources for the pilot program.

I should point out that these are not the only components we should consider and this is definitely not the only possible order. Rather, this is one example of how we can make use of the narrative arc, given what we know and the assumptions that

I've made. As one example of a riff on this—particularly if I'm not confident I can keep my audience's attention until the end, or if I think they may simply approve my request and I don't have to take the time to go through the details—I could opt for leading with the ending. I could start by saying, "I need $500 and 3 hours of a volunteer's time to launch a pilot program that I believe will increase adoptions: do you want to hear more?" (Note that this looks quite a lot like the Big Idea that we formed in Exercise 1.5!)

There is no end to how we can rearrange or add or take away and there are numerous different approaches that would lead to a successful communication. Paramount is that you give thought to how you do this to set yourself up for success.

Exercise 6.6: differentiate between live & stand-alone stories

There are two common scenarios when we communicate for explanatory purposes with data: (1) we are presenting live to our audience (in a meeting or presentation, whether in person or virtually via webex or similar) and (2) we send something to our audience (typically through email, though we may still encounter the occasional print-it-out-and-leave-it-on-someone's-desk situation).

In practice, we often create a single communication that is meant to meet the needs of both of these instances. We touched on this briefly in *SWD*: this gives rise to the "slideument." It is part presentation, part document and doesn't exactly meet the needs of either circumstance. Typically, our content created to meet both of these needs is too dense for the presented version and sometimes not detailed enough for the version that is consumed on its own without you present to support it.

There is an approach that I often recommend: build piece by piece for the live presentation, then end with a fully annotated slide. Let's do an exercise to practice and illustrate this concept.

Imagine you are a consultant to Company X. You've been brought in to analyze the hiring process. Your goals are both to bring greater understanding to how things have been functioning generally—given that no one has spent much time looking at this data before—and use this to facilitate discussions with the steering committee at Company X who has chartered the work to identify specific improvements. You've met with the steering committee several times already and developed a good understanding of the business context. Time to hire (the number of days once a job opening is posted that it takes to fill) is one metric in which people are highly interested and will be the focus of this exercise.

Figure 6.6a shows time to fill open roles (measured in days) for internal transfers and external hires for Company X. Spend a moment familiarizing yourself with this data, then complete the following steps.

Time to fill

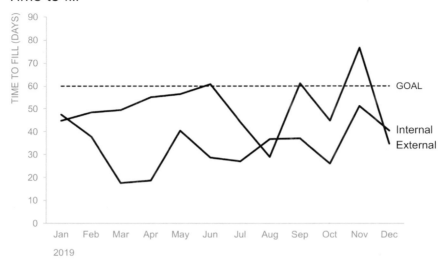

FIGURE 6.6a Time to fill

STEP 1: Let's say you will have an upcoming meeting with the steering committee. You have 10 minutes on the agenda to discuss time to hire. You'd like to take a couple of minutes to set the context by walking your audience through the data in Figure 6.6a and use that to facilitate a conversation. Take advantage of the fact that you'll be live in person with your audience: rather than simply show Figure 6.6a, consider how you might build the graph one or a few elements at a time. Create a bulleted list of what you would show, step by step. Feel free to liberally make assumptions.

STEP 2: Download the data and create the progression you outlined in Step 1 in the tool of your choice.

STEP 3: You anticipate the steering committee will want your visuals after the meeting. Rather than share the progression you went through, you've decided to build a single comprehensive graph (or slide). This will serve as a reminder of what you shared and will also be a good resource for anyone who misses the meeting. Create a visual to meet this need in the tool of your choice.

Solution 6.6: differentiate between live & stand-alone stories

STEP 1: My progression building this graph piece by piece could look like the following.

- **Start with a skeleton graph** that has x- and y-axis title and labels but no data. Use this to set the stage for my audience.

- **Add the Goal line**, sharing any known context about how it was set.

- **Build the External line**. Start with the first point in January, then add data through June and plan to talk through known context causing this trend. Then build the rest of the line, highlighting specific data I want to draw attention to as I do.

- **Build the Internal line**. Push the External line back so it doesn't compete for attention, then build the Internal line in a similar fashion, highlighting and planning to raise points of interest along the way.

STEP 2: The following shows how I would execute the steps I've outlined, along with my planned accompanying commentary. I've liberally made assumptions regarding the context for the purpose of illustration.

Let me take a few minutes to share with you recent data concerning time to hire. I'm going to use this to frame a conversation about some potential decisions you could make to impact time to hire going forward.

PRACTICE *with* COLE

First, let me set up for you what we'll be looking at before distracting you with any data. On the vertical y-axis, I'll be plotting time to fill. This is the average number of days from an open job being posted to a successful hire for hires made in the given month. On the x-axis, I'll plot time. We're looking at data from 2019, starting with January on the left and going through December on the right. (Figure 6.6b)

Time to fill

FIGURE 6.6b Skeleton graph

The company-wide goal is to fill roles within 60 days. (Figure 6.6c)

Time to fill

FIGURE 6.6c Introduce goal

Let's look at external hires first. Average time to hire in January was just under 45 days, well under our 60-day goal. (Figure 6.6d)

Time to fill

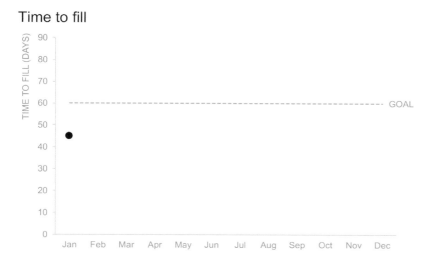

FIGURE 6.6d First point of external line

However, this increased steadily over the first half of the year. This coincides with increasing average number of interviews per candidate. As one may expect, the more interviews there are, the longer the hiring process. This led us to be just above goal in June, with average time to fill role of 61 days. (Figure 6.6e)

Time to fill

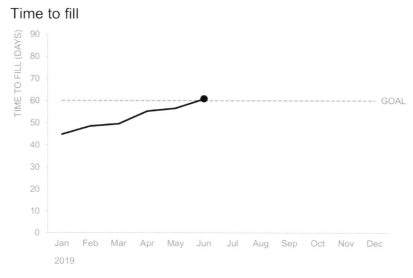

FIGURE 6.6e External time to fill increased in first half of year

Monthly time to fill for external hires varied quite a lot over the second half of the year. We found that those months having lower time to hire—denoted by blue markers—had fewer interviews per candidate on average. Both a greater quantity of interviews and interviewer vacation schedules likely contributed to the months above goal—designated by the orange markers. (Figure 6.6f)

Time to fill

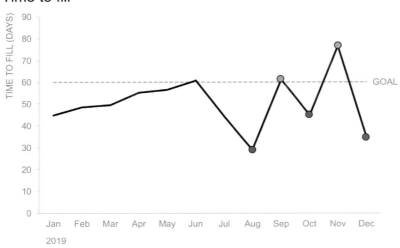

FIGURE 6.6f External time to fill varied in second half of year

Let's shift next to look at internal time to fill—these are those roles being filled by internal transfers. We started the year beating goal at 48 days to hire. (Figure 6.6g)

Time to fill

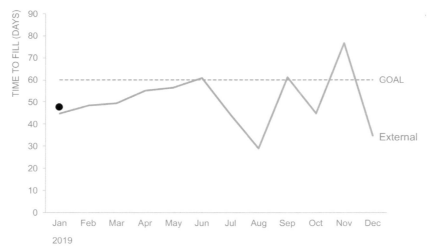

FIGURE 6.6g Add first point of internal line

Time to fill with internal candidates improved, decreasing the first few months of the year. In March and April, time to fill was under 3 weeks for internal candidates—this is impressively fast! (Figure 6.6h)

Time to fill

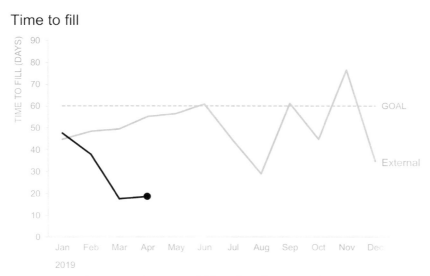

FIGURE 6.6h Internal time to fill low first few months of year

Time to hire increased in May. This coincided with an increase in the number of internal transfers, indicating that our processes might not be able to efficiently handle greater numbers of transfers. (Figure 6.6i)

Time to fill

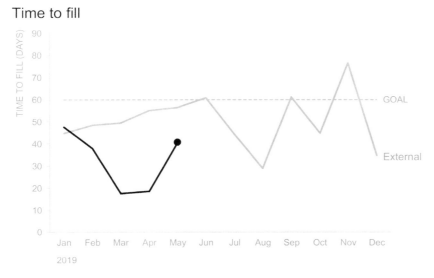

FIGURE 6.6i Increased April to May

After May, there was a slight dip followed by another increase. (Figure 6.6j)

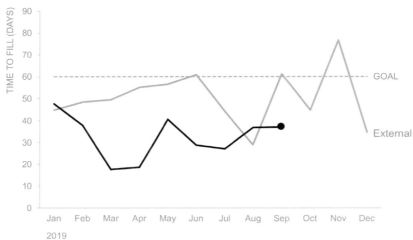

FIGURE 6.6j   Another dip and increase

September to November saw another dip then increase. (Figure 6.6k)

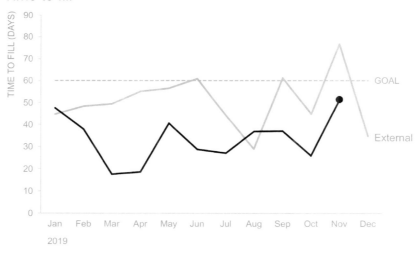

FIGURE 6.6k   Yet another dip and increase

Though down from November to December, internal time to fill was higher than external in December. Though a bit noisy month-to-month, there was a general increase in time to fill internal hires in the second half of the year. (Figure 6.6l)

Time to fill

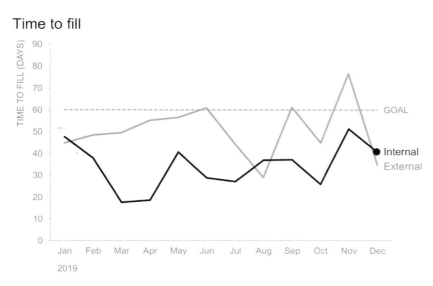

FIGURE 6.6l Internal ends the year above external

Let's look at the full picture and summarize. Both external and internal time to fill roles have varied over the past year. While both beat the 60-day target in most of the year, we have seen time to fill generally increase over the latter part of 2019. Probably not unexpectedly—more interviews lead to longer time to fill roles. Vacation schedules also contribute to delays. On the internal side, things take longer when we have more internal candidates, suggesting there could be some process improvements for better handling larger quantities.

Let's discuss: what does this mean for the coming year? Are there any changes you'd like to make? (Figure 6.6m)

Time to fill

FIGURE 6.6m Let's discuss the implications looking forward

STEP 3: I might summarize the progression illustrated in Step 2 with the following fully annotated visual. See Figure 6.6n.

Time to fill role discussion needed: where do we go from here?

Both External and Internal time to fill have varied in the past year. Understanding contributing factors—number of interviews, vacation schedules, and current internal transfer volume constraints—can help us better plan for the future.

Time to fill

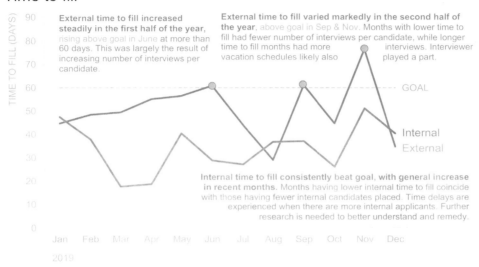

External time to fill increased steadily in the first half of the year, rising above goal in June at more than 60 days. This was largely the result of increasing number of interviews per candidate.

External time to fill varied markedly in the second half of the year, above goal in Sep & Nov. Months with lower time to fill had fewer number of interviews per candidate, while longer time to fill months had more interviews. Interviewer vacation schedules likely also played a part.

Internal time to fill consistently beat goal, with general increase in recent months. Months having lower internal time to fill coincide with those having fewer internal candidates placed. Time delays are experienced when there are more internal applicants. Further research is needed to better understand and remedy.

LET'S DISCUSS: Should we put stricter guidelines around maximum number of interviews? How can we keep vacation schedules from impacting time to hire? What can we do to improve efficiency of internal transfer process in order to better handle higher volumes?

FIGURE 6.6n Fully annotated view to be distributed

With Figure 6.6n, the audience processing it on their own—those who missed the meeting or need a reminder of what was covered—can read through a similar story to what I would walk through in a live setting.

Consider how this approach of building piece by piece in a live meeting or presentation, coupled with a fully annotated slide or two, could meet your needs for effectively telling your data stories.

Exercise 6.7: transition from dashboard to story

In Chapter 1 of *SWD*, I drew a distinction between exploratory and explanatory analysis. In a nutshell, exploratory is what you do to understand the data and explanatory is what you do to communicate something about the data to someone else.

I consider dashboards to be a useful tool in the *exploratory* part of the process. There is some data that we need to be looking at on a regular basis (weekly, monthly, or quarterly) to see where things are in line with our expectations as well as where they are not. The dashboard can help us identify where there might be something unexpected or interesting happening. However, once we've found those interesting things and want to communicate them, we should take that data *out* of the dashboard and apply the various lessons that we've covered.

Let's look at an example dashboard and practice how we can move from exploratory dashboard to explanatory story. Refer to Figure 6.7a, which shows the Project Dashboard. You'll see demand and capacity breakdowns by a variety of categories (by region and department). The metric being graphed across the dashboard is project hours.

This may feel familiar, as we've looked at some of this data already in Exercises 2.3 and 2.4. Spend some time studying Figure 6.7a, then complete the following steps.

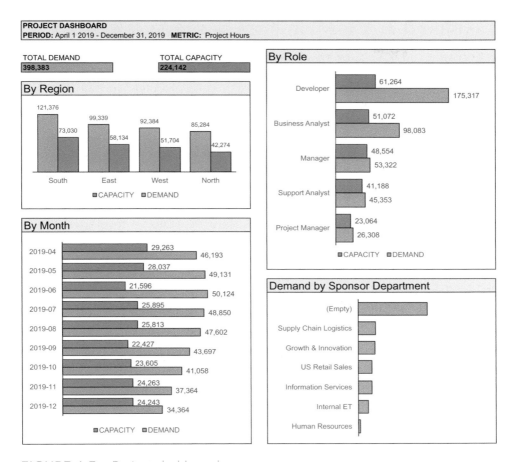

PROJECT DASHBOARD
PERIOD: April 1 2019 - December 31, 2019   **METRIC:** Project Hours

TOTAL DEMAND
398,383

TOTAL CAPACITY
224,142

FIGURE 6.7a Project dashboard

STEP 1: Let's start by practicing putting it into words. Write a sentence describing a takeaway from each component of the dashboard in Figure 6.7a.

STEP 2: Do we need all of this data? It may be important to look at project hours cut by each of these dimensions as part of our exploration of the data, but not all of the data is equally interesting when it comes to communicating it to our audience. Imagine you need to tell a story with this data: which parts of the dashboard would you focus on and which would you omit?

STEP 3: Create a visual story with the elements you selected to include in Step 2. Make assumptions as needed for purposes of the exercise. How would you show the data? How will you incorporate words? Decide whether you'll present live or send the information off to be consumed on its own. Optimize your approach for the scenario you've chosen.

Solution 6.7: transition from dashboard to story

STEP 1: I might summarize the main takeaway from the various components of the dashboard as follows.

- **Summary stats at top:** Demand far exceeds capacity in the period 4/1/19 to 12/31/19.

- **By Region:** Demand exceeds capacity across all regions in roughly similar magnitudes.

- **By Month:** The gap between capacity and demand, which was largest in June and generally quite high through Q2 and Q4, narrowed over the latter part of the year.

- **By Role:** Demand exceeds capacity the most for Developers; the gap between capacity and demand is also high for Business Analysts.

- **By Sponsor Department:** We are missing a lot of data related to the source of demand—or perhaps not all projects have a sponsor department?

STEP 2: I'll start by eliminating the things I don't want to include. Where things are pretty consistent or where we are missing data might be obvious aspects to omit (unless these vary from our expectations, in which case they may be interesting). There isn't a single correct answer: we are missing a lot of context, and have to make a number of assumptions. In real life, you'd want to build this context for yourself to make smart choices about where to focus your efforts, what is relevant, and which data to include or omit as you build your data story.

I do see some interesting things happening over time and by role, so I'll focus my attention there. In terms of changes to how the data is shown, I'll want to focus on the decreasing gap over time and also more clearly illustrate the difference between capacity and demand by role. I'll put more words around the data—both to make it clear what we are looking at, as well as to help walk my audience through the story.

STEP 3: I'll assume this is part of a year-end update and that the information is being sent off for my audience to consume on their own. Figure 6.7b illustrates what a single slide with the information I've chosen to concentrate on could look like (with my imagined context for illustration purposes).

Expect continued progress towards meeting demand

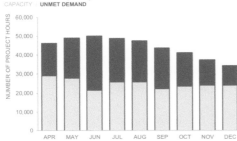

OVER TIME: GAP DECREASING, BUT PERSISTS

Demand continues to exceed capacity as of year end. In 2019, we reduced the gap between demand and capacity markedly, mainly by clearing backlog of requested projects that aren't possible given current team structure and competing priorities.

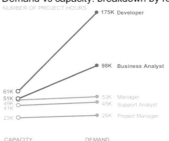

BY ROLE: BIGGEST GAP IN 2 AREAS

The biggest areas that have been over capacity are Developers and Business Analysts. Planned targeted hiring of these roles is expected to continue to reduce overall gap over time. We will continue to monitor and report.

FIGURE 6.7b Story on a single slide

Let's discuss some of my decision points in Figure 6.7b. I employed a takeaway title at the top that goes beyond the data shown to set an expectation for the future. I chose a two-sided layout for my send-away story. You'll see additional examples of this approach, as it tends to be my go-to structure when you have multiple visuals you want to put on a single slide. Two visuals is the magic number for me when you need to show more than a single graph, because you can still make the graphs large enough to read and also have space to lend context via text (for more than this, I recommend breaking into multiple slides).

In this example, the left-hand side focuses (through color and words) on the decreasing gap over time. I opted for the stacked bar out of the various iterations we looked at in Exercise 2.4 because I like how this shows both Capacity and Demand, with the ability to focus attention on the Unmet Demand. On the right-hand side, I showed the breakdown by role in a slopegraph. This view of the data, coupled with strategic use of color and words, makes the Developer and Business Analyst clear points of focus.

I've assumed the specifics in this scenario for purposes of illustration. I framed it more as an FYI, rather than any specific call to action, but a different spin on the details might necessitate something more pointed. Take note of how the steps we went through—putting our graphs into words, considering what to focus on and what to omit, graphing the data effectively and thoughtfully using color and words—help us transition from an exploratory dashboard to an explanatory data story.

Getting comfortable communicating with story takes practice. Let's identify the tension in a few real-world scenarios, then undertake additional exercises with the narrative arc to help us grab our audience's attention, build credibility, and spur action.

Exercise 6.8: identify the tension

As we've discussed, tension is a key component of story. Together, we practiced identifying the tension and a corresponding resolving action in Exercise 6.3. Here's an opportunity for you to do some additional practice on your own.

Read each of the following scenarios (some may be familiar from their use elsewhere). **For each, first identify the tension. Next, identify an action the audience can take to resolve the tension you've identified.**

SCENARIO 1: You are the Chief Financial Officer for a national retailer. Your team of financial analysts just completed a review of Q1 and have identified that the company is likely to end the fiscal year with a loss of $45 million if operating expenses and sales follow the latest projections. Because of a recent economic downturn, an increase in sales is unlikely. Therefore, you believe the projected loss can *only* be mitigated by controlling operating expenses and that management should implement an expense control policy ("expense control initiative ABC") immediately. You will be reporting the Q1 quarterly results at an upcoming Board of Directors meeting and are planning your communication—a summary of financial results in a PPT deck—that you will present to the board with your recommendation.

SCENARIO 2: Imagine you work for a regional medical group. You and several colleagues have just wrapped up an evaluation of Suppliers A, B, C, and D for the XYZ Products category. The data shows that historical usage has varied a lot by medical facility, with some using primarily Supplier B and others using primarily Supplier D (and only limited historical use of Suppliers A and C). You've also found that satisfaction is highest across the board for Supplier B. You've analyzed all of the data and realized there are significant cost savings in going with a single or dual supplier contract. However, either of these will mean changes for some medical centers relative to their historical supplier mix. You are preparing to present to the steering committee, where a majority vote will determine the decision.

SCENARIO 3: Craveberry yogurt is the new product that the food manufacturing company you are employed by is preparing to launch. The product team on which you work decided to do one more round of taste testing to get a final gauge of consumer sentiment. You've analyzed the results of the taste test and believe there are a couple of changes that should be made—minor things, but they could have major impact when it comes to consumer reception in the marketplace. You have a meeting with the Head of Product, who will need to decide whether to delay launch to allow time to make these changes, or to go to market with Craveberry as it is.

Exercise 6.9: move from linear path to narrative arc

Before arranging potential elements of our story along the narrative arc, it can sometimes be helpful to start with a more linear view. Specifically, the chronological path is one that business presentations default to frequently. This makes sense from the standpoint that this is the order that comes to us most naturally because it's the general path that we went through to get from the initial question we set out to solve to our proposed outcome or course of action.

However, the linear or chronological path isn't always the best path on which to take our audience. We should be thoughtful in how we organize the information through which we lead our audience. Rethinking things in light of the narrative arc can be one way to achieve this. Let's look at a linear storyboard we discussed in Chapter 1 about university elections and practice reimagining our potential communication path making use of the narrative arc.

You're a rising university senior serving on the student government council. One of the council's goals is to create a positive campus experience by representing the student body to faculty and administrators by electing representatives from each undergraduate class. You've served on the council for the past three years and are involved in the planning for this year's upcoming elections. Last year, student voter turnout for the elections was 30% lower than previous years, indicating lower engagement between the student body and the council. You and a fellow council member completed benchmarking research of voter turnout at other universities and found that universities with the highest voter turnout had the most effective student government council at effecting change. You think there's opportunity to increase voter turnout at this year's election by building awareness of the student government council's mission by doing an advertising campaign to the student body. You have an upcoming meeting with the student body president and finance committee where you will be presenting your findings and recommendation.

Your ultimate goal is a budget of $1,000 for an advertising campaign to increase awareness of why the student body should vote in these elections. To this end, your fellow councilmember created the following storyboard (Figure 6.9). Review the storyboard, then complete the following steps.

FIGURE 6.9 University elections colleague's storyboard

STEP 1: Review the sticky notes in the storyboard in Figure 6.9 and determine how you could align them to the components of the narrative arc. Specifically, list which points you would cover in each section of the arc: plot, rising action, climax, falling action, and ending (you may not use all of the ideas from the original storyboard).

STEP 2: Write the points you've outlined in Step 1 on your own stickies and arrange them in an arc shape. Continue to rearrange, add, remove, and change components of your story as you do this, making assumptions as needed.

STEP 3: Did the process of physically arranging ideas along an arc change your approach? Write a paragraph or two about your process and any learnings. Is this a strategy you can envision employing in the future? Why or why not?

Exercise 6.10: build a narrative arc

Let's make use of the narrative arc again. This time, we'll skip the storyboarding step and go straight from the scenario to creating our story arc using an example from Exercise 6.8 that was part of our tension identification practice. Refresh your memory by reading the following, then complete the subsequent steps.

Craveberry is the new yogurt product that your food manufacturing employer is preparing to launch. The product team on which you work decided to do an additional round of taste testing to get a final gauge of consumer sentiment before going to market with the product. The taste test collects data on what participants like or don't like across a number of dimensions: sweetness, size, amount of fruit, amount of yogurt, and thickness. You've analyzed the results of the taste test and believe there are a couple of changes that should be made—minor things that have the potential for major impact when it comes to consumer reception in the marketplace. Specifically, your recommendation will be to keep sweetness and size consistent. But people think the product is too thick and has too much fruit. Therefore, you recommend reducing the amount of fruit and increasing the amount of yogurt, which is expected to reduce the overall thickness. You have a meeting with the Head of Product, who will need to decide whether to delay launch to allow time to make these changes, or to go to market with Craveberry as it is.

STEP 1: Get some sticky notes and write down the components (pieces of content) that you believe will be part of your Craveberry story.

STEP 2: Arrange the stickies you've created in the shape of an arc, aligning your various ideas to the components of the arc: plot, rising action, climax, falling action, and ending. Feel free to add, remove, or change things as necessary to meet your needs, making assumptions for the purpose of the exercise.

STEP 3: Compare this process to that you experienced in Exercise 6.9. Did you find it easier to start with a storyboard or blank slate when it came to planning the components of your data story along the narrative arc? What are the resulting implications for the planning process you will undertake in the future? Write a paragraph or two outlining your observations and learnings.

PRACTICE on your OWN

Exercise 6.11: evolve from report to story

Dashboards and regular reporting (weekly, monthly, quarterly)—we can use these tools as one way to explore our data and figure out what could be interesting, worth highlighting, or digging into further. There can also be great value from a self-service standpoint of sharing reports with end users, who can then use them to answer their many individual questions, freeing up your time for more interesting analysis.

But too often, we share dashboards or reports meant for exploration when really we should be taking it a step further, making it clear to our audience what they should focus on and what they should do with the information we share.

Examine Figure 6.11, which shows a page from a monthly report on ticket volume and related metrics. Then complete the following steps.

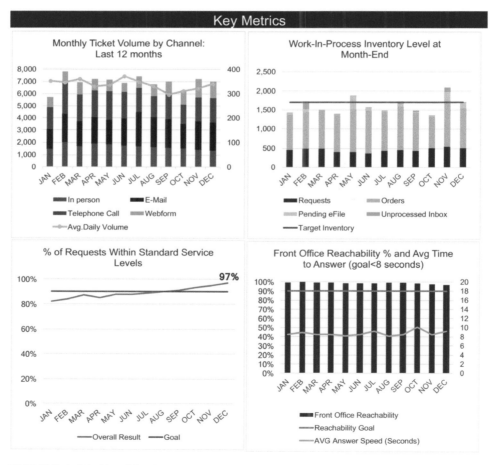

FIGURE 6.11 Key Metrics

STEP 1: Let's start by practicing putting it into words. Write a sentence describing a takeaway for each graph in the report shown in Figure 6.11.

STEP 2: Do we need all of this data? It may be important to look at all of these things as we are exploring the data, but not all of the data is necessarily equally interesting when it comes to communicating it to our audience. Imagine you need to tell a story with this data: which parts of the report would you focus on and which (if any) would you omit?

STEP 3: Download the data and create graphs and/or slides to tell a visual story with the elements you selected to include in Step 2. How would you show the data? How will you incorporate words? Create your preferred visuals. Decide whether you'll present live or send the information off to be consumed on its own. Optimize your approach for the scenario you've chosen, making assumptions as necessary for the purpose of this exercise.

PRACTICE on your OWN

PRACTICE at WORK

We'll undertake three targeted exercises to help get your data stories across to your audience—articulating your message in a repeatable way, answering the question "what's the story?" and leveraging the narrative arc.
Identify a project and get to work!

Exercise 6.12: form a pithy, repeatable phrase

Repetition helps form a bridge from our short-term memory to our long-term memory. We can make use of this in the actual words we use to communicate with data by articulating our main point in a pithy, repeatable phrase.

Identify a project you are working on to communicate with data for explanatory purposes. Have you crafted your Big Idea? If not, refer back to Exercise 1.20 and complete it. Next, turn your Big Idea into a pithy, repeatable phrase. This can help you get clear on your goal when communicating, and can also be incorporated into your actual materials to help increase memorability for your audience. The pithy, repeatable phrase is short and catchy and it may incorporate alliteration. It need not be cute. It does need to be memorable. (If you crave an example—allow me to foreshadow—you'll get a chance to practice and see this idea employed in Exercises and Solutions 7.4 and 7.6.)

In a live presentation, you can start with the pithy, repeatable phrase. You could also end with it, or you might weave it in different ways over the course of your presentation—so that when your audience leaves the room, they've heard it a few times. This means they are both more likely to remember *and be able to repeat it.*

When you are sending something around (not presenting live), the pithy, repeatable phrase can be written in words. You might opt to make it the title or subtitle of your deck. Or use it for the takeaway title of an important slide. Or put these words on the final slide your audience sees. In some situations, it may make sense to combine these ideas. Consider how you can use repetition in your words—whether spoken or written—to make your main point clear and memorable.

The next time you communicate with data, contemplate how you can make use of a pithy, repeatable phrase.

PRACTICE at WORK

Exercise 6.13: what's the story?

We ask ourselves and each other versions of this question frequently when look-ing at data: what's the story? When we ponder this, we generally don't mean story at all, rather we are trying to understand the key takeaway or point. Clearly answering the question, "So what?" is the *minimum* level of "story" that must exist any time we communicate with data for explanatory purposes. Too often, we leave it to our audience to figure this out on their own, and good work and improved understanding is missed as a result.

In the past, I've differentiated how we think about story as it relates to our data communications into two types. I refer to them as *story with a lowercase "s"* and *Story with a capital "S."* Let's discuss each of these, including tips for how to think about and make use of them at work.

story with a *lowercase* "s"

For every graph and slide you create, ask yourself: "What is the main point?" Put it into words, as we practiced in Exercises 6.2, 6.7, 6.11, 7.5, and 7.6. Once you've articulated your point, take intentional steps to make that point clear to your audi-ence. Employ a takeaway slide or graph title to set expectations for your audience (for a reminder of what this is or additional practice, refer back to Exercises 6.1 and 6.7). Focus attention as we practiced in Chapter 4. Use words—either in your spoken narrative or written physically on the page—to explain to your audience what they should see and what it means.

Never leave your audience wondering, "So what?" Answer this question clearly for them!

Story with a *capital* "S"

Clearly articulating the primary takeaway is a step in the right direction, but there is a whole other level of story that we can employ: Story with a *capital* "S." This is Story in the traditional sense. It starts with a plot, then tension is introduced. The tension builds to a point of climax. It is followed by a falling action, which brings us to the resolution. Well told stories get our attention, stick with us, and can be recalled and retold. We can make use of Story strategically when we communi-cate with data.

The tool I recommend for structuring your Story is the narrative arc. When we con-ceive our data story in the shape of an arc, it forces a couple of things. First, to create the rise, we must identify tension. As a reminder, this is not the tension that exists for us, but rather the tension that exists for our audience. It's not about mak-ing up tension—if tension didn't exist, you'd have nothing to communicate about in the first place. Viewing our path as an arc also encourages us to think about how one idea or component relates to the next. This is easy to skip when we arrange things linearly and can help us identify where we might need additional content or transitions to ensure smooth flow. The arc forces us to think about the path on which we take our audience. Perhaps more important than any of this, the narrative arc encourages us to think about things from our audience's perspective in a way that linear storyboarding simply doesn't facilitate in the same way. This is the most important shift I see happen when people move from how we typically communicate in a business setting to using the narrative arc and Story: with Story, we must step outside ourselves and think critically about what will work for our audience.

Consider how you can use *story with a lowercase "s"* and Story with a capital "S" the next time you communicate with data. When it comes to the latter, you'll find more specific steps for making use of the narrative arc in the next exercise.

PRACTICE at WORK

Exercise 6.14: employ the narrative arc

The stories we encounter in books, movies, and plays typically follow a path: the narrative arc. We can use the narrative arc to our advantage when telling stories with data as well.

Figure 6.14 shows the general narrative arc.

FIGURE 6.14 The narrative arc

Let's review each component of the arc, with some related thoughts and questions that you can use when communicating with data.

- **Plot:** What does your audience need to know in order to be in the right frame of mind for what you will be asking of them? Identify the tacit knowledge you have that would be helpful to communicate explicitly to ensure people are working from the same set of assumptions or understanding of the situation.

- **Rising action:** What tension exists for your audience? How can you bring that to light and build it—to the level appropriate given the circumstances—for your audience?

- **Climax:** What is the maximum point of tension? This isn't tension for you, but rather tension for your audience. Think back to the Big Idea and conveying what is at stake. What does your audience care about? How can you utilize that to get and maintain their attention?

- **Falling action:** This is perhaps the fuzziest of the components when it comes to application in a business setting. The main purpose is so that we don't go abruptly from the highest point of tension—the climax—to the ending. The falling action is a buffer to ease this transition. In our data stories, it can take the form of additional detail or further breakdown (here's how the tension plays out by product or region), or could be potential options you've weighed, solutions you may employ, or discussion you'd like to facilitate among your audience.

- **Ending:** This is the resolution, the call to action. The ending is what your audience can do to resolve the tension that you've brought to light. Note that it isn't typically so simple as "We found X; therefore you should do Y." Our data stories are often more nuanced than that. This ending could be a conversation you want to drive, options to choose from, or perhaps even input you need from your audience to fully flesh out your story. In any case, identify the action you need your audience to take and how to make it clear and compelling.

From my perspective, in a business setting, it's less important that your story follow the arc in this order exactly (we see stories in everyday life veer from this path often anyway through flashbacks, foreshadowing, and so on) and more important that each of these pieces are present. In particular, I find that when we go with the typical linear path for communicating information in a business setting, tension and climax can be missed entirely. As we've discussed, these are critical elements of story. By not bringing them to light, we are doing our data and the stories we want to tell with it a disservice.

That said, it can sometimes be difficult to make the jump from all we know about a given scenario to the arc. Storyboarding can be a good interim step. Refer to Exercise 1.24 for instructions on storyboarding. Once you have your storyboard, go through the process of arranging components along the arc. This is simply another tool in your communications toolbelt that you can use to your advantage in some situations. I find when I have something important to communicate, going through the process of arranging the pieces along the arc can highlight when I might be missing something to make the pieces fit together or not fully thinking about my audience, the tension, and how they can help resolve it.

Consider how you can use the narrative arc when communicating to tell a data story that will get your audience's attention, build credibility, and inspire them to act!

PRACTICE at WORK

Exercise 6.15: let's discuss

Consider the following questions related to Chapter 6 lessons and exercises. Discuss with a partner or group.

1. What is a takeaway title? How does it differ from a descriptive title? When, why, and where would you choose to use a takeaway title in your communications?

2. What role does tension play when communicating with data? How can you identify the tension in a given situation? Reflect on a current project: what is the tension? How might you incorporate this tension in your data story?

3. What are the components of the narrative arc? Can you list them? When and how can you make use of the narrative arc when communicating with data? Are any components of the arc fuzzy or confusing? Are there any you'd like to talk about more?

4. How should we order the various components of our data-driven stories? What should we consider when determining how to organize the information?

5. Do you anticipate resistance from your audience or other challenges using story to communicate in the ways outlined in *SWD* and illustrated in this chapter? How will you deal with it? When does it *not* make sense to use story to communicate?

6. How can we use repetition strategically in our data communications? Why would we want to do this?

7. What is different when you present live to your audience (in a meeting or presentation) compared to when you send something off to be consumed on its own? How should the materials you create differ? What strategies can you employ in each of these scenarios to help ensure success?

8. What is one specific goal you will set for yourself or your team related to the strategies outlined in this chapter? How can you hold yourself (or your team) accountable to this? Who will you turn to for feedback?

PRACTICE at WORK

practice more
with cole

While prior chapters have provided a piecemeal focus on the given lesson, this chapter takes a more comprehensive view of the entire *storytelling with data* process. Real-world based scenarios and related data visualizations are introduced and paired with specific questions to consider and solve. These are followed by step-by-step illustrations that give full insight into my thought process and design decisions.

I encounter many examples of data communications through our workshops. Clients share their work ahead of time and we use this as the basis of discussion and practice. These cross many topics and industries and there is something to be learned from each and every one. The process of creating data visualization makeovers from select examples to highlight *storytelling with data* lessons has been key to honing my own and my team's skills for critiquing, remaking, and sharing and discussing examples. In this section, you'll get an opportunity to practice just like the *storytelling with data* team—then you'll be walked through our solution as if you were a participant in one of our hands-on workshops.

Though the lessons in *SWD* and here could be taken as step-by-step instruction, my typical approach for moving from data to data story is more holistic, which is how you'll see it addressed in the forthcoming examples. Rather than go through all parts of the process each time, the various examples are used to highlight different components, exposing you to varied challenges and potential solutions. We will start out with some simple graph and slide redesigns and get increasingly comprehensive as we move through the case studies presented and solved in this chapter.

Let's practice!

Before we do, we'll review the main lessons we've covered so far.

SWD BOOK

FIRST, LET'S RECAP
The **STORYTELLING** with **DATA** PROCESS

STEP 1:

UNDERSTAND the CONTEXT

WHO is your audience?

WHAT do you need them to do?

HOW will data help make your point?

ARTICULATE your BIG IDEA

CREATE a STORYBOARD

→ brainstorm
→ edit
→ get feedback

STEP 2:

CHOOSE an APPROPRIATE VISUAL

DRAW IT!

then... CREATE it in your TOOL

iterate and look at your data different ways

SEEK FEEDBACK from others

STEP 3:

ELIMINATE CLUTTER

IDENTIFY UNNECESSARY ELEMENTS and REMOVE THEM

→ Leverage white space
→ Align elements
→ Avoid diagonal components

STEP 4:
DRAW ATTENTION *where you* **WANT it**

Use POSITION, SIZE, and COLOR to FOCUS your AUDIENCE's ATTENTION

Use the "where are your eyes drawn?" test

CLOSE EYES...

then OPEN EYES

WHAT do you SEE FIRST?

STEP 5:
THINK LIKE a DESIGNER

FIRST **FUNCTION** ⟶ **SECOND** **FORM**

think about what you want your audience to **DO** with the data

create a visualization that will make this easy

→ Affordances
→ Accessibility
→ Aesthetics
→ Acceptance

ANALYZE fine detail   VS.   COMMUNICATE key trends

STEP 6:
TELL a STORY

RETURN to your STORYBOARD

Where and how will data fit into the story?

Use the narrative arc to plan your story and form a pithy, repeatable phrase to help your message stick

PRACTICE MORE with COLE

7.1 new advertiser revenue	**7.2** sales channel update	**7.3** model performance
7.4 back-to-school shopping	**7.5** diabetes rates	**7.6** net promoter score

Exercise 7.1: new advertiser revenue

Imagine you are an analyst at a digital marketing company. A new feature was rolled out in 2015—let's call it Feature Z—that allows your company's clients to create better ads and will introduce a new revenue stream for your platform. The challenge is that Feature Z has a steep learning curve, so there's been some difficulty getting clients to utilize it. Overall, you have seen improvement over time, both in terms of clients using Feature Z and increased revenue from it. At a recent meeting when discussing this topic, the head of client support raised a question about what Feature Z adoption looks like for *new advertisers* specifically—those creating an advertisement on your platform for the first time. No one has sliced the data to look at this before, so you're working with a colleague to answer this question.

Your colleague put together the heatmap shown in Figure 7.1a. Spend a few moments studying it, then complete the following steps.

Advertisers are getting more sophisticated sooner

Advertiser Age (Full Qtrs)	Quarter of First Ad Create																
	2015Q1	2015Q2	2015Q3	2015Q4	2016Q1	2016Q2	2016Q3	2016Q4	2017Q1	2017Q2	2017Q3	2017Q4	2018Q1	2018Q2	2018Q3	2018Q4	2019Q1
0	15%	17%	14%	17%	16%	18%	17%	19%	21%	22%	24%	23%	24%	25%	26%	25%	28%
1	21%	18%	18%	18%	19%	21%	22%	23%	23%	25%	26%	23%	26%	31%	30%	33%	
2	20%	20%	20%	19%	20%	22%	24%	25%	22%	22%	23%	25%	29%	31%	32%		
3	20%	27%	26%	23%	23%	24%	23%	23%	24%	24%	27%	27%	33%	34%			
4	21%	26%	27%	26%	25%	24%	25%	23%	26%	28%	29%	30%	34%				
5	25%	33%	30%	26%	27%	25%	25%	23%	29%	29%	33%	32%					
6	28%	35%	31%	27%	28%	25%	29%	27%	31%	31%	34%						
7	29%	35%	32%	30%	28%	30%	33%	28%	35%	33%							
8	30%	37%	32%	33%	28%	32%	35%	32%	39%								
9	30%	38%	30%	35%	33%	32%	39%	34%									
10	31%	38%	33%	35%	37%	35%	41%										
11	35%	41%	37%	35%	39%	40%											
12	38%	43%	40%	39%	42%												
13	42%	46%	43%	43%													
14	44%	47%	43%														
15	47%	49%															
16	50%																

28% of new advertiser revenue in Q1 '19 came from Feature Z, up from 21% of new advertiser revenue in Q1 '17

FIGURE 7.1a   Advertisers are getting more sophisticated sooner

STEP 1: It's easy to jump to what's "wrong" when faced with someone else's data viz; let's pause first and reflect on positive points to share as feedback. What do you like about the current visual? Write a sentence or two.

STEP 2: What is not ideal in Figure 7.1a? Make a list.

STEP 3: How would you show this data? Download the data and iterate in the tool of your choice to create your preferred view.

STEP 4: What is the tension in this scenario? What action do you want your audience to take to resolve this tension?

STEP 5: You've been asked to provide a single slide that tells the story. Create this slide in the tool of your choice, making assumptions as necessary for the purpose of this exercise.

Solution 7.1: new advertiser revenue

STEP 1: There are a couple of things I like in this visual. Words are generally used well. The takeaway title at the top does a nice job setting up the story and starting to address the question posed. Axes are titled directly. I also like that there is annotation directly on the graph (in the grey text box on the right) that supports the takeaway title and also is connected directly to the data that is described so I don't have to search for it. That said, I don't love the arrows for creating this connection because they look messy and cover up some of the data. Oops, I've already jumped to what I'd do differently! Let's address that next.

STEP 2: There are a number of things that could be improved in this visual. The following are three primary aspects that are not ideal from my perspective.

- **The table feels like work.** I find the tabular data difficult to wrap my head around. The heatmapping helps, but it still requires effort to figure out what we're meant to see.

- **We've employed a problematic color scheme.** The red/green color scheme will be an issue for colorblind individuals in our audience. Beyond that, the red and green are competing for my attention, making it difficult to focus.

- **There is lack of alignment.** The various elements on the page aren't aligned. We see a mix of left-aligned, centered, and right-aligned text and numbers, without an apparent reason why. This creates an overall disorganized feel.

STEP 3: Iterating through multiple ways of graphing the data will likely be necessary to observe how variant views allow us to more or less easily see different things. We have time in a couple of ways in this example: by quarter for the first time an ad was created and by advertiser age. This means we could graph this data in lines two totally distinct ways. I'll start by creating a couple of quick and dirty graphs of the data (these are simply default charts; I'm not worrying at all about formatting at this step). See Figure 7.1b.

more PRACTICE *with* COLE

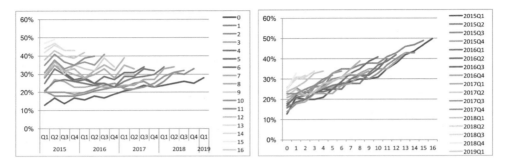

FIGURE 7.1b   Quick and dirty views of data

Let's consider what the visuals in Figure 7.1b allow us to see. In both cases, the y-axis represents the percent of total revenue driven by Feature Z. On the left-hand side, my x-axis is the date when the first ad was created. Each line represents advertisers of the given age group. This allows us to see that those in the first quarter (0) are less successful (the dark blue line for 0 quarters is at the bottom of the graph, where percent of revenue is lowest), though improving (the line for 0 increases as you move from left to right). Revenue goes up generally as age increases (the lines as we move upwards in age are increasingly high on the graph), with those in their 15th quarter appearing highest on the graph (we don't see a line for 16 quarters of tenure since there's only a single data point and you need two points to make a line). If you're reading this and thinking, Wow, this sounds complicated—you are correct. Let's shift our attention to the second graph.

The right-hand side plots advertiser age on the x-axis. Each line represents the quarter in which the first ad was created. Lines going upward to the right illustrate sophistication increasing with advertiser age. Lines moving upward on the graph shows sophistication increasing earlier—with more recent quarters at the top. Notice how much simpler that was to put into words compared to the left-hand side! This is going to be a good general view of the data given what we want to illustrate.

That said, this is still a lot of data to process. Do we need it all? Perhaps we could simplify by showing less. One way to do so would be to show fewer quarters of data. That said, I don't necessarily want to narrow our time window, since I'd like to be able to compare how things looked when Feature Z was introduced in 2015 and our recent data. But that still leaves me a couple of options. Given that the most recent data point is Q1 2019, I could elect to show just Q1 line for each year. Another approach could be to roll this data into annual cohorts. Look back to the right-hand side of Figure 7.1b and imagine we have just 5 lines of data (2015, 2016, 2017, 2018, 2019). Aggregating in this way would simplify things and allow us to clearly make our point: we're seeing more revenue sooner as advertiser sophistication gets better with both time (increasing as we move up the graph) and age (increasing rightwards). Bingo!

STEP 4: Let's step back from the data for a moment to identify the tension and resolution. I'd characterize the tension as: while we're generally seeing improvement in adoption of and revenue from Feature Z, we don't know how this plays out for our newbie advertisers. Are things okay? Are there issues we need to address?

The resolution is that things look good—no immediate action is needed. I often suggest that if we can't clearly articulate the action we want our audience to take, we should revisit the need to communicate in the first place. But here, our audience posed a question and though no action is needed, this isn't a reason not to answer it! Still, let's be clear on what we need our audience to do: they should be aware of this and they don't need to do anything right now. *We* can take the action to continue to monitor things from this perspective and alert them if this changes.

STEP 5: Figure 7.1c shows my single-slide story. Take a moment to study it and compare to what you created. Are there similarities? Where are there differences? Note what works well in each approach.

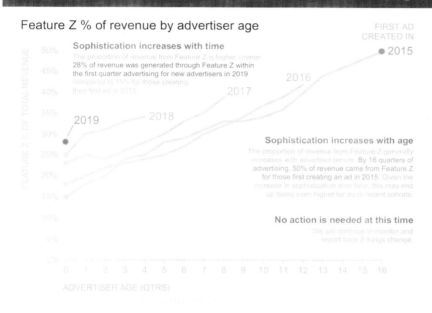

FIGURE 7.1c Sophistication increasing with time & age

We've reviewed a number of lessons over the course of this solution. Always ask yourself: do you need all the data? Determine what you want your audience to see, then select a visual that will facilitate that, iterating as needed to identify an effective view. Design thoughtfully, aligning elements to create structure, using color sparingly to direct attention, and titling and annotating effectively with words to help the data make sense.

Exercise 7.2: sales channel update

The following slide (Figure 7.2a) shows unit channel sales over time for a given product. Familiarize yourself with the details, then complete the following steps on your own or with a partner.

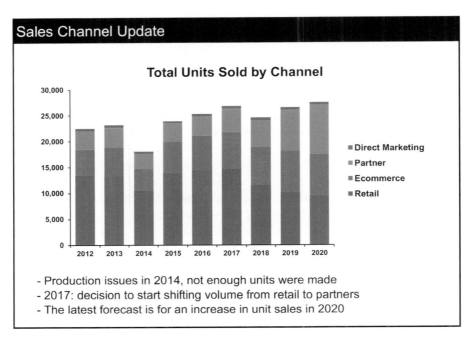

FIGURE 7.2a Sales channel update

STEP 1: Let's start with the positive: what do you like about this slide?

STEP 2: What questions can we answer with this graph? Where specifically do we look in the data for answers to these questions? How effectively are these questions answered? Write a couple of sentences outlining your thoughts.

STEP 3: What changes would you recommend based on the lessons we've covered? Write a few sentences or make a list outlining specific points of feedback and how you would resolve.

STEP 4: Consider how your approach would vary if you were (1) presenting this data live in a meeting and (2) sending it to your audience to be consumed on its own. How would the way you'd tackle this differ? Write a few sentences explaining your thoughts. To take it a step further, redesign this visual for these different use cases in the tool of your choice.

Solution 7.2: sales channel update

For me, this is a situation where we are trying to answer too many questions in a single graph. In doing so, we don't answer any single question effectively. Rather than pack a lot into one graph, we will be better off allowing ourselves to have multiple visuals.

STEP 1: What do I like about the original slide? I like that someone outlined some specific points of interest via the bulleted text below the graph. The general design of the graph is also pretty clean; there isn't a lot of clutter to distract from the data.

STEP 2: We can answer a couple of different primary queries with this graph: how have unit sales changed over time? How has the composition of sales across channels changed over time? We're meant to see the former by comparing the tops of the bars and the latter by comparing the pieces within the stack. Stacked bars are challenging, though, because when you stack things that are changing on top of other things that are changing, it becomes very difficult to see what is happening. The second point outlined via bullets says there was a decision made to shift sales from retail to partners. Does the data show that happening? Is this a success story or a call for action? It's tough to tell!

STEP 3: I have three major points of feedback that I will address in my makeover of this visual. Let's talk through each of these.

Use multiple graphs. The biggest change I will make is to use multiple graphs. I sometimes think of the stacked bar chart like a Swiss Army knife. You can do many things with it and sometimes constraints may necessitate its use. But you can't do any of these tasks quite as well as if you had the dedicated tool. Sure, the scissors on a Swiss Army knife work well enough to cut a loose thread, but for anything more I'd much rather have a pair of scissors. Instead of the stacked bar, I'll use two different graphs that each directly answer the questions outlined in Step 2. I'll walk you through the specifics in Step 4.

Tie text visually to data. In terms of additional changes, as mentioned in Step 1, I like that someone looked at this data and outlined takeaways. The challenge, though, is that when I read the text at the bottom of the slide, I have to spend time thinking and searching to figure out where to look in the data for evidence of what is being said. I'll want to solve for this—when someone reads the text, I want them to know where to look in the data. When someone sees the data, I want them to know where to look in the text for related context or takeaways. To connect the text and data, we should think back to the Gestalt principles. We can use proximity, putting the text close to the data it describes. We can use connection and physically draw a line between the text and data. We can use similarity, making the text the same color as the data it describes. I'll employ aspects of each of these approaches in my solution.

Clearly differentiate forecast data. If I take the time to read through all of the text, the final bullet raises something perhaps unexpected—not all of this data is real. The final point, 2020, is a forecast. But there's nothing done to the design of the data to indicate this to us. I'll want to change that and clearly indicate which points are actual data and which are forecast.

STEP 4: My makeover will address the points of feedback raised in Step 3. Let's first tackle the initial question—how have total unit sales changed over time? See Figure 7.2b.

Total units sold

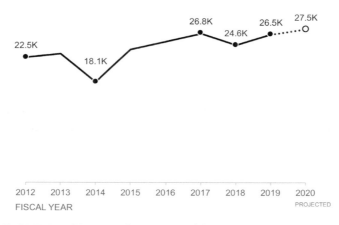

FIGURE 7.2b Visualize units sold over time with a line

I moved from bars to a line so the connection between points would allow us to more easily see the trend. I chose to omit the axis and instead labeled a few of the data points; why I chose the ones I did will become clear momentarily. I made a visual distinction between the actual data (solid line, filled points) and projected data (dotted line, unfilled point) and also added the descriptor text "Projected" to the x-axis tied through proximity to the 2020 label.

If I will be presenting this information in a live setting, that opens up additional opportunities. Any time we are looking at data over time, we have a natural construct for storytelling: the chronological story. In a live setting, I can build the graph piece by piece, talking through relative context as I do. See the following (Figure 7.2e - 7.2r) for an illustration of how I might do this, paired with my written voiceover.

Today, we'll be looking at unit sales over time. I'll start back in 2012, we'll look at actual data through 2019 and then our latest projection for 2020. (Figure 7.2c)

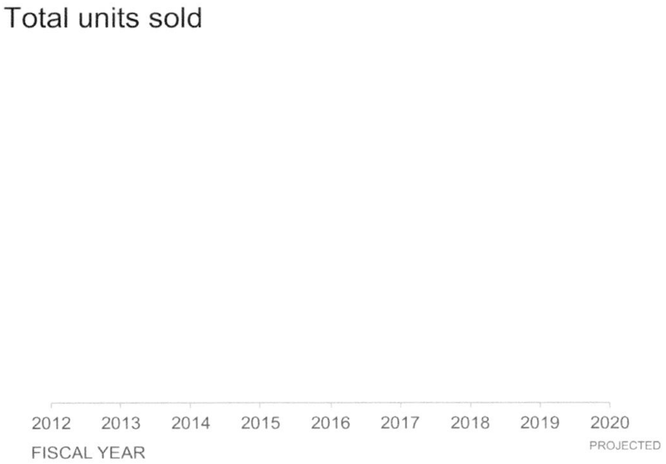

Total units sold

2012   2013   2014   2015   2016   2017   2018   2019   2020
FISCAL YEAR   PROJECTED

FIGURE 7.2c In a live progression, first set up graph

Our product hit the market in 2012. Sales that first year amounted to twenty-two and a half thousand units, which we were very happy with against our initial target of 18,000 units. (Figure 7.2d)

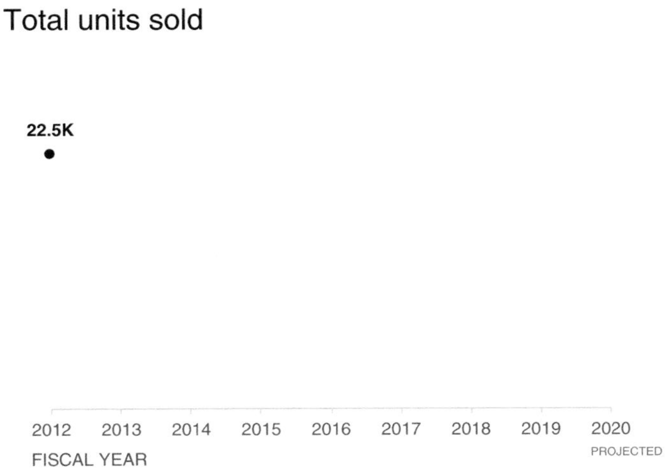

Total units sold

22.5K
●

2012   2013   2014   2015   2016   2017   2018   2019   2020
FISCAL YEAR   PROJECTED

FIGURE 7.2d Live progression

Sales increased slightly in 2013, to just over 23,000 units sold. (Figure 7.2e)

Total units sold

FIGURE 7.2e Live progression

But then in 2014, we encountered production issues. As a result, we weren't able to keep up with demand. Units sold plummeted. (Figure 7.2f)

Total units sold

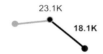

FIGURE 7.2f Live progression

We quickly recovered, fixing the issues and hitting nearly 24,000 in unit sales in 2015. (Figure 7.2g)

Total units sold

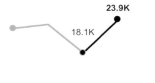

2012 2013 2014 2015 2016 2017 2018 2019 2020
FISCAL YEAR   PROJECTED

FIGURE 7.2g Live progression

Sales continued to increase through 2016 and 2017. (Figure 7.2h)

Total units sold

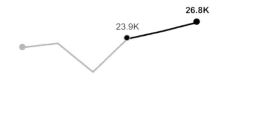

2012 2013 2014 2015 2016 2017 2018 2019 2020
FISCAL YEAR   PROJECTED

FIGURE 7.2h Live progression

In 2017, we made the decision to start shifting sales from retail to our partner channel. We saw sales in 2018 dip as a result of this. (Figure 7.2i)

Total units sold

23.9K   26.8K

2012 2013 2014 2015 2016 2017 2018 2019 2020
FISCAL YEAR   PROJECTED

FIGURE 7.2i Live progression

We recovered from this dip in 2019. (Figure 7.2j)

Total units sold

24.6K   26.5K

2012 2013 2014 2015 2016 2017 2018 2019 2020
FISCAL YEAR   PROJECTED

FIGURE 7.2j Live progression

We expect continued increasing sales in 2020. (Figure 7.2k)

Total units sold

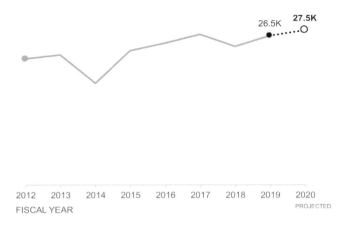

FIGURE 7.2k Live progression

If I weren't presenting live, I could annotate this context directly on the graph so that my audience processing it on their own would get the same sort of story I'd walk my audience through in a live setting. See Figure 7.2l.

Total units sold

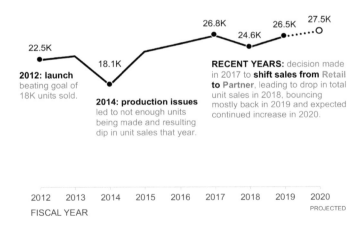

FIGURE 7.2l Annotated line graph

We'll look momentarily at how we could integrate a version of this graph into a slide. But before we get there, let's determine how we can answer the relative composition question in a live setting: with a 100% stacked bar. The 100% stacked bar does face some of the same challenges as the typical stacked bar, in that the middle segments are harder to compare. However, we also get some benefit.

With a consistent baseline both along the bottom *and* top of the graph, there are two data series that our audience can more easily compare over time. Depending on what we need to highlight and if we are smart about how we order the data, we can actually make this work quite well. Let's tune back into my live presentation:

Let's look next at the composition of sales across channels. (Figure 7.2m)

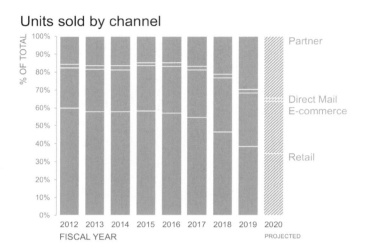

FIGURE 7.2m   Another view: channel breakdown

The retail channel has decreased as a proportion of total over time. (Figure 7.2n)

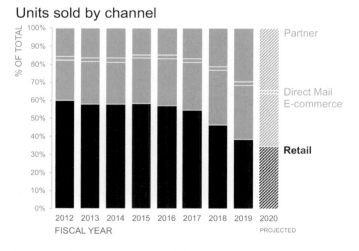

FIGURE 7.2n   Focus on retail

E-commerce has increased marginally since launch, but has made up a consistent proportion of total sales in recent years. (Figure 7.2o)

Units sold by channel

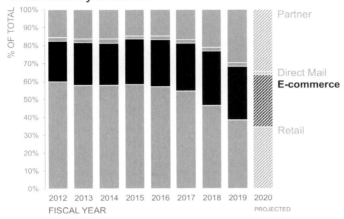

FIGURE 7.2o Focus on e-commerce

Direct mail is tiny, has always been tiny, and will stay tiny. (Figure 7.2p)

Units sold by channel

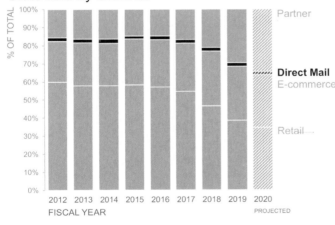

FIGURE 7.2p Focus on direct mail

Partner sales have increased as a percent of total. (Figure 7.2q)

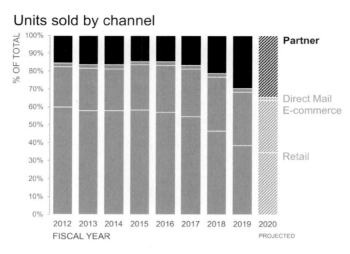

FIGURE 7.2q Focus on partner

Most noteworthy is the change we've seen in composition of sales by channel over time. In particular, since the decision was made in 2017 to shift sales from retail to partner: we've seen that change happen. Retail is making up a decreasing proportion of total sales, while the partner channel is making up an increasing proportion of sales over time. We expect this will continue in 2020. (Figure 7.2r)

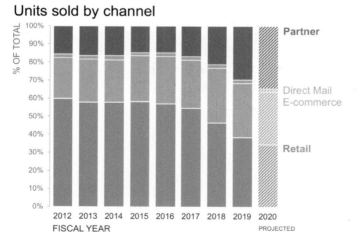

FIGURE 7.2r The desired shift in channels has happened: success!

This is a success story! If we need to pull that together in a way that can stand on its own to be sent around, I would opt for a single slide with takeaway titles, clear structure, and more written words to lend context. See Figure 7.2s.

Total sales increasing as channels shift

2020 EXPECT INCREASE IN SALES

The 2012 launch yielded 22.5K units sold, beating initial 18K goal by 25%. In 2014, production issues led to not enough units being made and resulting in a 22% drop in annual unit sales. Unit sales increased through 2017, when the **decision was made to shift channel sales** from retail to partners. This led to a drop in 2018, bouncing mostly back in 2019, and expected to continue to increase in 2020.

CHANNEL SHIFT OVER TIME

The relative composition of sales channels has shifted markedly over time. Unit sales from the **Retail** channel, which historically accounted for 60% of total sales, has decreased to 38% in 2019 due to intentional shift towards the **Partner** channel, where contribution to total unit sales has increased from less than 20% in our early years to 30% in 2019. We expect these trends to continue.

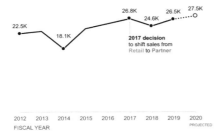

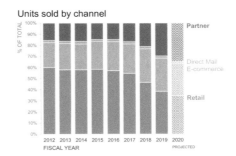

Data is from Sales Database through 12/31/19. 2020 projections assume no major market changes. For more details, reach out to Sales Analytics team

FIGURE 7.2s Single slide for distribution

By allowing ourselves to have more than one graph, we can effectively answer multiple questions. Note also the various ways in which text is used in the preceding visual, and the numerous ways words are visually tied to the data. When my audience reads the text, they know where to look in the data for the important things and vice versa. Not only will this be a more pleasant experience for my audience to process this data, but we can also get much more information out of it!

Exercise 7.3: model performance

You work at a large national bank managing a team of statisticians. One of your employees shares the following graph (Figure 7.3a) with you during their weekly one-on-one and asks for your feedback. Spend a moment analyzing it, then complete the following steps.

FIGURE A: Model Performance by LTV

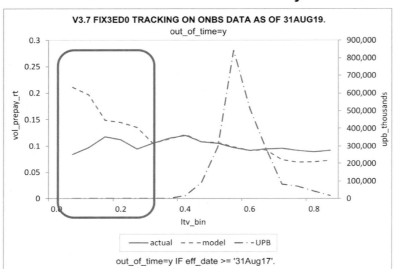

FIGURE 7.3a Model performance by LTV

STEP 1: What questions would you ask about this data? Make a list.

STEP 2: What feedback would you give based on the lessons we've covered? Outline your thoughts, focusing not just on *what* you would recommend changing, but also *why*. It's by grounding our feedback in underlying principles that we help improve not just a single graph, but also deeper understanding that can lead to better data visualization in the future.

STEP 3: How would you recommend presenting this? What is the story and how can it be brought to life? Make an assumption about whether this information will be presented live or sent around, and outline your recommended plan of attack in light of this assumption. Take things a step further by creating your recommended communication in the tool of your choice.

Solution 7.3: model performance

STEP 1: This is a difficult one! I have so many questions about the graph that it's hard to step back and consider what the data is showing. I would ask about the language used: what do the acronyms mean and what do the axes represent? Which data is meant to be read on the secondary y-axis on the right-hand side of the graph? Why have these particular choices for line style been made? What is the big red box meant to highlight?

STEP 2: After getting answers to my questions raised in Step 1, I would offer the following feedback.

Use more approachable language. This looks to me like output from statistical programming software (SAS or similar). If you are a statistician and you are communicating to your colleagues who are also statisticians, this is totally fine. If you are communicating to *anyone else on the planet*, you need to turn this into accessible language. Rather than put things like "vol_prepay_rt" (y-axis title in Figure 7.3a), we should translate it into voluntary prepayment rate. This is the proportion of people who are paying off their loan before it is due. The only reason I have any idea what's going on in this graph is because I used to work in Credit Risk Management, so I have enough banking subject matter expertise to make sense of it.

On the topic of comprehensible language, you should also spell out any acronyms. If someone in your audience doesn't know what an acronym means, they will usually be too embarrassed to ask—or they may make an incorrect assumption. In that event, you've lost the ability to fully communicate to everyone. Spell out acronyms on each page at least once. This can be the first time you use it or you can have a footnote at the bottom of the page defining acronyms or specialized language. This isn't about dumbing anything down, but rather not making things more complicated than necessary. By the way, "ltv_bin" on the x-axis represents the loan-to-value ratio. This is commonly referred to as LTV and represents the loan amount relative to the value of the property (typically expressed as a percent, but here we have it as a decimal). The higher the LTV, the riskier the loan, because the higher proportion the loan amount is relative to the value of the property. UPB is unpaid principal balance: the sum of total outstanding loans.

There is also some pretty convoluted language in the title of the graph and at the bottom of it. I guarantee you that the person who created this graph knows exactly what it all means. I can decipher enough to believe that it indicates the product in the title and what they used for their out of time sample to validate the model. Who our audience is will dictate whether and how prominently we need to present this. If we're reporting to a senior leadership team, we probably don't need to get into any of those details—they are going to trust that we know our stuff and have done it in a way that makes sense. If we're communicating to people who will care about the technical details, we may need to include some of this, but it's likely footnote material rather than things that are prominently called out as in the original.

Change up line style sparingly. Dotted lines are super attention grabbing. They also add some visual noise. If we think about a dotted line from a clutter standpoint, we've taken what could have been a single visual element (a line) and chopped it into many pieces. Because of this, I recommend reserving the use of dotted lines for when you have uncertainty to depict: a forecast, prediction, target or goal. In these cases, the visual sense of uncertainty we get with the dotted or dashed line more than makes up for the additional noise it adds. The blue model line in Figure 7.3a is the perfect use of a dotted line. When it comes to the green UPB line, though—I certainly hope we aren't estimating the volume of unpaid principal balance across our portfolio—we should know exactly what that is! Use thick, solid, filled in elements to depict actual data and thin, dotted, unfilled points to represent estimated data.

Eliminate the secondary y-axis. I recommend avoiding the use of a secondary y-axis, both in this specific example and in general. The challenge with a secondary axis is—no matter how clearly things are titled and labeled—there is always some work that has to be undertaken to figure out which data to read against which axis. I don't want my audience to have to do this work. Rather than use a secondary axis, you can hide the secondary y-axis and instead title and label the data that is meant to be read against it directly. As another alternative, you can create two graphs, using the same x-axis across each. Putting the data into separate graphs means you can title and label each of the data series on the left, so there's no question of "Do I look left or right to get the details that I need?"

The data that is meant to be read against the secondary axis is the unpaid principal balance. This is shown in an odd way in Figure 7.3a: thousands of thousands. A thousand thousand is a *million*. Changing our scale to millions will both make the graph easier to process and talk about the data it depicts.

It seems like the general shape of the data is more important than the specific numeric values. Given this, I'd recommend employing the second alternative raised previously: divide the data across two graphs, as shown in Figure 7.3b.

Model performance by LTV

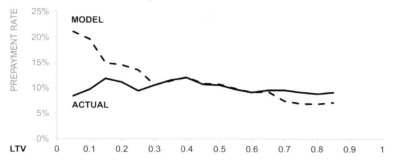

FIGURE 7.3b Pull the data apart into two graphs

In Figure 7.3b, I separated the visual into two graphs. The top graph shows Model and Actual prepayment rate. The LTV axis in the middle is meant to be read across both graphs (if you find this confusing, you could simply repeat it again below the second graph). The bottom graph shows the distribution of loans by Unpaid Principal Balance in our portfolio. We'll look at another potential option for presenting this data momentarily. First, let's continue my points of feedback.

The big red box doesn't highlight the right thing. Someone looked at this graph and thought, *I would like you to look here* and then they drew a red box around it. I appreciate the effort. However, I think this might be a red herring.

Now that we've hopefully answered a lot of the questions about this data, take a look back at the red box in Figure 7.3a. What are we meant to see? Can you state it in a sentence?

If I were to do so, my sentence would be: *our model overpredicts prepayment at low LTVs*. Is that an issue? Look back at Figure 7.3a. Do we have any loans in our portfolio at low LTVs? (Hint: look at the green dotted line to answer this question.)

No. We don't have any loan balance in that part of the portfolio. That's probably why our model isn't performing well there: we didn't have any loans to model on in this area. Beyond that, low LTVs represent our *least* risky loans. These are cases where the loan amount is low compared to the property value (so if someone doesn't pay and the bank needs to take the house, they will make their money back...and then some). This probably isn't cause for concern. That said, there is still something interesting here. We'll get to that momentarily.

STEP 3: Let me walk you through how I would present this data in a live setting, which—as we saw in the prior exercise—gives us some interesting options for communicating this data.

I can start by setting up the graph for my audience. *Today, we'll be looking at modeled versus actual prepayment rates by LTV. Prepayment rate is shown on the vertical y-axis. Loan to value, LTV, is depicted across the x-axis.* (Figure 7.3c)

Model performance by LTV

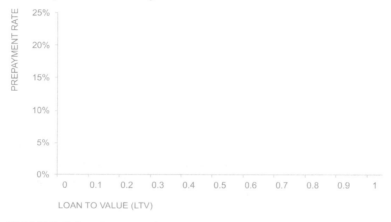

FIGURE 7.3c First, set the stage

Actual prepayment doesn't vary much by LTV: this line is pretty flat. (Figure 7.3d)

Model performance by LTV

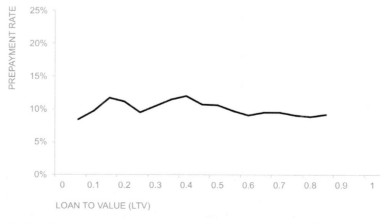

FIGURE 7.3d Actual prepayment doesn't vary by LTV

Our model, however, behaves differently. It overpredicts at low LTVs and under-predicts at high LTVs. (Figure 7.3e)

Model performance by LTV

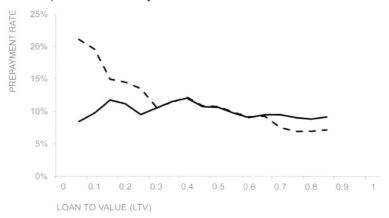

FIGURE 7.3e Model overpredicts at low LTVs and underpredicts at high LTVs

Next, I'm going to do something a little different. You might ask: how big of a deal is this? Where are loans concentrated in the portfolio? I'm going to replace prepayment rate on the y-axis with the unpaid principal balance of loans across our portfolio. That looks like this. (Figure 7.3f)

Model performance by LTV

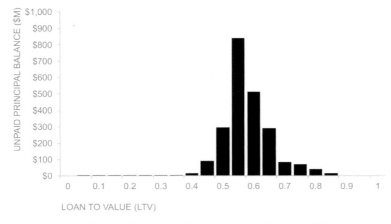

FIGURE 7.3f Distribution of loans across the portfolio

Here is how the loans are distributed across the portfolio. Let's pause and take note of the y-axis scale and how the data lines up against it: the biggest bar represents roughly $800 million in unpaid principal balance. That said, more import-

ant than the specific numbers is that we focus on the general shape of the data, so I'm going to get rid of this axis in my next step. At the same time, I'll push these bars to the background and layer the modeled and actual prepayment rates back onto the graph. (Figure 7.3g)

Model performance by LTV

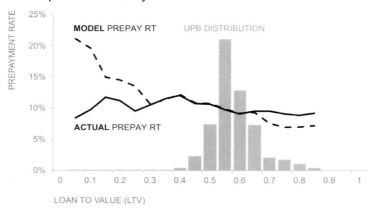

FIGURE 7.3g Add prepayment back to graph

This allows us to see that the model over-predicts prepayment at low LTVs—but we don't have any portfolio concentrated there. (Figure 7.3h)

Model performance by LTV

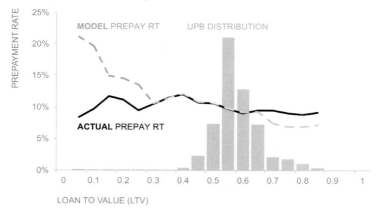

FIGURE 7.3h Model over-predicts prepayment at low LTVs

The model under-predicts prepayment at high LTVs—by the way, we do have loan balances in that part of the portfolio. We should watch this going forward. (Figure 7.3i)

Model performance by LTV

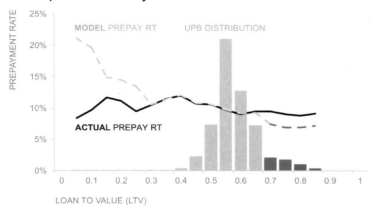

FIGURE 7.3i Model under-predicts prepayment at high LTVs

The preceding sequence would work well in a live presentation. If we need a single visual to send out to remind people what we discussed or for those who missed the meeting, I would annotate important points directly on the slide. This will make it clear to my audience what they are meant to take away and what it means. See Figure 7.3j.

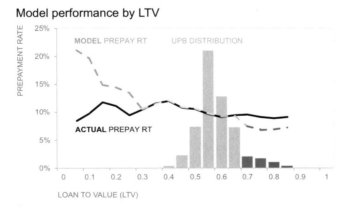

FIGURE 7.3j Annotate important points directly on slide

Lessons put into practice: use accessible language and don't overcomplicate. Highlight sparingly with color. Articulate your message clearly so your audience doesn't miss it!

Exercise 7.4: back-to-school shopping

As a data analyst at a national clothing retailer, you are gearing up for this year's back-to-school shopping season. You've analyzed survey data from last year's back-to-school shopping to understand customers' experience—what they liked and what they didn't like. You believe the data reveals some clear opportunities and want to use it to inform the strategy for this year's back-to-school shopping season across your company's stores.

This example may sound familiar; we've seen it before in Exercises 1.2, 1.3, 1.4, 1.7, 6.3 and 6.4. Refer back to these exercises and corresponding solutions to remind yourself how we thought about our audience, Big Idea, storyboard, tension, resolution, and the narrative arc for this scenario. Review Figure 7.4a and complete the following.

Back-to-school shopping survey results

	% FAVORABLE	
STORE OFFERS...	Our store	All stores
The store is well-organized.	40%	38%
Fast and easy checkout.	33%	34%
Friendly and helpful employees.	45%	50%
Good promotions.	45%	65%
I can find what I'm looking for.	46%	55%
I can find the size I need.	39%	49%
A nice atmosphere.	80%	70%
Latest technology for easy shopping.	35%	34%
Lowest sales prices.	40%	60%
A wide selection.	49%	47%
Items I can't find elsewhere.	74%	54%
The latest styles.	65%	55%

FIGURE 7.4a Back-to-school shopping survey results

STEP 1: What is the story here? How would you visualize the data in Figure 7.4a to lend insight into what we should focus on in this situation? Reflect on all of the lessons that we've covered and how you would apply them. Make assumptions about the scenario as needed. Download the data and create your preferred visual(s).

STEP 2: You will be walking your audience through this data in a meeting. How would you present the information to them? Develop your materials in the tool of your choice.

STEP 3: You anticipate that your audience will want you to send them content after the meeting. This will remind those who attended what was talked about as well as let folks who weren't able to attend know what was discussed. How would you design graphs or slides to meet this need? Create in the tool of your choice.

Solution 7.4: back-to-school shopping

STEP 1: Let's look at a few iterations of this data to see which can help us facilitate that magical "ah ha" moment of understanding what graphs done well can do. First, I'll try a scatterplot. See Figure 7.4b.

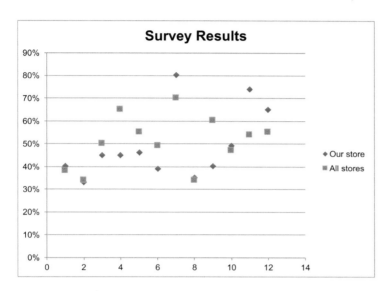

FIGURE 7.4b Scatterplot

The scatterplot seems to prompt more questions than it answers; it doesn't work well for this data. Let's try a line graph. See Figure 7.4c.

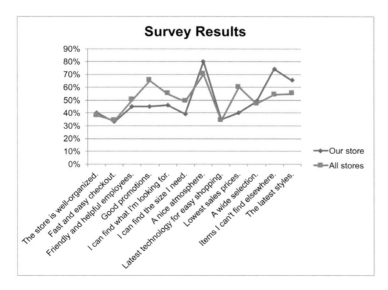

FIGURE 7.4c Line graph

Do lines work for us here? We can more easily pick out highs and lows than the prior view. But the lines are connecting categorical data in a way that doesn't make sense. Given that we have categorical data, let's try a bar chart. See Figure 7.4d.

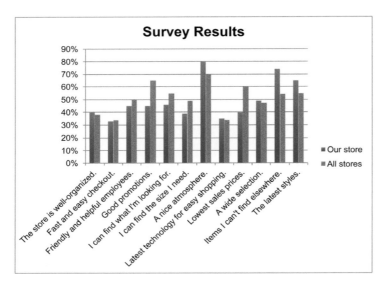

FIGURE 7.4d Vertical bars

The most frequent reason I find myself moving from a standard vertical bar chart to a horizontal bar chart is simply to get more space to write the x-axis labels. Diagonal elements are attention-grabbing. They are also messy: they create jagged edges, which look disorganized. Worse than any of that, though—diagonal text is slower to read than horizontal text. This is an easy fix: we can rotate our graph 90 degrees to a horizontal bar chart, which gives us more space to write the category names in a legible fashion. See Figure 7.4e.

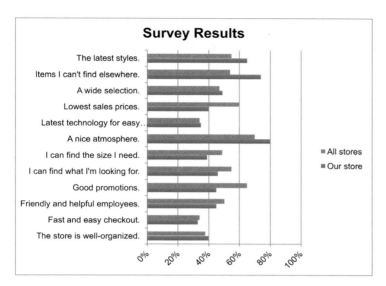

FIGURE 7.4e Horizontal bars

Any time we show data, we want to be thoughtful about how we order the data. Sometimes, there is a natural ordering inherent to our categories that we should honor. If we don't have a set order to our categories, then we want to order meaningfully by the data. In doing so, we should think back to that zigzagging "z" of processing: without other visual cues, your audience will start at the top left of your page or screen and do zigzagging "z's" with their eyes to take in the information. This means they encounter the top left of your graph first. If the small pieces are the important ones, we might put those at the top. See Figure 7.4f.

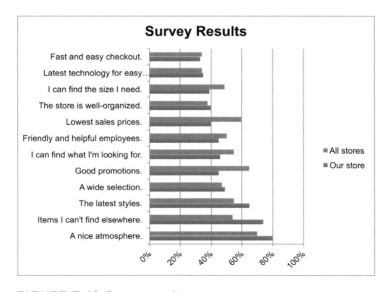

FIGURE 7.4f Sort ascending

However, if we step back and think about story progression, we'd be starting with where we perform the worst, which could be a bit abrupt. Perhaps we want to start with where we perform well and then move into the opportunities: we could put the large categories at the top and sort in descending fashion. See Figure 7.4g.

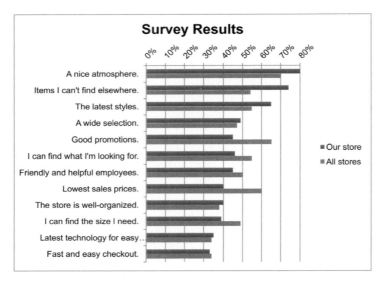

FIGURE 7.4g Sort descending

Excel moved my x-axis to the top with this reorganization in Figure 7.4g, which I like. It means my audience hits how to read the data before they get to the data.

In the spirit of applying the other lessons we've covered: next, let's declutter. Before reading on, spend a moment studying Figure 7.4g. What clutter would you eliminate? What other changes would you make to ease the processing of this data?

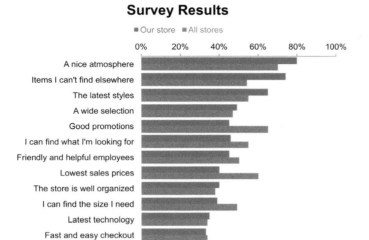

FIGURE 7.4h Decluttered graph

Figure 7.4h represents my decluttered graph. I removed the chart border and gridlines. I thickend the bars. I increased the x-axis maximum to 100% and reduced the frequency of x-axis labels so they would fit horizontally. I removed the y-axis line and tick marks. I eliminated the periods from the ends of the y-axis labels and shortened the second-to-last label so it would fit on a single line. I put the legend at the top of the graph, so my audience will encounter it before they get to the data and used similarity of color to visually tie it to the data it describes.

Before proceeding, look back at Figure 7.4h: where are your eyes drawn?

If you're like me, your response is: nowhere very clearly. This means we aren't currently using our preattentive attributes strategically to direct attention. Let's be more thoughtful in how we use our color and contrast. See Figure 7.4i.

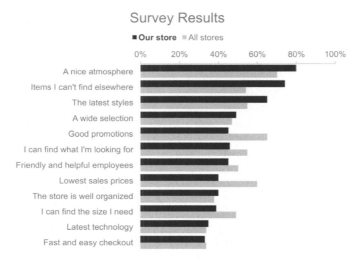

FIGURE 7.4i Focus attention

In Figure 7.4i, I've pushed most elements of the graph to the background by making them grey. I drew attention to Our Store by making it dark blue. We'll further focus attention in a few different places when we tell our story in a live progression momentarily. First, let's add the words that need to be present to ensure the data is accessible: see Figure 7.4j.

FIGURE 7.4j Add words

Stories have words. At minimum, we need descriptive words on the graph to help it make sense: a graph title and axis titles. We can take this a step further and use our words to tell a story. Let's do that next.

STEP 2: If I were presenting in a live meeting, I might go through a progression similar to the following.

I'll be making one recommendation today: that we invest in employee training to improve the in-store customer experience. (Figure 7.4k)

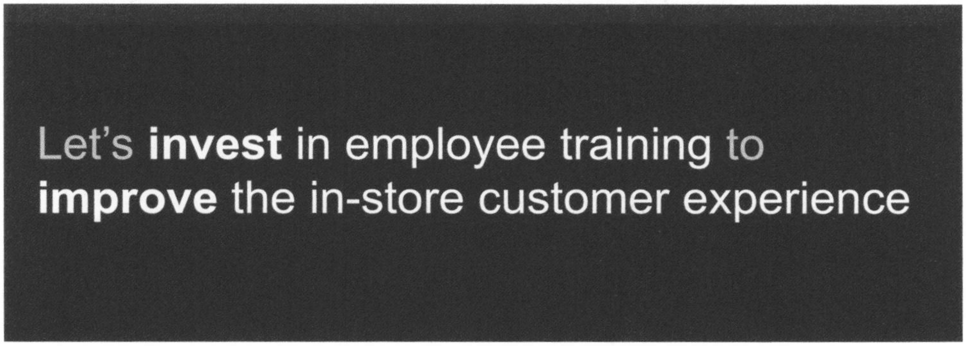

FIGURE 7.4k My Big Idea summarized in a pithy, repeatable phrase

Let me back up and set the plot. The back-to-school shopping season makes up nearly a third of our annual revenue, so is a huge driver of our overall success. But we've not historically been data-driven about how we've approached it. We allowed a one-off compliment or criticism at the store level drive how we did things. That worked okay when we were small, but clearly it doesn't scale. So we thought: let's get more data-driven about how we plan for this important part of our business. Coming out of last year's back-to-school shopping season, we conducted a survey of our customers and the customers of our competitors. The data collected lends important insight into both how we fare across different dimensions of our store experience, as well as how we stack up against the competition. (Figure 7.4l)

FIGURE 7.4l Back up and set the plot

Today I'll take you through those survey results and use them to frame up a spe-cific recommendation. I've already foreshadowed this: I believe we should invest in employee training to improve the in-store customer experience. (Figure 7.4m)

What we'll cover today

1 **Discuss what we've learned** from our survey analysis[1] and

2 **Suggest specific recommendations** on changes to make for the upcoming back-to-school shopping season to improve customer satisfaction and increase sales.

[1]Comprehensive details on survey methodology and related info can be found in the Appendix on pages 15-20.

FIGURE 7.4m   What we'll cover today

Before we get to the data, let me set up for you what we're going to be looking at. We asked people about a number of dimensions of the shopping experience—things like the store offers a nice atmosphere, items I can't find elsewhere, and the latest styles. For each of these dimensions, we'll be summarizing into percent favorable. This is the proportion of respondents who indicated positive sentiment on the given item. (Figure 7.4n)

Back-to-school shopping: **consumer sentiment**

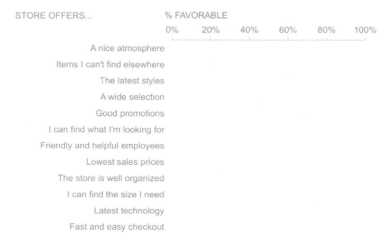

FIGURE 7.4n   Set up the graph

Let's add the data for our stores. You'll see there is variance in performance across the different items. (Figure 7.4o)

Back-to-school shopping: **consumer sentiment**

FIGURE 7.4o Focus on our business

Let's focus first on where things are going well. We score highest in three areas: a nice atmosphere, items people can't find elsewhere, and the latest styles. Verbatim comments echoed these points as well: people like the idea of shopping with us and they have positive brand association. (Figure 7.4p)

Back-to-school shopping: **consumer sentiment**

FIGURE 7.4p Focus on highest scoring items

But there is also another side of the story: items where we score lower. (Figure 7.4q)

Back-to-school shopping: **consumer sentiment**

FIGURE 7.4q Focus on lowest scoring items

Interestingly, when we layer on our competitor data—which I'll do next via grey bars—we score on par with the competition in these low scoring areas. So that's not where we recommend focusing. (Figure 7.4r)

Back-to-school shopping: **consumer sentiment**

FIGURE 7.4r Add competitor data

There are other items, however, where we score lower than the competition. (Figure 7.4s)

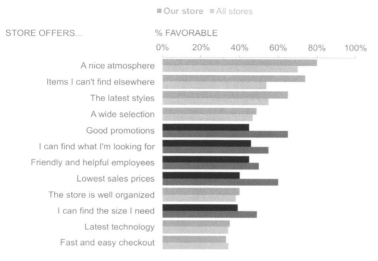

FIGURE 7.4s Highlight where we underscore competition

Next, I'm going to transition to a different view of the data. Rather than plot absolute percent favorable, I'm going to graph the difference between the bars. The left-hand side represents where we underperform—we score lower than—the competition. The right-hand side shows where we outperform—we score higher than—the competition. (Figure 7.4t)

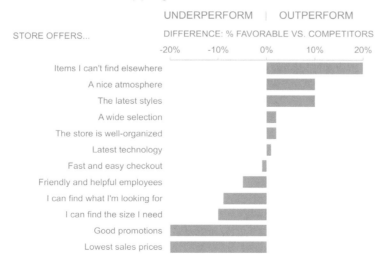

FIGURE 7.4t Shift from focus on absolute to difference

Let's refocus again, first on where things are going well. The three areas we out-
perform the competition the most—items that can't be found elsewhere, a nice
atmosphere, and the latest styles—these are the same three items we score high-
est on an absolute percent favorable basis. (Figure 7.4u)

Back-to-school shopping: **consumer sentiment**

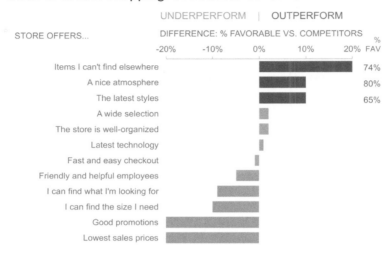

FIGURE 7.4u Focus on items we outperform

But there are also areas where we underperform the competition. (Figure 7.4v)

Back-to-school shopping: **consumer sentiment**

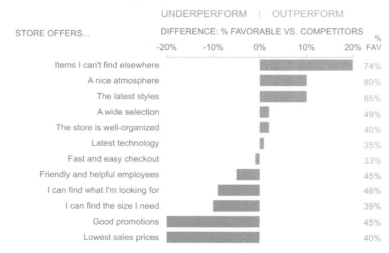

FIGURE 7.4v Focus on items we underperform

We underperform the most in items related to promotions and sales. These are areas we've intentionally avoided historically because of the brand dilution we expect may result. We don't recommend focusing here. (Figure 7.4w)

Back-to-school shopping: **consumer sentiment**

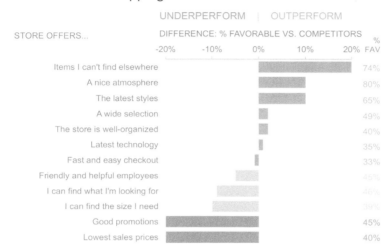

FIGURE 7.4w Underperform the most in promotions

Rather, look at these other areas where we underperform. Friendly and helpful employees, I can find what I'm looking for, and I can find the size I need—it is alarming that we underscore the competition so much in these areas. The good news is that these are all aspects of customer experience over which our sales associates have direct control. (Figure 7.4x)

Back-to-school shopping: **consumer sentiment**

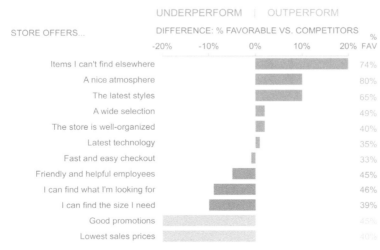

FIGURE 7.4x Recommend focusing on areas we can control

Let's invest in employee training to create a common understanding of what good service looks like to improve the in-store customer experience and make the up-coming back-to-school shopping season the best one yet! (Figure 7.4y)

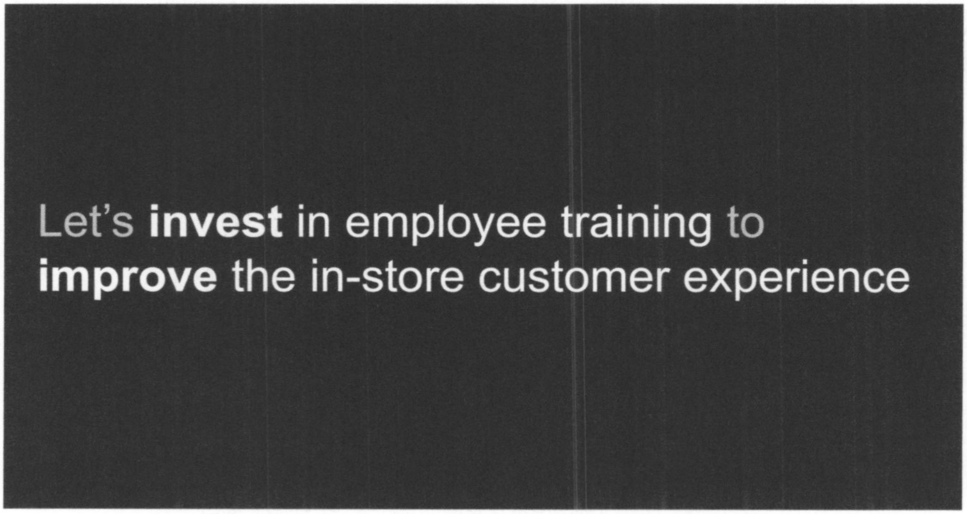

Let's **invest** in employee training to **improve** the in-store customer experience

FIGURE 7.4y Repeat my Big Idea summarized in a pithy, repeatable phrase

STEP 3: If I need something to send out after my live presentation, I would fully annotate a slide so that my audience processing it on their own would get a similar story to what I took my audience through in the live progression. See Figure 7.4z.

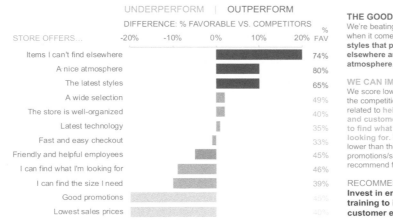

Action needed: invest in employee training

Back-to-school shopping: **consumer sentiment**

THE GOOD NEWS: We're beating the competition when it comes to **the latest styles that people can't find elsewhere and store atmosphere**.

WE CAN IMPROVE: We score low and lower than the competition in areas related to **helpful employees and customers being able to find what they are looking for**. We also score lower than the competition on promotions/sales, but don't recommend focusing here.

RECOMMENDATION: **Invest in employee training to improve customer experience.**

Data Source: 2019 Back-to-School shopping survey (represents 21,862 survey responses). Additional survey and methodology details available upon request. Reach out to Insights Team.

FIGURE 7.4z Final annotated version

This is a good illustration of the power of applying the many lessons that we've covered: building a robust understanding of the context, choosing an appropriate visual display, identifying and eliminating clutter, drawing attention where we want it, thinking like a designer, and telling a story. Don't just show data: make data a pivotal point in an overarching story!

Exercise 7.5: diabetes rates

The following case study was created and solved by storytelling with data *team member Elizabeth Hardman Ricks.*

Imagine you work as an analyst for a large health care system with medical centers in several states. Your role is to use data to understand trends in the patient base and communicate your findings to help administrators make organizational decisions. Your analysis has shown a recent rise in diabetes rates across all medical centers (A-M) in a given region. If this trend continues at its current rate, the centers may be understaffed to provide an appropriate level of care. Specifically, you've estimated the increase will be an additional 14,000 patients per year for the next four years. You want administrators to understand the trend in diabetes rates and use that information to determine whether additional resources are needed.

You're planning to share this analysis at an upcoming meeting. You've visualized the diabetes rates four different ways, as shown in Figure 7.5a. Spend a moment familiarizing yourself with the data then complete the following steps.

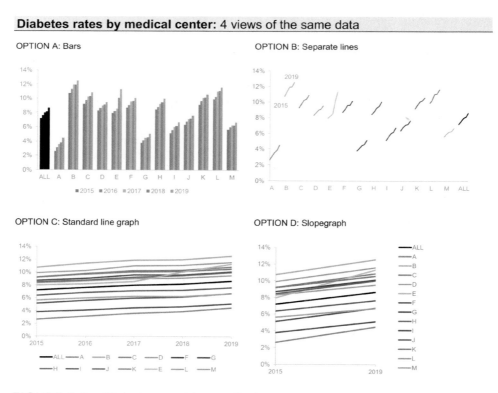

FIGURE 7.5a Diabetes rates by medical center

STEP 1: Let's start by considering our audience. The decision maker is a senior administrator. Because this is an anonymized example, we won't aim to pinpoint the needs of a specific person; rather, we can think *generally* about what motivating factors someone in this role may have. What would keep them up at night? What might motivate them? Spend a few minutes brainstorming and make a list.

STEP 2: Create the Big Idea for your communication (if helpful, refer to the Big Idea worksheet in Exercise 1.20). Feel free to liberally make assumptions as needed for the purpose of the exercise.

STEP 3: Next, let's think about the narrative arc. What tension exists for the audience? What does your analysis suggest that resolves this tension? What pieces of content will you need to provide your audience? With this in mind, create a storyboard (if helpful, refer to Exercises 1.23 and 1.24) and arrange your pieces of content along the narrative arc (see Exercise 6.14).

STEP 4: Review the four graphs in Figure 7.5a. Analyze each and observe what it allows you to most easily see in the data. Write a one-sentence observation for each graph. Think back to the Big Idea you crafted in Step 2: which of these approaches reinforces your message best?

STEP 5: Assume you have a tight timeline to communicate your findings. A key stakeholder has asked for an update by the end of the day today. Refer to the graph you identified as working best in Step 4. Assume you don't have time to change anything about the layout of the graph. How could you use color and words to make the main takeaway clear? Download the data and make these changes to your selected graph.

STEP 6: Your visual from Step 5 was well received (nice work!). Administrators would like to discuss the data at an upcoming meeting where your manager will present the full analysis, including your forward-looking projections that diabetes rates will continue to increase. Create the deck that your manager will use in your tool of choice to tell a story with this data. Provide the accompanying narrative as speaker notes for each slide.

PRACTICE with COLE (more)

Solution 7.5: diabetes rates

STEP 1: In brainstorming what my audience might care about, I set a timer and wrote down as many ideas as I could in five minutes. When I stepped back and looked at my list, I realized I could group what I'd come up with into five categories:

1. **Financial:** controlling operating expenses, hitting revenue targets

2. **People:** recruiting providers, managing and retaining talent to deliver quality patient care

3. **Accreditation and standards:** remaining within certain benchmarks, navigating government regulations

4. **Suppliers:** maintaining reimbursement levels from insurance companies, negotiating contracts, purchasing medical equipment

5. **Competitors:** maintaining a superior level of patient care and/or cost compared to other facilities and patient options

STEP 2: As I worked through the Big Idea worksheet, the motivating factors from my list in Step 1 helped me narrow in on what's at stake for my audience in this specific circumstance. My audience stands to lose revenue (reimbursement from payers) and fall below accreditation standards if the patient care does not meet a certain threshold. To mitigate this risk, I will ask them to think about hiring additional resources to meet the growing demand for diabetes care.

My Big Idea for my communication is:

We should consider hiring additional staff to care for the projected increase in diabetic patients so that we don't lose revenue and remain within national accreditation standards.

STEP 3: While my audience has tension coming from several places (from my list in Step 1, it's a wonder they sleep at night!), I'd consider the financial implications to be a *strong* source of tension. Without revenue coming in, eventually the system would shut down. This analysis shows one way to remain afloat: staff accordingly to provide the appropriate level of care.

My initial storyboard is shown in Figure 7.5b. Notice I arranged these stickies chronologically. This feels most natural to me because it mirrors the steps I followed in my analytical process.

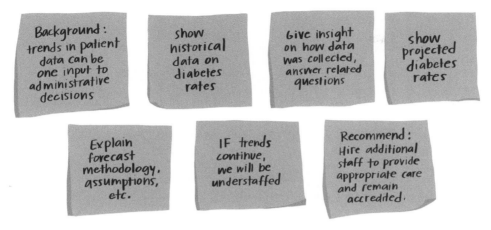

FIGURE 7.5b My initial storyboard

However, I'll want to consider my audience's perspective. I can use the narrative arc to arrange these stickies to align to how the data resolves their tension, as shown in Figure 7.5c.

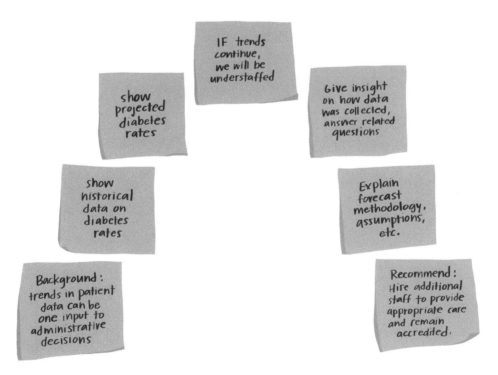

FIGURE 7.5c My storyboard arranged along the narrative arc

STEP 4: When I look at the four graphs in Figure 7.5a, it's interesting how different views enable us to see certain things about the data more clearly. Here are my one-sentence observations about each graph:

1. OPTION A: Center A has the lowest rate while B has the highest rate.

2. OPTION B: Every line is sloping upward with varying degrees of change.

3. OPTION C: Every line is sloping upward with Center A lowest (about 3%) and a marked increase in Center E between 2017-2019 (roughly 8% to 11%).

4. OPTION D: Center E increased the most (from roughly 8% in 2015 to 11% in 2019); Center A remains lowest (slightly above 4% in 2019).

Which graph will help my audience understand my Big Idea the best? I selected Option C, the standard line graph, for three primary reasons (although I'll definitely need to make some design changes—namely color and clutter—before presenting it). First, this view provides sufficient historical context, which I'll need my audience to see to ground them in what has happened and how this affects future expectations. Second, the line graph makes sense for this data over time and will feel familiar to my audience, so there won't be any obstacles to understanding the graph. Finally, I want to highlight the line indicating the diabetes rate across all of our medical centers in my final communication and show the projection going forward. This visual, with some modifications, will allow me to easily do that.

STEP 5: Time constraints are real. Fire drill requests happen, so I'll need to prioritize what changes I can make for the biggest impact. Due to time constraints, I'll skip making any modifications to the layout of the graph, but instead will make changes when it comes to color and use of words. Figure 7.5d shows what this could look like.

Diabetes rates have increased
Do we need additional staff to remain within standards?

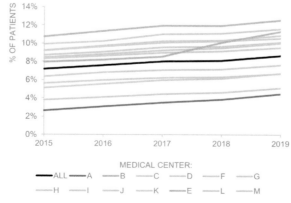

CENTERS OF CONCERN: Center B has the highest rate (12.5%); Center E has increased the most in the past four years. Next steps: further investigate specifics through demographic analysis at the medical center level and create action plans.

OVERALL: The diabetes rate across our medical centers has increased steadily to 8.6% in 2019. If this pace continues, we estimate an **additional 14,000 diabetic patients per year for the next four years.**

THE GOOD NEWS: Diabetes rate among our patients remains lowest in Center A. Next steps: further analysis to understand relative level of care and what we might make use of in other areas.

FIGURE 7.5d My visual completed for end-of-day fire drill request

I chose orange to emphasize the negatives: where diabetes rate is highest and in which center it increased the most. I utilized black to tie my title ("Diabetes rates have increased") to the data it describes (All). The subtitle acts to both illuminate the tension and suggest how the audience can resolve it. I picked blue to accentuate the positive: it's not all doom and gloom! I added text at the right (tied through both proximity and similarity of color to the data it describes) with some additional context and to help my audience understand why I've drawn attention as I have.

In a time-constrained environment, the contextual considerations we took in Steps 1 and 2 become even more valuable. Because I'd already done these thought exercises, I was able to create the visual in Figure 7.5d in under 15 minutes.

STEP 6: Figures 7.5e - 7.5p show the materials I would build and speaker notes for my manager to present this data story.

Today, I'd like you to contemplate an alarming number: 14,000. This is the number of additional diabetic patients per year we'll have if the increasing current trend in diabetes rates across our medical centers continues. I'll walk you through the details of how we arrived at that number momentarily, but keep in mind that our primary goal today is to discuss whether—given this anticipated increase in patient needs—we should consider hiring additional staff to remain within accreditation standards of appropriate care. (Figure 7.5e)

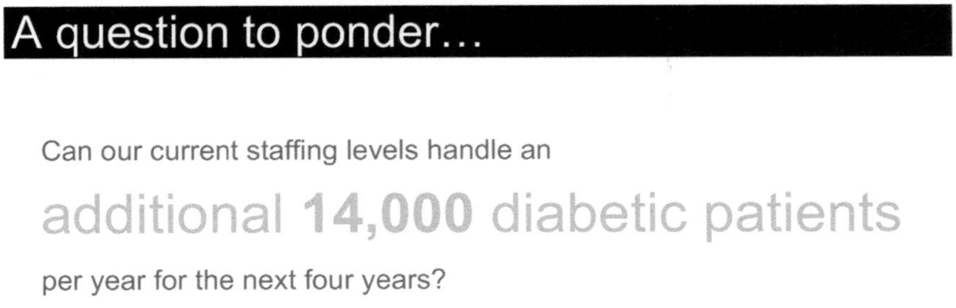

A question to ponder…

Can our current staffing levels handle an

additional **14,000** diabetic patients

per year for the next four years?

FIGURE 7.5e A question to ponder

Let me first talk you through the historical trends. We'll be looking at diabetes rates—expressed as a percent of our total patient base—at the medical center level from 2015 through 2019. (Figure 7.5f)

Let's set the stage

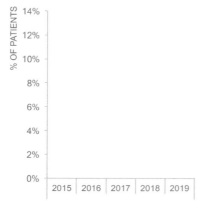

Diabetes rates by medical center

FIGURE 7.5f Start by setting the stage

Let's look across all of our medical centers: overall diabetes rate among our patients in 2015 was 7.2%. (Figure 7.5g)

Across all medical centers: 7.2% in 2015

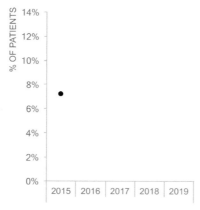

Diabetes rates by medical center

FIGURE 7.5g Overall diabetes rate was 7.2% in 2015

At that point, there were eight centers with higher diabetes rates (Figure 7.5h)

FIGURE 7.5h There were 8 centers with rates higher than overall

...and five centers with lower diabetes rates. (Figure 7.5i)

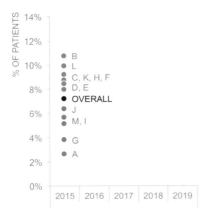

FIGURE 7.5i There were 5 centers with relatively low diabetes rates

We've seen a steady increase in the overall diabetes rate in our patients over the past five years. Today, it is 8.6%. (Figure 7.5j)

Across all medical centers: now 8.6%

Diabetes rates by medical center

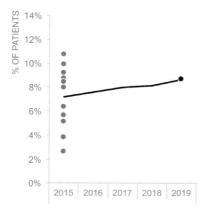

FIGURE 7.5j Diabetes rate across our medical centers is 8.6% in 2019

Over this period, all eight of the higher medical centers have increased. (Figure 7.5k)

Increase: high centers

Diabetes rates by medical center

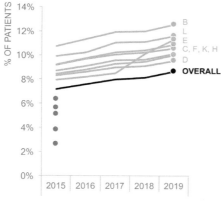

FIGURE 7.5k Medical centers having relatively high diabetes rates increased

Those with relatively lower diabetes rate also all increased. (Figure 7.5l)

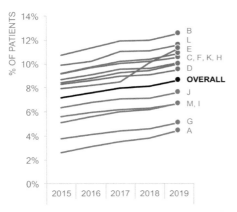

FIGURE 7.5l Those centers having lower diabetes rates also increased

The overall rate has increased roughly 0.5 percentage points per year. (Figure 7.5m)

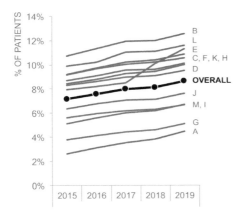

FIGURE 7.5m This is a consistent rise of 0.5 points per year

We forecast diabetes rates forward at the medical center level. I'm happy to talk about our methodology more specifically if there's interest in that. But the overall takeaway is that if a similar pace of increase continues, we project the diabetes rate across our medical centers will be 10% by the year 2023. In other words, one out of every ten patients across our clinics will be diabetic. (Figure 7.5n)

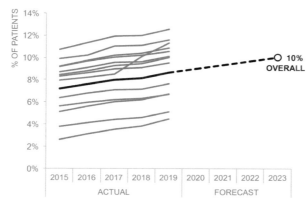

FIGURE 7.5n We project a continued increase

That translates to an additional 14,000 diabetic patients per year for the next four years. Given these projections, what should we do to prepare for this? Our initial recommendation is to consider hiring additional staff to be able to handle these numbers without any dip in patient care. What other options should we be thinking about? Let's discuss. (Figure 7.5o)

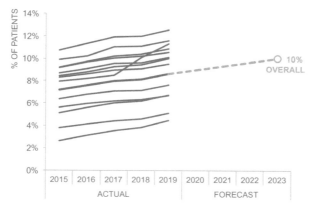

FIGURE 7.5o This implies 14,000 more patients with diabetes per year

If I needed something that would be sent around, I could have a single fully annotated slide that could stand on its own. Figure 7.5p shows what that might look like.

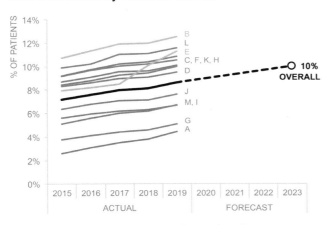

Rising diabetes rates: **do we need additional staff?**

Diabetes rates by medical center

Center B has the highest rate (12.5%) and Center E has seen a marked increase between 2017 (8.5%) and today (11.3%). What factors are influencing these levels?

The diabetes rate across all centers has increased from 7.2% in 2015 to 8.6% in 2019. At the current pace, this will increase to 10% by 2023. **This implies an additional 14,000 patients per year** for the next four years.

The good news is that we have an opportunity to learn what factors are influencing **Center A, which has the lowest rate and top patient care**. Next steps: Let's determine if these factors can be applied broadly.

FIGURE 7.5p Annotated slide to distribute

In this scenario, we've pulled from practice exercises in Chapters 1, 2, 4, and 6 to
craft a compelling story that should resonate with our audience and help us direct
a discussion focused on action!

Exercise 7.6: net promoter score

Imagine you work as an analyst on the customer insights team in your organization, which has three primary products. There is a monthly update meeting where the product team reviews data related to one of the products (cycling through so each product is focused on once per quarter). Your team has a dedicated 15-minute spot on the agenda to present voice of customer data related to product of focus for the given month. This is done through the Customer Feedback Analysis slide deck, which always follows the same format: a slide each for title page, data and methodology, analysis, and findings.

As a bit of background on the customer insights-related data you track, customers rate your products on a 5-star scale. You categorize 1-3 stars as "detractors" (those not likely to recommend the product); 4 stars are "passives"; 5 stars are "promoters" (those likely to recommend the product to others). The primary metric of focus is Net Promoter Score (NPS), which is the percent of promoters minus the percent of detractors, expressed as a number (not a percent). You typically look at NPS over time and compared to your competitor set for a given product. Customers rating your products also have the option of leaving comments, which your team categorizes into themes.

The product you focus on—an app—is on the agenda this month. You've updated the data and have found something interesting: while NPS has generally increased over time, underlying feedback has become increasingly polarized, with both promoter and detractor populations increasing as a proportion of total over time. Analysis of customer comments indicates a theme of latency and speed concerns among detractors. You'd like to bring this to light and use it to frame a recommendation to prioritize latency improvements for the product. This seems like the perfect situation in which to employ the various lessons we've reviewed and practiced over the course of this book!

The graphs presented on the Analysis slide of your typical deck are shown in Figure 7.6a. Study it in light of the scenario described, then complete the following steps.

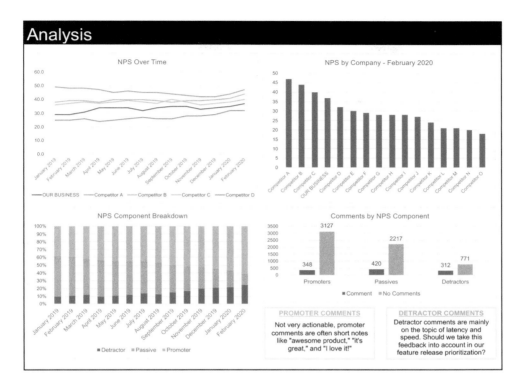

FIGURE 7.6a Typical graphs presented in monthly meeting

STEP 1: Form your Big Idea for this situation. Remember the Big Idea should (1) articulate your point of view, (2) convey what's at stake, and (3) be a complete sentence. Write it down. If possible, discuss it with someone else and refine. Create a pithy, repeatable phrase based on your Big Idea.

STEP 2: Let's take a closer look at the data. Write a sentence or two about each graph that describes the primary takeaway.

STEP 3: Time to get sticky! Get some sticky notes. In light of the context described, the Big Idea you created in Step 1, and the takeaways you outlined in Step 2, brainstorm the pieces of content you may include in your slide deck. After you've spent a few minutes doing this, arrange the pieces along the narrative arc. What is the tension? What can your audience do to resolve it?

STEP 4: It's time to design your graphs. Download the original graphs and underlying data. You can either modify the existing visuals or create new ones. Put into practice the lessons we've covered on choosing appropriate visuals, decluttering, and focusing attention. Be thoughtful in your overall design.

STEP 5: Create the deck you will use to present using the tool of your choice. Also outline the accompanying narrative of what you'll say for each slide. Even better: present this deck, walking a friend or colleague through your data-driven story.

Solution 7.6: net promoter score

STEP 1: My Big Idea could be something like, "We will continue losing users unless we improve the latency of our product: let's prioritize this in the next feature release."

For my pithy, repeatable phrase, I'll want something simple that doesn't feel overly salesy given the audience and typical meeting approach. Plus, I anticipate they will have additional context to lend as we together determine whether my recommendation is the best course of action. I can use something like, "Let's learn from our detractors." I could title my deck with this and weave it into my call to action.

STEP 2: Looking back at Figure 7.6a, my takeaways could be as follows.

- Top left: NPS has increased steadily recently, and as of February 2020, is at a 14-month high of 37 (NPS was 29 at this point in time last year, the lowest it's been over the time period observed).

- Top right: We currently rank 4th in NPS across our competitive set. Our 15 competitors have NPS ranging from a high of 47 (Competitor A) to a low of 18 (Competitor O).

- Bottom left: There has been a shift in makeup across promoters, passives, and detractors over time. Our users are becoming increasingly polarized, with the proportion of passives shrinking as the proportion of promoters and the proportion of detractors increases.

- Bottom right: A high proportion of detractors leave comments, and their primary concern is latency.

STEP 3: Figure 7.6b shows a basic narrative arc for this scenario.

PRACTICE with COLE
more

FIGURE 7.6b Narrative arc

STEPS 4 & 5: The following progression shows how I could weave everything together into a data-driven story with thoughtfully designed visuals, employing the various lessons covered in *SWD* and this book.

Today, I want to tell you a story. It's the story of what we've learned from our analysis of recent customer feedback. Let me offer a sneak peek—as indicated by my title, detractors play an important role—and we can learn from them in ways that may influence the go-forward strategy for our product roadmap. (Figure 7.6c)

Let's learn from our detractors

Monthly NPS Update

Presented by: Customer Insights Team
Date: March 1, 2020

FIGURE 7.6c Title slide

I have two primary goals today. First, to bring you up to speed on what we've learned from our analysis of recent customer feedback and related data. It turns out looking at NPS alone doesn't tell the whole story. Detractors are increasing. Second, I'd like to use the feedback from detractors to frame a conversation on how we can address their concerns. This will likely play into the product strategy and possibly impact the upcoming feature release schedule. (Figure 7.6d)

Goal today

1 **Build a common understanding of recent feedback.**
Though NPS has been flat to increasing over time, analysis of components reveals increasingly polarized customer base, with a **marked recent increase in detractors**.

2 Revisit product strategy given detractor feedback.
Detractor comments are on one theme above all others—latency. This should influence how we prioritize the various planned product improvements. **Determine whether and what changes to make**.

FIGURE 7.6d   Goal today

Let's take a look at the data. NPS has generally increased over time and has consistently increased in the past four months to 37 as of last month. (Figure 7.6e)

NPS: flat to increasing over time

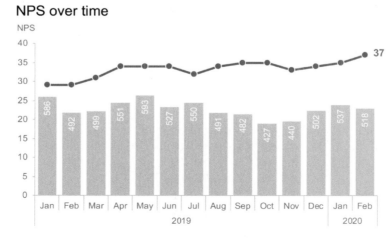

FIGURE 7.6e   NPS: flat to increasing over time

This 37 NPS puts us in 4th place relative to the competition. We anticipate that learning from our detractors and addressing their concerns will ultimately improve our positioning among competitors. (Figure 7.6f)

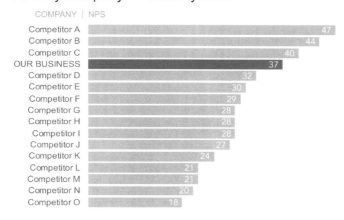

FIGURE 7.6f   We rank 4th against the competition

But as I mentioned, NPS alone doesn't tell the full story. Let's take a look at the components. As a reminder, we categorize customers based on their ratings of our product. Those rating us 1-3 stars are categorized as "detractors" (those not likely to recommend the product); 4 stars are "passives"; 5 stars are "promoters" (those likely to recommend the product to others). NPS is the percent of promoters minus percent of detractors. NPS provides a good aggregate measure but doesn't give us insight into how the breakdown across its components are changing over time. So next, let's take a look at those components.

Before I add the data, let me talk you through what we're going to be looking at. The y-axis represents the percent the given component—detractors, passives, and promoters—make up of total. We have time on our x-axis, ranging from January 2019 on the left to our most recent point of data, February 2020, on the right. (Figure 7.6g)

FIGURE 7.6g   Let's look at NPS components

I'm going to do something a little different here and build this graph from the middle out. These grey bars represent the proportion of total made up by passives. You see the proportion of passives is shrinking markedly over time: the height of these grey bars is getting smaller. (Figure 7.6h)

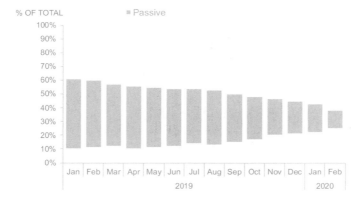

FIGURE 7.6h   Proportion of passives decreasing

Some of this change is good news: we've seen an accompanying increase in the proportion of promoters; the dark grey bars at the top are getting bigger over time. (Figure 7.6i)

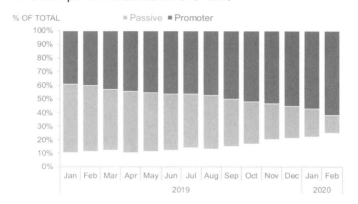

Proportion of **promoters increasing**

NPS component breakdown over time

FIGURE 7.6i Proportion of promoters increasing

But as you can probably anticipate based on the empty part of my graph and my commentary so far, the detractor population is also increasing as a percent of total. (Figure 7.6j)

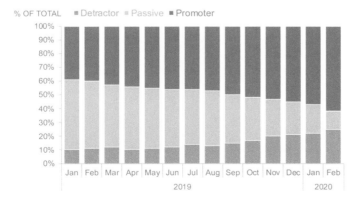

Proportion of **detractors increasing**

NPS component breakdown over time

FIGURE 7.6j Proportion of detractors increasing

And actually, let's put a couple of numbers on the graph to help understand the magnitude of this increase. Detractors made up 10% of those giving feedback at the beginning of 2019. This increased marginally, to 13% of total, over the first half of last year. Since then, the detractor population has nearly doubled as a percent of total. As of February this year, detractors make up 25% of those leaving us feedback about our product. (Figure 7.6k)

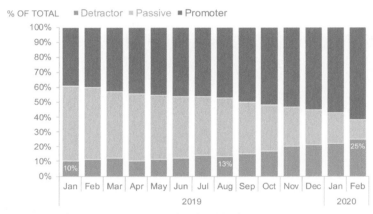

FIGURE 7.6k Detractors: nearly doubled since Aug

In addition to numerical ratings, customers also have the option of leaving comments that lend further context. Overall, 15% of those rating our product leave a comment. Relatively fewer promoters leave comments and they tend to be pretty general and less actionable: things like, "It's great!" and "I really like it!" But we get some incredibly rich detail from our detractors. Relatively many more leave comments—29% of those rating us 1-3 stars share additional detail. (Figure 7.6l)

Detractors: relatively **more comments**

Comments by NPS component

	% OF TOTAL COMMENT | NO COMMENT	# OF RATINGS
Total	15%	7,195
Promoters	10%	3,482
Passives	16%	2,624
Detractors	29%	1,089

FIGURE 7.6l Detractors: relatively more comments

Our detractor comments focus on one topic more than any other: speed and latency concerns.

Let me read you a sample verbatim comment: "My frustration in a single word: latency. It takes forever for the app to open. When it works, it works great. But I spend too much time waiting and wondering whether it's ever going to load. It often hangs when opening."

It is disheartening to read comments like this from our users. We've been focused on adding more features but it seems something that might help more is making sure the basics work seamlessly. (Figure 7.6m)

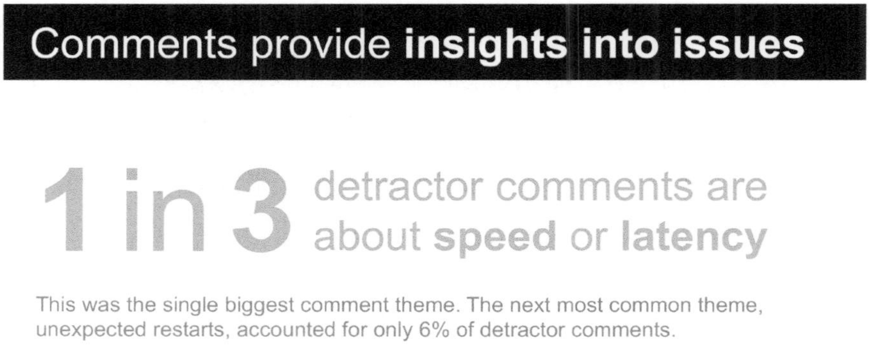

Comments provide **insights into issues**

1 in 3 detractor comments are about **speed** or **latency**

This was the single biggest comment theme. The next most common theme, unexpected restarts, accounted for only 6% of detractor comments.

FIGURE 7.6m Comments provide insights into issues

Now, I fully recognize that there is other context to consider. But I want to make sure to bring this customer insight data to light so that we can take it into account in our overall product strategy. Improving the latency of our product can help us reverse the increase in detractors and simply make for happier users. How should this play into our product strategy and upcoming release schedule? Let's discuss. (Figure 7.6n)

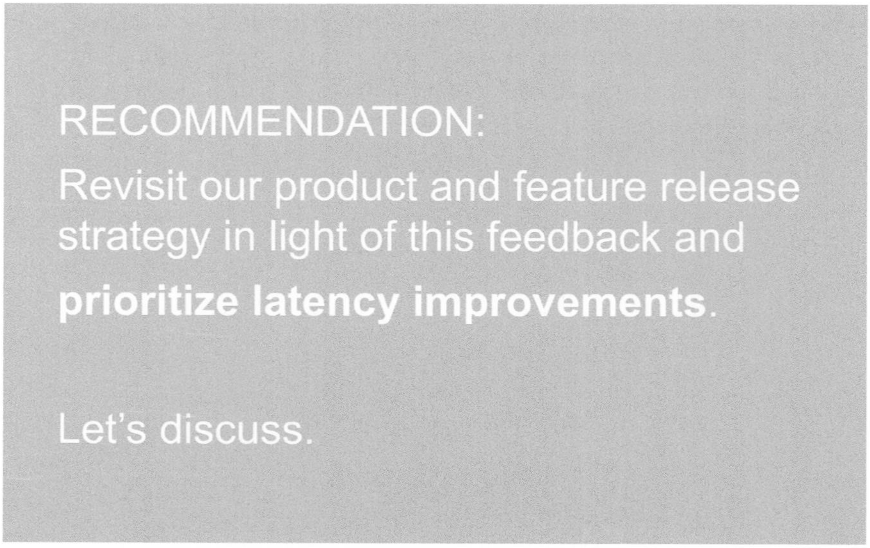

RECOMMENDATION:
Revisit our product and feature release strategy in light of this feedback and **prioritize latency improvements**.

Let's discuss.

FIGURE 7.6n Recommendation

Consider how the path we just took our audience along differs from the typical linear approach of methodology-analysis-findings that was outlined in the onset of this scenario. We can use data storytelling to capture and maintain our audience's attention and frame a productive data-driven discussion. Leaving the room after this meeting, you'd know the analysis you undertook will help influence decision making.

Will your audience always do what you want them to? Of course not. There are likely competing priorities or maybe speeding the app up is actually a really complicated thing. The great thing is, framing things in terms of a recommendation—thus giving the folks in the room something specific to react to—will drive conversation that will bring additional relevant context to light. Presenting a data story does not mean you know all the details or have all the answers. But it does mean thinking about the data and how we communicate it in a deeper way. When we are thoughtful about how we do this, we can influence richer debates and smarter decisions. Success!

We've practiced the holistic process of data storytelling together a handful of times. Next up you'll find additional examples and case studies to work through on your own.

PRACTICE more with COLE

practice more
on your own

While Chapter 7 posed problems *and* offered solutions, Chapter 8 has a number of unsolved exercises: to answer them, you will need to draw on the various lessons we've covered over the course of *SWD* and this book. These can be used as assignments, individual or group projects, or incorporated into tests or exams. They will also be useful for those simply wanting additional opportunities to apply the *storytelling with data* lessons.

The exercises in this chapter can be worked through on your own or with a partner or small group. They grow in nuance and complexity as you move through them. For topics or data that don't feel immediately relevant to your work, I still encourage you to complete the exercises. Continued rehearsal of lessons helps them become ingrained and enables you to refine your skills in a low-risk setting. Additionally, practicing in different contexts frees you up from the constraints of normal day-to-day work, which may bring to light more creative approaches. After completing an exercise, get feedback and consider what components of your solution you might employ in your work.

A number of exercises invite you to execute the recommendations you outline in the tool of your choice. This additional application helps you better learn your tools and further hone your data visualization and data storytelling skills.

For those assigning exercises from this chapter, feel free to take liberties. There is no end to the number of assignments you can create by mixing and matching specific discussion points or instructions across the various examples. You might use similar exercise framing with your own visuals to create custom exercises.

Let's practice **more on your own**!

But before you dive in, let's review some common myths in data visualization.

FIRST, LET'S REVIEW
COMMON MYTHS in DATA VIZ

MYTH:
LINE GRAPHS are for CONTINUOUS DATA ONLY

The LINES that CONNECT the POINTS HAVE to MAKE SENSE

Example:
SURVEY DATA SLOPEGRAPH
(a line graph w/ only two points)

EMPLOYEE SATISFACTION

these are comparisons across groups/ categories

OVERALL ORG   SALES ORG

MYTH:
BARS are ALWAYS BETTER

BARS are a GOOD PLACE to START... but NOT ALWAYS the BEST
Ask "what do I want my audience to see?"

Try other types of charts and decide what meets your needs

MYTH:
GRAPHS * MUST have a ZERO BASELINE

* THIS is TRUE for BAR CHARTS

 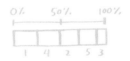

MYTH:
PIE CHARTS are EVIL

When USING a PIE, ASK yourself WHY?

Studies prove that people read pies & donuts by comparing AREA, not ANGLE

If you think pies make sense for your data & audience, test them out to see!

MYTH:
UNBIASED DATA EXISTS

We are BIASING our DATA at EVERY STEP of the PROCESS

 RULE! DON'T LIE with DATA

WHAT we choose to measure

HOW we aggregate and compare

HOW we show things

MYTH:
MORE DATA is ALWAYS BETTER

BEFORE CHASING after MORE DATA, ask "WHAT will it HELP us DO or DECIDE?"

Audience & context are important when it comes to the right amount of data

MYTH:
AVERAGES ALWAYS WORK to SUMMARIZE DATA

YOU NEED to UNDERSTAND the DISTRIBUTION, SPREAD, and VARIABILITY

ANNUAL   MONTHLY   DAILY

Averages can mislead by hiding a spread in a single number

MYTH:
THERE is a SINGLE RIGHT ANSWER when VISUALIZING DATA

YOU SHOULD ALWAYS CONSIDER when SHOWING DATA: WHAT is your GOAL?

INFORM   GOALS   INNOVATE

ENGAGE   ENTERTAIN

EXPLORE

PRACTICE MORE on your OWN

8.1 diversity hiring	8.2 sales by region	8.3 revenue forecast
8.4 adverse events	8.5 reasons for leaving	8.6 accounts over time
8.7 errors and complaints	8.8 taste test data	8.9 encounters by type
8.10 store traffic		

Exercise 8.1: diversity hiring

Your organization recently implemented a diversity hiring initiative for its "ABC Program." You're interested in understanding the relative success of the initiative. Familiarize yourself with Figure 8.1—a slide showing related data—then complete the following steps.

2019 ABC Program Hiring Highlights

Hiring Overview – 2019 Incoming Interns and Analysts
131 hires made across all ABC Programs. 3.60 GPA goal was slightly exceeded.

Program	Intern	Analyst	Intern MBA	Full Time MBA	Subtotal	% of Total Hires
			2019 Hires by LOB and Position Type			
ABXL	40	36	8	3	87	66%
ARC	20	5	2	0	27	21%
EMA	6	5	0	0	11	8%
REP	4	0	0	0	4	3%
QB	2	0	0	0	2	2%
Total	72	46	10	3	131	100%

2019 Hire Average GPA
3.66

Diversity Hiring Overview – 2019 Incoming Interns and Analysts
Female hiring target of 25% was exceeded (26%). Achieved ethnic diversity goal of 40%; however, five ethnically diverse candidates reneged on their offers. Ratio of diverse to non-diverse hires is 1:1.

Category Type	# Hires	% All Hires
Ethnic Female	12	9%
Ethnic Male	30	22%
Non-Ethnic Female	23	17%
Non-Ethnic Male	66	49%
Hired TBD	0	0%
Open	0	0%
Reneged	5	4%
Total	136	

Program	EF	EM	NEF	# Div	% Div	Non-Div	% Non-Div
		2019 Diversity Hires by LOB and Type					
ABXL	7	25	15	47	54%	40	46%
ARC	2	3	6	11	41%	16	59%
EMA	2	1	1	4	36%	7	64%
REP	1	0	1	2	50%	2	50%
QB	0	1	0	1	50%	1	50%
Total	12	30	23	65	50%	66	50%

Diversity Category Type Key: EF = Ethnically Diverse Female, **EM** = Ethnically Diverse Male, **NEF** = Non-Ethnically Diverse Female, and **Non-Div** = Caucasian Male

FIGURE 8.1 Program hiring highlights

STEP 1: Let's start with the positives: what do you like about this slide?

STEP 2: What is not ideal about Figure 8.1? Make notes or discuss with a partner.

STEP 3: What is the primary takeaway? Is this a success story or a call for action? Articulate in a sentence or two the point(s) you would focus on if you were presenting this data.

STEP 4: Assume you need to present this data and have been told it has to be in tabular form (a table or set of tables). Are there improvements you can make to the way the data is shown given this constraint to better focus on the takeaway you formed in Step 3? Draw (or if you prefer, download the data and create in your tool) the table or tables you would use and detail where and how you would direct attention.

STEP 5: Assume you have more liberty to make changes. How might you present the data? How would you tell a data-driven story about diversity hiring in the ABC Program? Outline your planned approach, then create your ideal materials in the tool of your choice.

Exercise 8.2: sales by region

Imagine that you are the Sales Manager of the Northwest (NW) region at your company. You've pulled the following slide (Figure 8.2) from a monthly report and want to cover it at an upcoming offsite with your sales team. You're preparing content together with your Chief of Staff. Let's consider two scenarios:

SCENARIO 1: The offsite is tomorrow, and both you and your Chief of Staff have a number of other items to tackle in the meantime. You don't have time to fully redesign the visual in Figure 8.2. Assume you can spend at most five minutes making changes. What would you do? How would you present the information?

SCENARIO 2: The offsite is a week away, and your Chief of Staff has volunteered to redesign the information shown in Figure 8.2. Before doing so, she's asked for your feedback. What aspects do you like about the current visual that you would want to be preserved? What changes would you suggest based on the lessons we've covered?

Make notes or discuss with a partner.

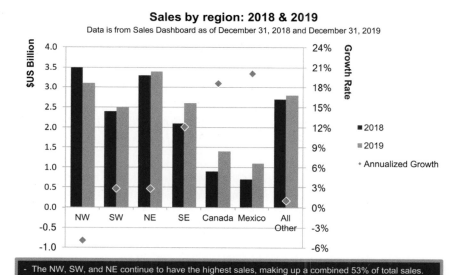

FIGURE 8.2 Sales by region

(margin note, left side) more PRACTICE on your OWN

Exercise 8.3: revenue forecast

Study Figure 8.3, which depicts gross and net revenue over time, then complete the following steps.

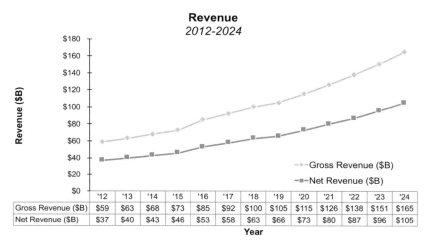

FIGURE 8.3 Revenue forecast

STEP 1: What do you like about this visual?

STEP 2: Reflect on the use of the data table. Do you find this effective? If so, explain why. If not, how might you approach it differently?

STEP 3: What other changes would you make? Take notes or talk with a partner.

STEP 4: Let's envision two distinct circumstances for communicating this data: (1) presenting in a live meeting and (2) emailing it to your audience. What would you do differently in these two situations? To take things a step further, download the data and create your preferred visuals in the tool of your choice, making assumptions as needed.

STEP 5: Select a data visualization tool that you have not previously used (see the Tools section of the Introduction for a partial list). Re-create your visual in this new tool. What did you learn from this experience? Write a paragraph or two outlining your insights.

Exercise 8.4: adverse events

Imagine that you work at a medical device company. A colleague approaches you with the following slide (Figure 8.4) summarizing a couple of points from a recent study and asks for your feedback. Spend a few moments examining it, then complete the following steps.

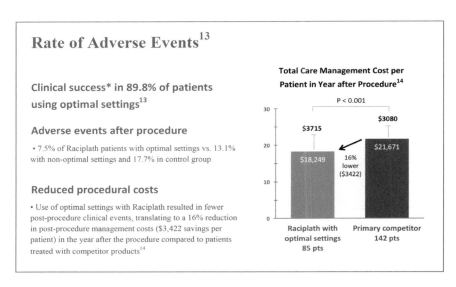

FIGURE 8.4 Adverse events

STEP 1: Before jumping into constructive criticism, it can be nice to point out what has been done well. What do you like about this slide?

STEP 2: What questions would you ask your colleague? Make a list.

STEP 3: What changes might you recommend based on the various lessons we've covered? Outline your thoughts, focusing not just on *what* you would recommend changing, but also *why*.

STEP 4: How would your recommendations change if you knew this information was going to be presented to a non-technical audience?

STEP 5: To take things a step further, download the data and create your revamped slide, incorporating the changes you've outlined in prior steps in the tool of your choice. Make assumptions as needed.

Exercise 8.5: reasons for leaving

Imagine that you are Chief of Staff for the Chief Marketing Officer (CMO) at a large company. Your boss, the CMO, has asked you to work with your Human Resources Business Partner (HRBP) to understand what is driving attrition—people leaving the company—across the marketing organization and present your findings. Your HRBP digs into the data, then emails you the following visual, Figure 8.5.

Spend a few minutes processing this data, then complete the following steps.

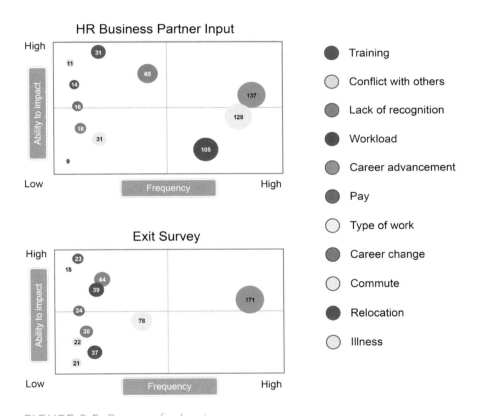

FIGURE 8.5 Reasons for leaving

STEP 1: What is being shown here? Write a few sentences explaining this data: how do we interpret this visual? Make assumptions as necessary for the purpose of this exercise.

STEP 2: What is confusing or not ideal about the visual in its current form? What questions would you ask or feedback might you give your HRBP? On a related note, assume your HRBP spent a lot of time creating this visual—how can you frame your feedback so they don't take offense?

STEP 3: Let's draw! Come up with three different ways to show this data. What are some advantages and shortcomings of each? List them. Which view do you like best and why?

STEP 4: Download the data and create your preferred visual in the tool of your choice.

STEP 5: It's time to present this data to the CMO. Make an assumption about whether you'll walk through it live or send it to be consumed on its own. Create your recommended communication in light of this assumption in the tool of your choice.

more
PRACTICE *on your* OWN

Exercise 8.6: accounts over time

You are an analyst in a sales organization and your team has been asked to summarize a current campaign, assessing how things are going against the goal of increasing the number of accounts. You have actual data through September 2019 and a forward-looking forecast through the end of 2020. Your colleague has pulled together the following summary (Figure 8.6) and asked for your feedback. Spend a couple of minutes examining the visual, then complete the following steps.

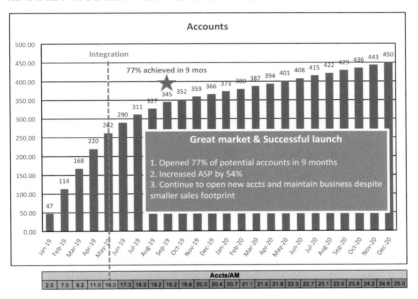

FIGURE 8.6 Accounts over time

STEP 1: What questions do you have about this data? Make a list.

STEP 2: Let's declutter: make a list of the elements you would remove.

STEP 3: What is the story—is this a success or call to action? What is the tension in this scenario? What action do you want your audience to take to resolve this tension?

STEP 4: How would you recommend showing this data? Draw or download the data and iterate in the tool of your choice to create your preferred design.

STEP 5: Consider how your approach would vary if you were (1) presenting this data live in a meeting and (2) sending it to your audience to be consumed on its own. How would the way you'd tackle this differ? Write a few sentences explaining your thoughts. To take it a step further, redesign this visual for these different use cases in the tool of your choice.

Exercise 8.7: errors & complaints

In this scenario, you are an analyst working at a national bank. At the beginning of each year, your team compiles a year-end review for each portfolio. This contains data from many parts of the lending process—from originations to collections. You've been tasked with analyzing data and creating content on the topics of quality and satisfaction in the Home Loans portfolio. You started by pulling the slide that was used for this in the prior year's review and updated it with the latest year's data. The resulting graphs are shown in Figure 8.7.

Instead of having a page of graphs, you'd decided to use this opportunity to tell a data story.

Spend a few minutes studying Figure 8.7, then complete the following steps.

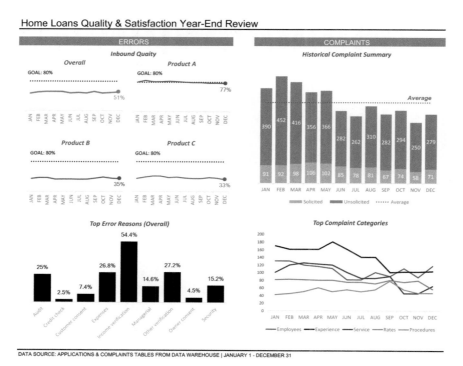

FIGURE 8.7 Errors & complaints

STEP 1: What questions would you ask about this data? Make a list. Next, answer each of these questions, making assumptions for the purpose of this exercise.

STEP 2: Write a sentence or two about each graph that describes the primary takeaway.

STEP 3: What story or stories would you focus on here? Which data would you include? Is there any data you would omit? Will it all work on a single slide, or do you believe it would be best to use more? Sketch your planned approach on blank paper.

STEP 4: How would you visualize the data in Figure 8.7 to lend insight into what we should focus on in this situation? Consider all of the lessons that we've covered and how you would apply them. Download the data and build your materials using the tool of your choice to tell the story with this data.

STEP 5: Imagine you draft your slide(s) and get feedback from your manager that the audience will expect a page of graphs, like they've seen in the past. How will you respond to this? Write out your thoughts.

more
PRACTICE on your OWN

Exercise 8.8: taste test data

Craveberry is the new yogurt product that your food-manufacturing employer is preparing to launch. The product team on which you work decided to do an additional round of taste testing to get a final gauge of consumer sentiment before going to market with the product. You've worked with your team to analyze the results. You are getting ready to meet with the Head of Product to discuss whether to potentially make changes before going to market. (If this sounds familiar, it's because we introduced it in context of the narrative arc in Chapter 6.)

Your colleague puts together the following visual (Figure 8.8) summarizing the taste test results and asks for your feedback. Spend a moment studying it, then complete the following steps.

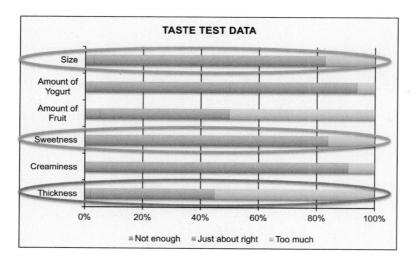

FIGURE 8.8 Taste test data

STEP 1: Let's start with the positives: what do you like about this slide?

STEP 2: What feedback would you give based on the lessons we've covered? Outline your thoughts, focusing not just on *what* you would recommend changing, but also *why*.

STEP 3: Let's step back and think about story. Reflect on the various components of the narrative arc: plot, rising action, climax, falling action, ending. List these components and what you would cover within each for this scenario. Even better: write out the points of your planned story on sticky notes and arrange them in the shape of the narrative arc. Edit as needed to outline the story you would tell with this data. What is the tension? What can your audience do to resolve it?

STEP 4: Download the data and create the data-driven story you outlined in Step 3 in the tool of your choice. Also outline the accompanying narrative of what you'll say when you present to the Head of Product.

Exercise 8.9: encounters by type

The following situation may sound familiar; we've seen it once before in Exercise 6.3. Read through the scenario to refresh your memory, then examine the data and complete the following steps.

You work as a data analyst at a regional health care center. As part of ongoing initiatives to improve overall efficiency, cost, and quality of care, there has been a push in recent years for greater use of virtual communications by physicians (via email, phone, and video) when possible in place of in-person visits. You've been asked to pull together data for inclusion in the annual review to assess whether the desired shift towards virtual is happening and make recommendations for targets for the coming year. Your analysis indicates there has indeed been a relative increase in virtual encounters across both primary and specialty care. You've forecast the coming year and expect these trends to continue. You can use recent data and your forecast to inform targets. You believe seeking physician input is also necessary to avoid setting overaggressive targets that could inadvertently lead to negative impact on quality of care.

Figure 8.9 shows the data you'll use to build your story.

| Encounters over Time by Type | | 2015 | 2016 | 2017 | 2018 | 2019 | 2020 (Proj) |
Per 1000 Patients							
In Person	Total	3,659	3,721	3,588	3,525	3,447	3,384
	Primary Care	1,723	1,735	1,681	1,586	1,526	1,500
	Specialty Care	1,936	1,986	1,907	1,939	1,921	1,884
Telephone	Total	28	39	138	263	394	535
	Primary Care	26	34	125	212	295	375
	Specialty Care	2	5	13	51	99	160
Video	Total	0.3	0.5	1.6	2.8	3.4	4.5
	Primary Care	0.2	0.3	0.4	0.8	1.2	2.0
	Specialty Care	0.1	0.2	1.2	2.0	2.2	2.5
Email	Total	1,240	1,287	1,350	1,368	1,443	1,580
	Primary Care	801	831	852	856	897	950
	Specialty Care	439	456	498	512	546	630
TOTAL	Total	4,927	5,048	5,078	5,159	5,287	5,504
	Primary Care	2,550	2,600	2,658	2,655	2,719	2,827
	Specialty Care	2,377	2,447	2,419	2,504	2,568	2,677

FIGURE 8.9 Encounters over time by type

PRACTICE on your OWN

STEP 1: It's difficult to see what's going on with the data in tabular form, so let's start by visualizing it. You can sketch it, or download the data in Figure 8.9 and create graphs in the tool of your choice. Do this to build a better understanding of the data and what we can learn from it. As part of this, you'll likely want to answer the following questions:

(A) How have the total number of encounters changed over time?

(B) How do encounters break down across the various types? Is the desired shift towards virtual channels (telephone, video, and email) happening?

(C) Is there a difference between Primary and Specialty Care when it comes to use of virtual channels?

(D) What targets would you recommend for Primary and Specialty Care virtual encounters based solely on the data?

STEP 2: Consider the provided context along with what you learned in Step 1. You anticipate that you'll have to present this data live. Create a low-tech outline of your data story. You may do this in written form, putting the various takeaways into words and creating a bulleted list. You could also make use of some of the tools we've discussed—sticky notes, storyboarding, and the narrative arc. Or perhaps you have other ideas. Plan your data story in the way that works best for you.

STEP 3: Create the data story you outlined in Step 2 using the tool of your choice.

STEP 4: In addition to the live progression, you'll need a one-pager to be shared with those who missed the meeting or as a reminder of what was covered. Create this visual in the tool of your choice.

Exercise 8.10: store traffic

You are an insights analyst at a large national retailer. You have just completed an analysis of recent store traffic and purchase trends. You've visualized the data and believe there is a compelling story to tell.

Store traffic has decreased since last year, both overall and across all regions. Traffic decreased the most in the Northeast—this makes sense, as your company closed several stores there in the past year. Many of those stores' customers are now shopping with your competitors. The decrease in traffic is also more marked for your most important customer group, which your organization calls "Super Shoppers." This year-over-year gap has increased in recent months. But traffic—the number of people shopping—is only one piece of the puzzle. To understand how changes in traffic manifest in changes in sales (something management cares deeply about), you also have to take into account how much people spend while at your store. You measure this by "basket," which is made up of unit purchases (the number of items bought) and the price per item.

The data shows that customers—and Super Shoppers in particular—are generally buying fewer items; however, the average price of those items has increased. This is likely due to targeted promotions your stores offered with luxury brands in the past year. Because of the positive impact of the promotions, you'd like to recommend to senior management to further investigate the financial implications of running additional Super Shopper promotions, both to further test this hypothesis and—more importantly—in hopes of turning around the undesirable trends you're seeing in the data.

You were talking through the visuals you created as part of this analysis with your manager. In doing so, you realized that the graphs you used to figure out the story may not work well for getting that information across to your stakeholders. Your manager has asked you to revamp the graphs and pull together a short slide deck to communicate your findings and recommendation to senior management. You've decided to take a step back and use this as an opportunity to employ the various lessons we've covered over the course of *SWD* and this book.

more PRACTICE on your OWN

Figure 8.10 shows your original graphs. Spend some time studying these, then complete the following steps.

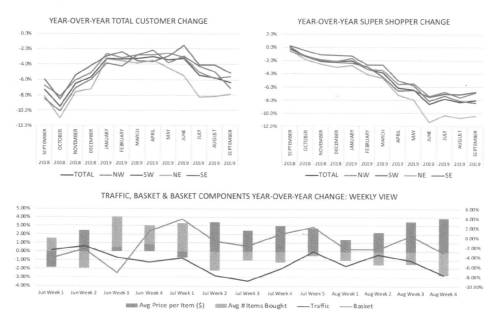

FIGURE 8.10 Your original graphs

STEP 1: Form your Big Idea for this scenario. Remember the Big Idea should (1) articulate your point of view, (2) convey what's at stake, and (3) be a complete sentence. Refer to the Big Idea worksheet in Exercise 1.20 if helpful. After crafting it, discuss it with someone else and refine. Do you think it makes sense to form a pithy, repeatable phrase based on your Big Idea? If so, create one, referring to Exercise 6.12 as needed.

STEP 2: Let's take a closer look at the data. Write a sentence or two about each graph that describes the primary takeaway.

STEP 3: Time to get sticky! Get some sticky notes. In light of the context described, the Big Idea you created in Step 1, and the takeaways you outlined in Step 2, brainstorm the pieces of content you might include in your slide deck. After you've spent a few minutes doing this, arrange the pieces along the narrative arc. What is the tension? What can your audience do to resolve it?

STEP 4: Next, spend some time with the data and design your graphs. Download the original graphs and underlying data (you'll find some additional data there, too, which may be useful). You'll likely need to iterate through a few different views of the data. Consider drawing your ideas as part of your iterating and brainstorming process. Put into practice the lessons we've covered on choosing appropriate visuals, decluttering, and focusing attention. Be thoughtful in your overall design.

STEP 5: Create the deck you will use to present using the tool of your choice. Also outline the accompanying narrative of what you'll say for each slide. Even better: present this deck, walking a friend or colleague through your data-driven story.

STEP 6: Let's take a few minutes to reflect. Compare the original graphs with what you've created. Do you believe your solution will be more effective? Why? How did this overall process feel? Which parts were most helpful and why? How can you envision applying components of what you've done in this exercise to your work in general? Write a paragraph or two outlining your thoughts.

You've made it: you've learned by example! You've practiced a ton. You've honed your data storytelling skills. Congrats! If you haven't already started, you are definitely now ready to practice at work. Let's move on to some final exercises designed to give you the skills and confidence you need to succeed telling stories with data in your day job.

PRACTICE on your OWN

practice more
at work

The final chapter of exercises focuses on how to apply the *storytelling with data* lessons at work. You've encountered a good amount of this guidance already and I encourage you to refer back to the *practice at work* exercises throughout this book when facing a specific project: the initial exercise in this chapter will help you do just that.

Additionally, you'll find guidance for further integrating the *storytelling with data* process into your and your colleagues' day-to-day work. This will help you examine and practice the totality of the lessons we've covered over the course of *SWD* and this book. You'll be provided with resources and guides for facilitating group learning and discussion and assessment rubrics that can be used to evaluate your own or others' work. We'll review the important role of feedback and how to best give and receive it, as well as setting—and helping others set—good goals for continuing to improve your data storytelling skills. There is no such thing as an "expert" in this space; regardless of skill level, there is always room for further growth. We can all continue to refine our abilities and become more nuanced in how we communicate with data.

Awesome work completing the exercises so far (and if you haven't completed them all, that's okay—it means you have more to go back to!). Next, **let's practice some more at work**!

To be helpful, let's first review some ideas for setting you and your team up for success.

FIRST, LET'S REVIEW
DEVELOPING your TEAM

WHAT ABOUT ME?

NOBODY WORKS in a VACUUM

Managers & leaders can benefit from building team capacity for telling stories with data

As well as individuals wanting to influence people around them

TYPICAL TEAM SET UPS

CROSS-FUNCTIONAL GROUPS

TECHNICIAN   DESIGNER   MANAGER   ANALYST

Most teams don't have a data visualization specialist rather this is a part of the analyst's role

BALANCING STRATEGIC & TECHNICAL

It's MUCH MORE than "MAKING DATA PRETTY"

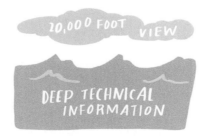

20,000 FOOT VIEW

DEEP TECHNICAL INFORMATION

Even the most brilliant analysis can be a wasted effort if it is not communicated effectively

FOR MANAGERS

FOSTER a CULTURE of LEARNING

Make data VIZ & communication an expected part of analytical role

Identify who has a natural proclivity and interest and support their growth to become an expert

FOR SMALL TEAMS

EMBRACE the CONSTRAINTS

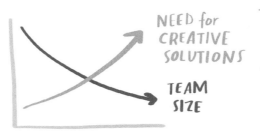

NEED for CREATIVE SOLUTIONS

TEAM SIZE

→ Encourage practicing and testing out new approaches

→ Utilize free resources online

→ Look externally for mentorship & guidance

FOR INDIVIDUALS

Do good work

Ask for feedback

Share tips without being preachy

small successes build confidence & credibility

PRACTICE MORE at WORK

9.1
create your plan of attack

9.2
set good goals

9.3
give & receive effective feedback

9.4
cultivate a feedback culture

9.5
refer to the SWD process

9.6
make use of an assessment rubric

9.7
facilitate a BIG IDEA practice session

9.8
conduct an SWD Working session

9.9
set yourself up for successful data stories

9.10
let's discuss

Exercise 9.1: create your plan of attack

You've seen a number of *practice at work* exercises already in Chapters 1- 6. You'll find all of these listed below. When facing a project where you need to communicate with data or present a story, scan through this list. Determine what combination of exercises will work best for your needs, then complete them!

1.17   get to know your audience
1.18   narrow your audience
1.19   identify the action
1.20   complete the Big Idea worksheet
1.21   solicit feedback on your Big Idea
1.22   create the Big Idea as a team
1.23   get the ideas out of your head!
1.24   organize your ideas in a storyboard
1.25   solicit feedback on your storyboard
2.17   draw it!
2.18   iterate in your tool
2.19   consider these questions
2.20   say it out loud
2.21   solicit feedback on your graph
2.22   build a data viz library
2.23   explore additional resources
3.11   start with a blank piece of paper
3.12   query *do you need that?*
4.9   test *where are your eyes drawn?*
4.10   practice differentiating in your tool
4.11   figure out where to focus
5.9   make data accessible with words
5.10   create visual hierarchy
5.11   pay attention to detail!
5.12   design more accessibly
5.13   garner acceptance for your designs
6.12   form a pithy, repeatable phrase
6.13   answer *what's the story?*
6.14   employ the narrative arc

PRACTICE *at* WORK *more*

Exercise 9.2: set good goals

I am a huge proponent of goal setting. When you articulate something you would like to happen and then plan the steps you can take to make it so, that thing is simply more likely to be accomplished! Setting good goals is one way to help ensure ongoing focus on further developing and honing your data storytelling skills.

At its core, the way to do this is simple. Isolate the skill or aspect of your work you want to advance. Then list the specific actions you can undertake to do it. Create a sense of urgency by making the actions time sensitive. Post this list somewhere you can see it for a regular reminder. Share with a manager or colleague to create additional accountability. If you're like me, the feeling of being able to check off completed things that lead you closer to your goal is super gratifying. Even more powerful is how these actions help you refine your skills and increase your expertise as you accomplish your initial goals and set increasingly ambitious ones.

If you crave a more specific structure for goal setting, I'll walk you through one momentarily. First, a caveat that if you have a current process that works, I encourage you to continue to use it. At *storytelling with data*, I set annual big-picture goals for the company. On a quarterly basis, all individuals (including me) follow a goal-setting and assessment framework that I learned at Google. I'll outline our process in case useful as you are setting—or helping your team set—goals.

We document and measure our quarterly **Objectives and Key Results** (OKRs) to maintain focus and accountability on goals that support the business. The *objectives* define what the individual wants to accomplish. These should be significant and communicate action. The *key results* describe how the given objective will be met. Key results should be aggressive yet realistic, measurable, limited in number, and time-bound (with target frequency or completion date). Individuals typically have 3-5 objectives for the quarter, each supported with 2-3 key results. For illustration, here is an example objective and associated key results:

OBJECTIVE: Thoughtfully integrate story into my presentation of pilot program XYZ, gaining approval for the resources needed to officialize and expand the program.

- KEY RESULT 1: Complete *SWD: let's practice!* exercises 1.17, 1.20, 1.21, 1.23, 1.24, 6.12, and 6.14 for two different projects by Jan 31st.

- KEY RESULT 2: Plan and create separate materials by Jan 15th optimized for the given setting: live presentation and email summary. Solicit and incorporate feedback from Key Stakeholder A by Jan 31st.

- KEY RESULT 3: Give three practice presentations this quarter to colleagues and integrate their feedback to improve my content, flow, and delivery style.

PRACTICE at WORK
more

Once an individual's OKRs are finalized, we publish and make them available to the broader team. This sort of transparency around what we're each trying to accomplish increases everyone's odds for success.

About a week after each quarter, we **review and grade** the past quarter's OKRs. The reflection piece is helpful both to pause and celebrate successes as well as evaluate where not as much progress as planned was made. Grading—one of the most important steps in OKRs—takes this part of the process a step further. We rate ours on a simple 0-10 scale, with zero indicating no progress and 10 indicating the key result was completely achieved (for example, if the key result was to create 12 graphs with a new tool you're learning and you created 12, you score 10; if you created 6, you score 5, and so on).

I find assigning a number helps us each be honest with ourselves and ensures adequate accountability. It's easy to say, "I could have done more." But when I score myself a zero or two (for example), that causes a different level of introspection: why didn't I do more? Did priorities change and is that okay? Or if not, what's keeping me from doing it? How do I change that in the future? I have these conversations with myself (and my husband, who also used to work at Google and helps keep me accountable!) about my own OKRs and with the individuals on my team about theirs. We aggregate each objective score by averaging the scores of the key results for that objective. Averaging the respective objective scores gives a summary for the overall quarter. In sum, reviewing the prior quarter's OKRs and corresponding scores helps drive really useful conversations around where things are going well, competing priorities, challenges, and potential solutions. All of that then feeds into the next OKR setting process for the current quarter and we do it all over again.

I credit the OKR process as having helped me personally continue to improve my skills and create and expand a successful business. I appreciate the disciplined thinking it enforces and the way it officializes accountability. It establishes indicators for measuring progress: at any point, we each know how far along we are, where we're missing what we set out to do, and where we're being successful. As my team has grown, it also helps ensure everyone knows what is important and can align their individual objectives so we are all working towards the same goal.

Your turn! What is a specific goal you have related to cultivating your skills for effectively visualizing or communicating with data? Write it down. Next, identify 2-3 key results that will help you achieve this objective. Discuss it with your manager. Post it somewhere you will regularly see it. Congrats, you've just written your first OKR. Next, complete it!

For more on goal setting in general and the OKR process in particular, check out Episode 13 of the *storytelling with data* podcast (storytellingwithdata.com/podcast), which focuses on goal setting.

more PRACTICE at WORK

Exercise 9.3: give & receive effective feedback

Getting feedback and iterating is an incredibly important part of the process for evolving our skills. We all know this. Yet it can be understandably difficult to open yourself up to critique. When receiving feedback, it's easy to become defensive rather than really listen and absorb. Here are a few thoughts related to this to help you get—and give—more effective feedback. The next time you find yourself in need of input, refer to the following.

Determine who to ask. Spend some time thinking about who will be well positioned to give you feedback based on your specific needs. We often think first of someone who is familiar with the situation, but pause to reflect on what type of feedback will serve you best. Lack of context can be a good thing because it ensures a totally fresh perspective. This can be especially useful if your audience isn't close to the work you are doing, as it will help point out inaccessible language, assumptions you may unknowingly be making, unfamiliar types of visualizations, or other issues that could inhibit successful communication. That said, expert feedback is sometimes warranted. This can be useful, for example, when facing a technical audience and needing to make sure you're well prepared for anticipated scrutiny, or when some level of context is necessary in order to offer useful feedback.

Time it right. This temporal aspect is important both for you as well as for the people you ask to spend time providing feedback. When it comes to timing for you—the earlier in the process you can get input, often the better. At this point you've put in less effort, which means you're less attached to a particular path or output and can more easily change directions. Particularly if you have strongly opinionated stakeholders, starting the process of feedback early on can help reduce iterations over the course of a project. That said, there will be different aspects of the work that people can better evaluate in a completed form compared to early stage (something mocked up or hand-drawn, for example), so getting feedback at multiple points in the process can be helpful for highly critical projects. When it comes to timing from the critiquer's standpoint: be respectful of their schedule and try to time your requests for feedback at points that are convenient for them. If you find it difficult to get someone's feedback when you need it, set up time to do this live, where you can review and get the needed input over the course of a meeting. Be appreciative towards those who provide you feedback.

Be clear on the focus. Do you want to understand if the graph is easy to read, if your point comes across efficiently, or something else? Be as specific as you can about where you need input so that you get useful feedback in the right places. Consider as part of this whether it will be helpful to share the context of who the audience is, what they care about, or what knowledge they have. It can also be useful to convey what constraints you faced as part of the process—or what constraints you will face for incorporating feedback. For example, if it's late in the game and you just need a second opinion on whether something works, you can make this clear: "Tell me what you think of this. I have to send it out today, so I'm looking for anything that's unclear, or issues I can hopefully resolve quickly so I can meet my 5 p.m. deadline. Given that, what reactions can you share?" On the other hand, if you have ample time, you can be broad in your request for feedback: "Really, everything is fair game. I'm trying to understand broadly what's working well and how I might further refine."

Listen, don't talk. When someone raises a point of constructive criticism, it is natural to want to respond and justify your decision with all the reasons you approached something the way you did. Refrain from doing this, as it may shut down the conversation. Instead, listen with an open mind and without judging the feedback. Acknowledge that you've heard. Take notes. Encourage the person giving the feedback to keep talking. Ask probing questions to better understand this alternative point of view. If needed to help drive the conversation, refer to the following questions.

After listening: ask questions. If you need more feedback after you've listened, use the following discussion prompters.

- Where do your eyes go first on this page?

- What is the main takeaway or message?

- Talk me through how you process the graph: what do you pay attention to first? Next?

- Are there things you would have done differently? Why?

- Is anything distracting from the message?

- Set it aside. Can you tell me the main point or story? What else do you remember?

Weigh the input you receive. Not all feedback is equal and you will sometimes receive bad advice. Who it is coming from will typically be the dictating factor for whether it must be followed or can be ignored. That said, if you find you're being met with resistance, step back and really try to take any feelings or attachment to what you've created out of it to figure out what's not working. If you're unsure about the feedback you've received, seek another opinion. If this backs up the first, don't assume the issue sits with those providing feedback—assume it's something about the design. Take time to understand this so you can identify and address the root issue.

Provide good feedback to others. Getting good at *giving* feedback can have positive benefits for framing the feedback you'd like from others. It can also help you sharpen your thinking in ways that ultimately improve your own work. Refrain

more **PRACTICE** *at* **WORK**

from dogmatically identifying aspects as right or wrong or good or bad. When giving feedback, be thoughtful about how you frame it: the person likely spent time creating what they are sharing with you and they are putting themselves in a position of vulnerability when they ask for feedback. They also probably faced constraints to which you don't have visibility. Ask them to be clear on what feedback they want so you can direct your comments accordingly. Always make the feedback about the work, not the person. Before offering ideas for changes, point out what is executed well. On this note, I've heard of one team's approach for giving each other feedback is by completing the following sentences: "I like…," "I have questions about…," and finally, "I'd suggest…" Another similar feedback framework is analyze-discuss-suggest, where you start by analyzing the graph or slide or presentation. After you've spent time doing so, discuss. Only after all of that do you make suggestions.

Impromptu input can be helpful, too. While sometimes the process of getting feedback is formalized—for example, one of the ideas in forthcoming Exercise 9.4 is to organize a group feedback session—that won't always be the case. When you find yourself wondering whether something works, print it out or have a colleague peer over your shoulder at your computer and share their thoughts. You can pull ideas from this exercise in these more impromptu scenarios, too. Get input from others to iterate and refine your work from good to great!

Beyond seeking feedback for your own work, there are steps that can be taken to help build a culture where feedback is part of the norm for your broader team or organization. We'll talk more about this in the next exercise.

PRACTICE more at WORK

Exercise 9.4: cultivate a feedback culture

As we've discussed, getting input from others is hugely important to understand what is working and when further iteration is warranted as you hone your data storytelling skills. Creating an open culture where feedback is part of the norm across your team or organization is a critical part of this—and often means taking intentional steps to cultivate.

Simply telling people they need to solicit or provide feedback likely isn't enough to create the right sort of enriching environment. At work, stakes are often high. This sometimes causes individuals to be hesitant to admit they need feedback. If the culture isn't right or the feedback isn't delivered well, it can be taken as a personal attack rather than constructive criticism—which can be more detrimental than beneficial. That said, if you find yourself or your team facing challenges in this area, there are plenty of things you can do to shift the culture and help people practice and develop confidence when it comes to giving and receiving feedback. Here are a few ideas:

- **Introduce "present & discuss" time in your regular team meeting.** Reserve ten minutes of a recurring team meeting for a team member to present something they are working on or have recently completed. Then have a conversation where each person shares a positive point about the work and a suggestion for further improvement. Rotate who shares each time.

- **Assign "feedback buddies."** Pair up people on your team (or across teams) and set expectations around at what points in a project people should seek and provide feedback, or with what frequency over a given time period (for example, twice weekly over a 1-month period). Managers can help hold people accountable by asking about the feedback received and incorporated during one-on-ones or project updates. After a predetermined amount of time (a month or a quarter), shuffle the partners. This can help forge stronger relationships among your team or across teams and also integrate regular feedback into the process.

- **Hold a feedback "speed dating" session.** Invite those who have a specific graph or slide on which they'd like feedback. Instruct them to print out a copy and bring it with them to the session. Organize tables in opposing rows so that individuals face one another in pairs. Identify a timekeeper with a loud voice to manage the session. At the first "Go!," have each duo exchange the printed work product they brought and allow one minute to quietly review. Each person should then spend two minutes asking questions and giving suggestions (with the timekeeper watching the clock, alerting everyone when to change focus). Each pair will be together for a total of five minutes (one-minute review + two-minute suggestions to Person A + two-minute suggestions to Person B). After five minutes, have those on one side of the table move seats by one position (the person on the end fills the now empty spot on the opposite side). Repeat until you run out of people or time. If your organization does lunch-and-learn or other less formal gatherings, this can be a fun team or cross-team activity to integrate.

- **Conduct a formal feedback session.** Schedule an hour. Each person should bring a physical copy of something on which they'd like feedback (a storyboard, a graph, a slide, a presentation). Set expectations for the session and share tips for giving effective feedback (see Exercise 9.3). Divide people into groups of three. Within these triads, each person should spend five minutes lending context to what they've brought to share and the specific feedback they seek, followed by ten minutes of group discussion and suggestions. Rotate so that each person in the group has an opportunity to share their work and get feedback (for a total of three 15-minute segments, one each focused on Person A, Person B, and Person C's work). End with a full-group debrief on what worked well, whether you'll do it again, and what you would do differently next time. This can be a standalone session or also works well as part of a team offsite.

It can also be useful to create non-work-centric forums for presenting and exchanging feedback. This takes away some of the pressure, making it easier to give and receive critique. As people become practiced exchanging feedback in a low-risk setting, they start to build a habit that can better enable them in the work environment. This can be a particularly smart approach if you're trying to change the culture in an environment that hasn't historically been conducive to open feedback. Here are a couple of ideas related to this:

- **Introduce "review & critique" time in your regular team meeting.** This is similar to the "present & discuss" idea raised previously, but focuses on publicly available examples rather than work-specific ones. This takes pride and potential for taking criticism personally off the table entirely. Assign a team member ahead of time to source a graph, slide, or data visualization from the wild (for example, the media). Spend a few minutes talking through it, then have each person share a positive point about the work and a suggestion for what they might do differently. Rotate who picks the example each time. There can be a tendency to look for non-effective examples, which is fine, but evaluating good examples in this manner can make for productive conversations and help people identify finer points of feedback, too.

- **Create a team monthly #SWDchallenge.** See Exercise 2.16 or storytelling-withdata.com/SWDchallenge for more on our monthly challenges. As a team, you can participate in a live challenge, pick one from the archives, or create your own. In the first week of the month, set the specific challenge and encourage participants to identify non-work data of interest. Over the course of the rest of the month, individuals or partners should create their respective data visualizations. At the end of the month, schedule time in person or virtually and invite those who participated. Have each person or duo present their creation and get feedback from others. This idea is inspired by Simon Beaumont (Global Director of Business Intelligence at Jones Lang LaSalle), who has been doing something similar with his team. Simon observed that, over time, this has led to both improved data visualization and more productive feedback exchange among his team in general. Additionally, they record their webinar feedback sessions and make them broadly available so others at the organization can watch and learn as well.

If your team could benefit from cultivating a culture of feedback, step back and think about how you can best do that and whether one of these ideas might help. Take liberties to design something that will work well for your team based on the environment. Learn and iterate and determine how to evolve the ways in which you facilitate feedback over time. Doing this well can help everyone hone their skills and create better data communications!

more
PRACTICE at WORK

Exercise 9.5: refer to the SWD process

Over the course of this book, we've covered six lessons to set you up for success-ful data communications. It can be helpful to revisit these with a specific project in mind. When you find yourself needing to communicate with data, read the following for a reminder of the main lessons we've covered and some thought starters to reflect on for the project you face (each of these corresponds to a chapter of the same number). Refer back to the *practice with Cole* solutions within each chapter for illustrations and examples and the *practice at work* exercises for additional guidance on applying the various lessons.

(1) **Understand the context.** Who is your audience? What motivates them? What do you want to communicate to your audience? **Articulate your Big Idea.** The Big Idea has three components, it (1) articulates your point of view, (2) conveys what's at stake, and (3) is a complete sentence. **Create a storyboard** of the components you'll cover with your audience to help them understand the situation and con-vince them to act. Determine what order will work best; arrange sticky notes to create the desired narrative flow. You now have a plan of attack to follow. Get client or stakeholder input at this point if possible.

(2) **Choose an appropriate visual.** What do you want to communicate? Identify your point and how you can show your data in a way that will be easy for your audience to understand. This often means iterating and looking at your data a number of different ways to find the graph that will help you create that magical "ah ha" moment. **Draw it!** Consider what tools and other resources you have at your disposal to realize your drawing and then **create it**. Ask for feedback from others to learn whether your visual is serving its intended purpose or give you pointers on where to iterate.

(3) **Eliminate clutter.** Is there anything that isn't adding value? **Identify unneces-sary elements and remove them.** Reduce cognitive burden by visually connecting related things, maintaining white space, cleanly aligning elements, and avoiding diagonal components. Use visual contrast sparingly and strategically: don't let your message get lost in the clutter!

(4) **Focus attention.** Where do you want your audience to look? Determine how you can draw your audience's attention to what you want them to see through position, size, and color. Use color sparingly and strategically, considering tone, brand, and colorblindness. **Employ the "Where are your eyes drawn?" test** to understand whether you're using preattentive attributes to effectively direct your audience's attention.

(5) **Think like a designer.** Words help data make sense. Clearly title and label graphs and axes and **employ a takeaway title** to answer the question, "So what?"

Create visual hierarchy of elements to ease the processing and make it clear how to interact with your visual communications. **Pay attention to details:** don't let minor issues distract from your credibility of message. Make your visual designs accessible. Spend time on the finer details of your design: your audience will appreciate it, heightening the odds for successful communication.

(6) Tell a story. Refer back to your Big Idea: **create a pithy, repeatable phrase** from it. Revisit your storyboard and arrange the components of your story along the **narrative arc**. What is the tension? How can your audience act to resolve it? Where and how does data fit into the narrative? How will your materials for a live presentation vary from those that are sent out to be consumed on their own? Create a data story that captures your audience's attention, drives a robust discussion, and influences action!

Want to hang the preceding list at your desk for easy reference? A downloadable version can be found at storytellingwithdata.com/letspractice/downloads/SWDprocess.

How do you know if you've applied these lessons well? Refer to Exercise 9.6 for an assessment rubric that can be used for this.

Exercise 9.6: make use of an assessment rubric

I don't tend to use rubrics in the context of visualizing and communicating data. People like rules, and they are too easy to turn into a formulaic approach when more nuanced thinking is warranted. That said, I understand the desire to have a way to assess the effectiveness of your own or others' work. Consider the following framework to be a starting point to address this need.

I'm intentionally not going to be prescriptive or formulaic in how this should be used. I'll outline a couple of options, but I encourage you to give thought to what makes sense given the specifics of your situation. Are you a manager giving feedback to an individual or multiple individuals on your team? An instructor needing to grade assignments? Or an individual wanting to judge your own work?

For those simply seeking a structured way to assess your own or others' work, you can use the following as a checklist, or apply some simple labels (I personally like the three-category scale of "nailed it!," "good," and "more attention needed"; you can also sometimes have a fourth category of "not applicable"). A numeric score will be helpful if you need to assess across multiple individuals or see changes over time (for example, grading). You could use a simple 1-3 scale that aligns with the descriptors above, or a 1-10 scale if you crave a finer level of detail or find this more intuitive.

Component	Assessment
I understand how to read the graph(s).	
The choice of visual(s) makes sense given the data and what is being communicated.	
An appropriate amount of context is present about the data/methodology/background.	
Words are used well to title, label, annotate, and explain.	
Visual clutter is minimized/absent.	
It is clear where I should focus first.	
Color is used effectively.	
The communication is free of misspellings, grammar mistakes, and math errors.	
The overall design is well structured: elements are aligned, white space is used well.	
The order of content makes sense.	
The main message and/or call to action is clear.	
Materials are optimized for how the content will be delivered.	
Overall success: the communication created solves the need it set out to.	

FIGURE 9.6 Example assessment rubric

PRACTICE *more* at WORK

The preceding list should be adjusted given what you are assessing. Is it a graph? A slide? An entire presentation? There might be some components that don't make sense for your scenario. There could be others you should add to have the full picture. I invite you to modify the rubric to best meet your needs. The final lines are intentionally blank to encourage you to think through what additional components may make sense given the specifics of what you are trying to assess.

I'll close this exercise by pointing out that there are a number of intangibles that are harder to evaluate in a structure like this. These are little things that sum up to create a good or not-so-great experience. There is something about the manner in which this is achieved that plays into overall success as well. For example, one aspect to consider is whether and how time was optimized given the relative importance of what needs to be accomplished. You do not need to apply the entire *storytelling with data* process every time you touch data—be smart about where and how you apply the various lessons we've covered for maximum benefit with minimal additional work. That sort of efficiency and prioritization should be recognized.

Use Exercise 9.5, which outlined the SWD process, as you work through a current project. Once finished, run through this rubric as a final assessment to ensure all components were addressed.

You can download this rubric and adjust for your own needs at storytellingwithdata.com/letspractice/downloads/rubric.

Exercise 9.7: facilitate a Big Idea practice session

Before spending time visualizing data or creating content, pause to understand the context, consider your audience, and craft your message. Devoting thought to these important aspects can yield massive payback in being able to better meet your audience's needs, get your message across, and drive the action you seek. One way to encourage and kickstart this process across a team is to organize and conduct a Big Idea practice session.

This guide should give you what you need to introduce the concept of the Big Idea and facilitate an exercise with individual, partner, and group discussion components. The overarching goal is to help participants practice articulating the Big Idea and giving and receiving feedback to refine.

Prep work: what to do ahead of time
Read through this guide. Also review the Big Idea-related exercises in Chapter 1. Explain the Big Idea to someone else and have them ask you questions. The resulting conversation will help you get comfortable talking about this concept,

PRACTICE *more* *at* WORK

which will better prepare you for facilitating it with a group (do this a couple times with different people if possible!).

When it comes to the logistics for the session, decide who will attend. Book a room and send a calendar invite for 60 minutes. It's ideal if everyone can attend in person (if not possible, pair those joining remotely and have everyone tune into the main room for the introduction and debrief). Print a copy of the Big Idea worksheet per person (you can make copies from Exercise 1.20, or download from storytellingwithdata.com/letspractice/downloads/bigidea). If people tend to use laptops for everything, grab a handful of pens: this exercise is best done in a low-tech manner (encourage people to leave their laptops behind!).

Example agenda (HH:MM)
00:00 - 00:10 Introduce the Big Idea, talk through an example
00:10 - 00:20 Hands-on exercise (Big Idea worksheet)
00:20 - 00:30 First partner discussion
00:30 - 00:40 Second partner discussion
00:40 - 01:00 Group discussion

A scenario to introduce the Big Idea
Introduce the Big Idea by presenting the three components—remember, the Big Idea should:

1. Articulate your unique point of view,

2. Convey what's at stake, and

3. Be a complete sentence.

To illustrate, introduce the following scenario (excerpted from *storytelling with data*, Wiley, 2015), then demonstrate the example Big Idea. Alternatively, you can use a scenario and corresponding Big Idea from one of the *practice with Cole* exercises in Chapter 1 or create your own.

SCENARIO: A group of us in the science department were brainstorming about how to resolve an ongoing issue we have with incoming fourth-graders. It seems that when kids get to their first science class, they come in with this attitude that it's going to be difficult and they aren't going to like it. It takes a good amount of time at the beginning of the school year to get beyond that. So we thought, what if we try to give kids exposure to science sooner? Can we influence their perception? We piloted a learning program last summer aimed at doing just that. We invited elementary school students and ended up with a large group of second- and third-graders. Our goal was to give them earlier exposure to science in hopes of forming positive perception. To test whether we were successful, we surveyed the students before and after the program. We found that, going into the program, the biggest segment of students, 40%, felt just okay about science, whereas after the program, most of these shifted into positive perceptions, with nearly 70% of students experiencing some level of interest towards science. We feel that this demonstrates the success of the program and that we should not only continue to offer it, but also to expand our reach with it going forward.

Let's imagine that we are communicating to the budget committee who has control over the funds that we need to continue our program. **The Big Idea** could be: *The pilot summer learning program was successful at improving students' perception of science; please approve our budget to continue this important program.*

This Big Idea:

1. Articulates our point of view (we should continue this important program),
2. Conveys what's at stake (improved student perception of science), and
3. Is a complete (and single!) sentence.

After introducing the Big Idea and talking through an example, it's time to turn it over to participants to practice.

Hands-on exercise: the Big Idea worksheet
Ask each participant to identify a project. This can be any example where they need to communicate something to an audience (something they can talk about openly, as they will be sharing with others). Pass out the Big Idea worksheet and ask participants to work through it for the project they have identified.

Allow about **10 minutes** for this. As participants are working their way through the Big Idea worksheet, wander the room to monitor progress and answer any questions. After approximately 10 minutes or when you see that nearly everyone has completed writing their Big Idea (and hopefully every person has at least started), you can begin the partner discussion.

Partner discussion
It's okay if not everyone is totally done with their Big Idea, as they will still have a chance to refine as they confer with partners. Next, ask them to partner up and take turns sharing their Big Idea and giving each other feedback. I usually give a couple of specific directions related to this:

- If there are people in the room who are more familiar with what you're going to be talking about and others who are less so, partner first with someone who is *less* familiar. If this requires standing up and moving around the room, please do so.

- Receiving partner, your job is very important. Your job is to ask the person reading their Big Idea a ton of questions, helping them get clear and concise on their message.

MORE PRACTICE at WORK

Allow **10 minutes** for this initial partner discussion. Wander the room to answer any questions that arise. After about 5 minutes, check in with each group to make sure they've moved on to the second person so both partners have a chance to share and get feedback.

After about 10 minutes, direct participants to switch and partner up with a new person and repeat the process of taking turns to share and receive feedback. Again, check in with each at the five-minute mark to make sure people are shifting to the second person so both people in each partner group have a chance to share and receive feedback. Allow 10 minutes for this second iteration of partner feedback. Then direct participants to come back together for group discussion.

Facilitate the group discussion

The group discussion that you guide after the individual and partner work is important for reinforcing content and helping address any questions or challenges that may have arisen as part of the Big Idea exercise.

The following are questions to spark ideas (pause after each of these and let the conversation take its natural course, helping to reinforce the main points below):

- Did you find this exercise easy or challenging?
- What was hard about this exercise?
- How did you get it down to a single sentence?
- Show of hands: how many people found partner feedback to be helpful?
- What was helpful about partner feedback?

Points to make as part of the conversation:

- **Getting it down to a single sentence is hard.** Concision is surprisingly difficult, especially when it's work that we are close to—it's hard to let go of all those details! The Big Idea won't be the only thing you communicate; rather, supporting content will come into play.

- **There are various strategies that can help you get it down to a single sentence.** It can sometimes be useful to write a few sentences first, then trim. The Big Idea worksheet can also be helpful, since it breaks each component apart so you can deal with them one at a time. By the time you get to the end, you have the pieces and it's like a puzzle that you can work to put together in a way that makes sense.

- **Getting it down to a single sentence is important.** The sentence restriction is arbitrary, but it is purposefully short. This forces you to let go of most of the details. You probably also have to do some wordsmithing. This is important: clarity of thought happens through this wordsmithing process.

- **Saying it out loud is helpful.** When we say things out loud, it ignites a different part of our brain as we hear ourselves. If you find yourself tripping up when reading your Big Idea, or something just doesn't sound right, these can be pointers on where to iterate. Because of this, there is a benefit to saying the Big Idea out loud, even if it's to yourself in an empty room. Even better if someone is present to react to what you've said, which brings us to the next point.

- **Partner feedback is critical.** As we get close to our work, we develop tacit knowledge: things that we know that we forget others don't know (specialized language, assumptions, or things we take as given). Talking to a partner can be a great way to identify these issues and adjust as needed. The dialogue you have with a partner helps you get solid on the point you want to make and find the words that will help you make it clearly.

- **The partner need not have any prior context.** It can be helpful if your partner doesn't have any context, because of the kinds of questions this will prompt them to ask. Simple questions like, "Why?" can be very useful, both because it helps point out something that is obvious to us but not to someone else and also because of the logic this forces us to articulate when it comes to answering. Your audience will never be as close to your work as you are, so soliciting feedback from someone less familiar can be really useful for identifying the right words to make your overall point accessible and understandable.

- **Clearly articulating the Big Idea makes creating your communication easier.** If you can't clearly get your point across in a single sentence, how will you put together a slide deck or report that will do so? Too often, we go straight to our tools and start building content, without having a clear goal in mind. The Big Idea is that clear goal—the guiding North Star, directing the process of generating supporting content. Once it's been formulated, it is the built-in litmus test for any bit of content up for consideration for inclusion: does this help me get my Big Idea across?

Best of luck facilitating the Big Idea session!

more
PRACTICE at WORK

Exercise 9.8: conduct an SWD working session

I often facilitate working sessions with teams after conducting a *storytelling with data* workshop. I never cease to be amazed by the amount of progress people are able to make with a few low-tech tools and some dedicated time. Grab some colleagues, read *SWD* or this book, then use the guide outlined on the following pages to run your own *storytelling with data* working session.

Prep work: what to do ahead of time
Send a calendar invite for three hours to your team and book a conference room with plenty of table space and whiteboards. Stock up on supplies: colored markers, flip-charts, and multiple sizes of sticky notes (the 6x8-inch ones are awesome, as they are the same dimensions as a standard slide and can be used to mock up an entire presentation in a low-tech manner; also have some smaller ones on hand for those who may want to do higher level storyboarding and focus on general topics and flow before getting into the details).

Use the following instructions in combination with the *storytelling with data* process in Exercise 9.5 to organize a working session where everyone can have time and space to put lessons into practice, present, and receive feedback. The example agenda that follows works best for groups of 8-10 (enough time for everyone to present and give/receive feedback), but can be expanded for larger groups by adding more time to the present back portion (plan about 6-7 minutes per person or group). Instructions for participants are shown on the following pages; a downloadable version to print can be found at storytellingwithdata.com/letspractice/downloads/SWDworkingsession.

For the actual session, nominate someone to be timekeeper. They should keep an eye on the clock during project work time and alert participants when they are halfway through and when 20 minutes remain to ensure everyone has a chance to prepare low-tech content to present. During the present back, they should watch the clock and move discussion along as needed to make sure everyone has time to share and get feedback from the group.

Example agenda (HH:MM)
00:00 - 00:15   Recap lessons, discussion/Q&A, set expectations for the session
00:15 - 01:30   Project work time
01:30 - 01:45   Take a break!
01:45 - 02:45   Present back
02:45 - 03:00   Debrief, discussion/Q&A, wrap up

The following pages contain instructions for participants.

Project work: how to focus your time
Choose a project to focus on today. This can be on your own or in a group. Read through the *storytelling with data* process. Determine how you'd like to spend the next 75 minutes when it comes to putting one or more of the *storytelling with data* lessons into practice. Spend time sketching this out.

Here are some ideas of how you might use your time:

Lesson 1: understand the context
Articulate the Big Idea or craft a storyboard.

Lesson 2: choose an appropriate visual
Draw various views of your data and identify which will enable you to best make your point.

Lesson 3: eliminate clutter
Is there anything that isn't adding value? Identify unnecessary elements and remove them.

Lesson 4: focus attention
How will you indicate to your audience where you want them to look? Plan your use of position, size, color, and other means of contrast to strategically direct your audience's attention.

Lesson 5: think like a designer
Final polishing will take place in your tools—your mock-up design can be rough. Still, give thought to how you'll organize elements to create structure and use words to make data accessible.

Lesson 6: tell a story
Sketch out the components of your story along the narrative arc. Where and how will data fit in? How can tension and conflict help you capture and maintain your audience's attention? What pithy, repeatable phrase could you create to help your message stick with your audience?

Keep it low-tech: pens and paper are at your disposal (but please keep laptops closed!). Use your colleagues in the room as brainstorm partners or to solicit feedback from as you go along. Be creative and have fun!

Present back: share with group
You will have roughly five minutes to share a piece of what you've crafted or planned with the group. We will continue to be low tech: hand write or draw visuals to support what you'd like to present to the group for feedback.

PRACTICE more at WORK

Your present back should include:

1. **A brief explanation of the background.** This should incorporate the intended audience, overall goal/objective, key decision(s) to be made, and what success looks like.

2. **How you've applied a *storytelling with data* lesson to your project.** This could mean focusing on any of the following: your Big Idea, storyboard, ideas of how to best visualize the data, a comparison of how you had been looking at data and what changes you'll make, how you'll focus attention, or the overarching story you'll tell. This doesn't have to be fully executed; rather, well-formed ideas on what changes you'll make or the approach you plan to take are fine. Draw and make use of the pens/paper/stickies so everyone can see what you're envisioning. Frame the specific feedback you'd like from the group to help you continue to refine.

Debrief: discussion and Q&A
After everyone has had an opportunity to present and receive feedback, spend a few minutes discussing the following:

*   How did this session feel? Was the time spent useful?

*   What did you find most helpful?

*   Are there changes we should make if we do it again in the future?

*   What challenges do you anticipate applying SWD lessons in our work?

*   What additional steps can we take to improve how we communicate with data?

Publicize the outcome of this session to other teams who might benefit (either by participating in something similar themselves or by virtue of being on the receiving end of the materials planned in your working session) and your management. Share success stories. Identify any aspects of the session that didn't work as you'd anticipated, try to isolate why, and adjust.

Do everything you can to help make folks aware and supportive of everyone's efforts: both the dedicated time planning and willingness to try new strategies for improving data-driven communications. Create champions who can help promote the power of data done well. This will lead to increased recognition on this important piece of the process, which will hopefully manifest as patience with you and your team for the ongoing time and resources it will take to do it well.

PRACTICE *more* at WORK

Exercise 9.9: set yourself up for successful data stories

When it comes to using story to communicate data, there are steps you can take to help improve your odds of success. The following outlines some specific things to consider when crafting and delivering data stories.

Try new things in low-risk places first. Don't go into your next board or exec meeting and say, "Today, folks, I'm going to do something a little different—today, I'm going to tell you a story." That's not a recipe for success! Especially if anything feels counter-cultural for your organization or markedly different from what you've done in the past, try it out in a low-risk setting first. Learn and refine. Get feedback. Small successes will build your confidence and credibility for making bigger changes over time.

Order thoughtfully. For anything we want to communicate, there are typically many options for how to order the content and there is no single correct approach. Think about how you can organize things—whether elements in a graph, objects on a slide, or slides in a presentation deck—in a way that will make sense for your audience to create the overall experience you seek. Get feedback from someone less familiar with the content as a means to assess whether the way you've ordered your materials is likely to work for your ultimate needs.

Optimize materials for *how* you are communicating. Presenting live opens up a different set of opportunities for building our data stories. As we've seen through a number of examples, one strategy is to build visuals piece by piece for our audience in a live setting. Pair this with a fully annotated slide or two for the version that gets sent around so that those consuming it on their own get the same story that you walk through in a live progression. Give thought to the specifics of how you will be presenting and create materials that will serve you well.

Anticipate how it could go wrong. How might things go off the rails? How can you equip yourself to deal with that if it happens? Identify and pressure test your assumptions. Make sure you've investigated alternative hypotheses. Ask colleagues to play devil's advocate and poke holes or play a snarky audience member. Anticipate questions and be well prepared to answer them. The time you spend prepping for how to respond to surprises will help you be more equipped to deal with them eloquently if they arise.

Answer the question, "So what?" Never leave your audience wondering why they are looking at what you've put in front of them. Don't make them figure it out on their own. Make the purpose clear. Why are they here? What do you have to tell them? Why should they listen to you? Consider how you can use the various lessons we've covered to get your audience's attention, establish credibility, and lead them to a productive conversation or decision.

PRACTICE at WORK more

Be flexible. Rarely do things go exactly as planned. If you can anticipate that things are likely to head in a direction not entirely in your control, be thoughtful about how you organize your approach and materials to be able to deal with this. In some circumstances, a "choose your own adventure" story may be warranted. Demonstrating willingness to be flexible and adjust to your audience is one fantastic way of establishing credibility and can help you turn a potential nightmare situation into a successful one.

Seek feedback. We've talked about feedback as you prepare your data stories, but it's also important to solicit feedback after you've presented. Get input from your audience or colleagues on what worked well and what you could adjust in the future to best meet their needs (and through that, your own).

Learn from successes and failures. After each time you send off a report or present data, pause to reflect on how it went. For successful scenarios, think about why things worked and which aspects you can make use of in your future work. We can often learn even more from the cases that *don't* go as well. What caused issues? What is in your control that you can change in the future? Share success and failure stories so that others can learn as well. In this way, we can all help each other improve.

The meta theme underlying all of these tips is to be thoughtful. Consider what success looks like and try to position yourself to make that happen so that the data stories you tell will have the impact you seek.

PRACTICE *more* at WORK

Exercise 9.10: let's discuss

Consider the following questions related to everything we've covered over the course of this book and how you'll apply them in your work. Discuss with a partner or group. If you've been undertaking the exercises in this book with others on your team (or even if you haven't!), these will make for an excellent team conversation on how to integrate the *storytelling with data* lessons into everyone's work.

1. What is *one thing* you will commit to doing differently going forward?

2. Reflect on the lessons covered in *SWD* and this book: (1) understand the context, (2) choose an appropriate visual, (3) declutter, (4) focus attention, (5) think like a designer, and (6) tell a story. Which lessons are most critical to do well in your work? Why is that? Which areas do you—or your team—need to develop the most? How can you do this?

3. Consider how you will apply the various lessons we've reviewed: where could things go wrong? How can you prepare for this or take steps to help ensure success? What other challenges do you anticipate? How will you overcome them?

4. Are there additional resources that would be helpful for your overall success when it comes to effectively visualizing and communicating with data?

5. What is your biggest takeaway from this book? How do you anticipate this will manifest in your day-to-day work?

6. Where do gaps exist between how you work today and how you'd like to be working when it comes to data storytelling? How can you address those?

7. Do you anticipate you will face resistance for the things you'd like to do differently? Who do you think it will come from? What can you do to overcome it?

8. We always face constraints when we work. What limitations do you face? How might these impact when and how you apply the *storytelling with data* lessons? How can you embrace these constraints to generate creative solutions?

9. What steps can you take to help others on your team or in your organization recognize the value of data storytelling and improve their skills?

10. What specific goals will you set for yourself or your team related to the strategies outlined in this book? How will you hold yourself (or your team) accountable to these goals? How will you measure success?

more PRACTICE at WORK

chapter ten

closing words

We have practiced a great deal over the preceding nine chapters! You should feel well-equipped to integrate the various lessons, tips, and strategies into your work. That said—you are not done practicing.

Communicating effectively with data is like trying to solve a puzzle. Pieces of the puzzle include a gamut of different considerations, things like: audience, context, data, assumptions, biases, credibility, how you'll present, the physical space, the printer or projector, interpersonal dynamics, and the action sought. We have to fit all of these things together in a way that works. To complicate things, the puzzle pieces are different every time!

But it's not a jigsaw: there isn't only one way. There isn't a single design or technique that works. This sometimes frustrates people. But it's actually a really awesome thing. Many different approaches *could* work. There's no end to how you can mix and match the lessons and strategies illustrated with your own twists to come up with potentially effective solutions. How fun is that?

You've practiced. But your practice is not complete. We can all keep learning. We can continue to hone our data visualization design. We can become increasingly nuanced in how we tell stories with our data and use it to inspire others.

And that is what I hope you will do. Put into practice what you've learned. Share it with others. Tell stories with your data that will influence positive change.

My support and encouragement doesn't end here. Visit storytellingwithdata.com/learnmore for information on the next phase of learning and advancement from the SWD team.

Thanks for practicing with me!

sʍD CLOSING THOUGHTS

START SMALL...

MAKE SWD a PART of your EVERY DAY

SWD IDEAS & OPPORTUNITIES

RISK

START HERE!

EFFORT

Over time, little bits add up

LOW-HANGING FRUIT:

COLOR and WORDS — TITLES, ANNOTATIONS, LABELS

PRACTICE and PRIORITIZE

Keep at it!

LEARN GUIDELINES

(Then break them thoughtfully when it makes sense)

SWD Podcast

... then
TAKE it
UP a NOTCH!

MOVE BEYOND INFORMING to INFLUENCING

Drive change
THOUGHTFULLY

FOCUS on YOU as the PRESENTER

Building storytelling
muscles takes time

— Know your data
— Believe in your story
— Practice to calm
   your nerves

PLAN TIME for THIS

STORY

ANALYSIS   SHARE

It always takes
more time than
you think it should

CHECK OUT RESOURCES at
storytellingwithdata.com
(more coming!)

index

A

Acceptance by audience of designs
    garnering acceptance exercise for, 231–232
    thinking like a designer and, 191, 193, 220, 231–232
Accessibility
    alt text for, 229–230
    colorblindness and, 136, 154,160, 191, 218, 230, 291, 388
    data accessibility with words exercise and, 225–226
    guidelines for, 230
    practice at work exercise for, 229–230
    thinking like a designer and, 191, 193, 220, 229–230
"*accessible data viz is better data viz*" (Cesal), 229
Accounts over time exercise, 365
Action for audience to take
    ending in narrative arc and, 253, 255
    identifying, 43
    storytelling and, 237
    tension in story and, 249, 251, 272
Adverse effects exercise, 362
Aesthetics, and design, 191, 193, 220
Affordances, and design, 191, 192, 220
Alignment of elements. *See also* Centering; Justification
    axis titles and, 121, 131, 198, 199, 202
    detail in graphs and, 208, 228
    effectiveness of graphs using, 112
    eliminating clutter and, 120–122, 140, 286
    horizontal elements and, 108
    justification of text and, 121, 131
    logos and, 216
    market size over time graph and, 112

    physician prescription patterns graph for, 120–122
    practice on your own and, 140
    practice with Cole and, 120–122
    text boxes and, 121, 216
    text in titles and, 198
    visual order and, 108
All caps
    axis labels with, 198, 202, 214, 228
    branding text with, 217
    making things stand out using, 154
    rectangular shape using, 133, 198, 202
    short phrases using, 133
Alt text, 229–230
Analysis
    explanatory vs. exploratory, 2, 188, 268
    storyboarding with, 36
    types of, 2
Animation, to focus attention, 171
Area graphs
    attrition rate exercise for, 79
    moving from stacked charts to, 246–247
    practice with Cole on, 79, 246–247
Arrows, for directing attention, 165
Assessment rubric, 389–391
Attention, focusing. *See* Audience attention, focusing
Attrition rate over time exercise, 76–80
Audience
    acceptance of designs by, 191, 193, 220, 231–232
    Big Idea and
        Big Idea worksheet, 10, 12
        critiquing, 19
        refining and focus, 14
    critical role of words in communicating data to, 195, 197, 199
    deciding on right amount of data and needs of, 357
    deciding what you need them to do, 2

defining who they are, 2
detail in graphs and assumptions
    made by, 208
determining what data is needed for, 2
different perspectives and different
    interpretations of text by, 197
getting to know
    checking with colleagues about
        assumptions made, 41
    data overview for new HR head
        exercise, 5–6
    identifying specific actions to take, 41
    practice at work, 41
    practice on your own, 28
    practice with Cole, 5–6
    tactics used, 9
    talking with colleagues about
        audience needs, 6
graph familiarity of, 101
identifying action to take, 43
identifying during planning, 1
narrowing
    back-to-school shopping
        exercise, 7–9
    having specific audience in mind, 7
    possible questions to ask, 7–8
    practice at work, 42
    practice on your own, 29
    practice with Cole, 7–9
    primary audiences, 7, 29, 42
    time factors in defining audience, 9
    planning process and, 1
    tying words to graphs for, 113,
        114, 119, 229
Audience attention, focusing, 147–189, 388
    arrows for, 165
    bars exercise for, 184
    bold type and, 158
    cat food sales graph for, 156–163
    circling information for, 165–166
    color used for, 135–137, 158, 159,
        160, 161, 162, 164, 169, 176,
        177, 188
    combining preattentive attributes for,
        173–174
    consecutive comprehensive graphs
        for, 162–163
    data labels for, 158, 172–173

data markers for, 172, 173
detail in graphs and, 208
discussion questions at work and, 189
eliminating data for, 171
end markers and labels on lines for, 173
figuring out where to focus in, 188
financial savings graph for, 175–177
grey for background data and, 176
highlighting key elements for, 154–155
hue changes for, 170
line color intensity and, 169
line style and, 168
line thickness and, 167–168
motion (animation) and, 171
multiple ways of directing attention
    exercises
        practice on your own, 183
        practice with Cole, 164–174
overview of (main lessons from *SWD*
    book), 148–149
position and, 169
practice exercises for, 150–189
    overview, 159
    practice at work, 185–189
    practice on your own, 178–184
    practice with Cole, 151–177
practicing strategies on your tool for,
    186–187
pithy, repeatable phrase and, 278,
    287, 389
preattentive attributes and, 147, 148,
    164, 173–174
seeing with your brain and, 148
starting place in graphs and, 149
storytelling and, 287
SWD working session on, 397
tabular data exercise and, 182–183
time to close deal graph for, 135–137
title text and, 158, 160, 170
transparent white boxes for, 166–167
types of memory and, 148
visual hierarchy and, 227
visualizing *all* data exercise in,
    175–177
where eyes are drawn
    in graphs, 156–163, 174, 287, 388
    in pictures, 151–155
    practice at work, 185

practice on your own, 178–181

practice with Cole, 151–163

in tables, 57

testing, 149, 151

Average time to close a deal exercise,
91–92

Axes. *See* x-axis; y-axis

Axis labels and titles

alignment of, 121, 131, 198, 199, 202

all caps format of, 198, 214, 228

color of, 176, 198, 216

consistency of content of, 208

date format in, 125, 126, 128,
209–210, 211–212

decluttering of, 319

dropping trailing zeros from, 125

effective visuals with, 66

guidelines for, 199, 208, 225–226

horizontal vs. vertical bar chart and
space for, 316

intuitive, 208

labeling data directly vs. using, 105

necessity of having, 199, 225

placement of, 66, 198, 228

progression building of graph and,
259

proximity principle and, 112

selective labeling fo long text, 208

streamlining redundant information
in, 145

word choice for clarity of, 197, 198,
320

Axis lines, color of, 216, 218

B

Background information, in storyboarding,
36

Background of graphs

branding and, 218

practicing out loud with graphs to
find elements to push to, 102

visual hierarchy and, 228

Back-to-school shopping exercise, 7–14,
2   0–23, 314–329

Bank branch satisfaction exercise, 84–86,
175–177

Bar charts

attrition rate exercise for, 80

axis labels on, 316

choosing a graph exercise with,
94–95

color in, 115–116

connection principle and, 126

data label placement on, 127

demand and capacity by month
exercise for, 71, 72–73

focusing on bars in, 184

improving, 87–90

labels on, 82, 127–128, 189

line charts vs., 129

meals served over time exercise for,
64, 65–66, 67

myth about, 356

NPLs and loan loss reserves exercise
for, 87–90

overlapping bars on, 72–73

practice with Cole on, 59–60, 64,
65–66, 67, 71, 72–73, 80

stacked bars on, 69, 73

thickening bars in, 126–127

tying words to, 113–119

using two charts for comparison,
59–60

weather forecast exercise for, 81–83

zero baseline on, 53, 83, 356

Beaumont, Simon, 387

Benefits or risks definition, in refining Big
idea, 13, 14, 30

Bias, in data, 357

Big Idea, 10–19, 388

articulating point of view using, 10, 18

back-to-school shopping exercise for,
13–14

comparing and contrasting, 13

components of, 10, 18

conveying what's at stake using, 10, 18

crafting and refining during planning,
1, 10

creating as a team, 46

critiquing your initial ideas for, 18–19

facilitating practice session for,
391–395

forming, using Big Idea worksheet, 12

forming pithy, repeatable phrase exercise and, 278
function of, 10
pithy, repeatable phrase created from, 278, 321, 328, 343, 389
refining and reframing
positive and negative framing exercises, 13–14, 30, 35
practice on your own, 30, 35
practice with Cole, 13–14
revising, with feedback, 45
single sentence summary of, 10, 18
soliciting feedback on, 35, 45
vaccine rate exercise for, 17–18
Big Idea worksheet
completing
back-to-school shopping exercise, 10–12
CFO's update exercise, 31–32
pet adoption pilot exercise, 16–17
university elections exercise, 33–35
working as a team, 46
description and function of, 10
practice at work, 44
practice on your own, 31–35
practice with Cole, 10–12, 15–17
reasons to use, 10
sample worksheet, 11, 16, 32, 34, 44
Bold font
differentiating text elements using, 186
focusing attention using, 154, 158, 167
highlighting using, 227
label text with, 158, 159
line labels with, 71–72
logos with, 216, 217
sparing text use of, 115
title text with, 158, 217
visual hierarchy and, 227
Borders
branding graph with, 216–217
closure principle and, 112, 123, 124
decluttering by removing, 123, 124, 145, 202, 319
setting apart columns and rows using, 57
Boxed data, to focus attention, 166–167
Brain, seeing with, 148
Brainstorming, in storyboarding, 3, 286

back-to-school shopping exercise for, 20, 22
CFO's update exercise for, 37–38
good number of ideas for initial list in, 20, 24
overview of process in, 3
pet adoption pilot exercise for, 24, 26
practice at work and, 46
when to perform, 46
Branding, 214–219, 223–224
Coca Cola example of, 217–218
market size over time graph and, 214–219
practice on your own exercise, 223–224
United Airlines example of, 216–217
Butler, Jill, 227

C

Call breakdown over time graph, 242–248
Capitalization. *See also* All caps; Case
axis titles and, 198, 202
logos and, 216
short word sequences with, 227
titles and, 227, 241
when to use, 227
Car sales over time graph, 200–205
Case. *See also* Capitalization
all caps vs., 133, 198, 228
titles and, 227, 241
visual hierarchy and, 227
Cat food sales graph, 156–163
Centering
of labels, 74, 121
of logos, 216
of text, 57, 121, 131, 208, 216, 217, 291
of titles, 202
Cesal, Amy, 229
Chart Chooser, 104
Chartmaker Directory, 104
Charts. *See* Bar charts
Checklist, for assessment, 389–391
Chief Financial Officer (CFO)'s financial update exercise, 31–32, 37–38
Chronological (linear) path
data event over time and, 296–297
moving to narrative arc from, exercise, 273–274

as narrative path of story, 237
storyboard example using, 332–333
Circling data, to focus attention, 165–166
Climax, in narrative arc, 252, 253, 254, 255
Closure principle, 109, 111
    decluttering and, 124, 139
    description and use of, 112
    heavy line removal and, 124
Clutter, identifying and eliminating,
            107–146, 388
    alignment and white space exercises
            practice on your own, 140
            practice with Cole, 120–122
    audience needs and, 113, 114, 119
    axis labels and, 319
    clutter as enemy in, 108
    cognitive burden and, 108, 138, 141,
            142, 143, 145
    connection principle and, 118–119,
            126, 139
    contrast, nonstrategic use of, 109
    declutter exercises
            practice on your own, 141–143
            practice with Cole, 123–137
    deleting noncritical data and, 227, 277
    discussion questions at work on, 146
    drawing exercise for, 144
    enclosure principle and, 116–117, 139
    Gestalt and
            overview, 109
            practice on your own, 138–139
            practice with Cole, 111–112
            tying words to graphs, 113–119
    iterations in, 133–134
    lack of visual order and, 108
    market size over time graph and,
            111–112
    monthly voluntary exercise rate
            graph and, 113–119
    overview of (main lessons from *SWD*
            book), 108–109
    physician prescription patterns graph
            for, 120–122
    practice exercises for, 110–146
            overview, 110
            practice at work, 144–146
            practice on your own, 138–143

    practice with Cole, 111–137
    proximity principle and, 114–115,
            130, 139
    questions to ask yourself and, 145
    reducing redundancy in labels and, 209
    similarity principle and, 115–116, 117,
            119, 139
    storytelling and, 286
    SWD working session on, 397
    time to close deal graph for, 123–134
    tying words to graphs exercise, 113–119
    visual hierarchy and, 202, 227–228
Coca Cola brand, 217–218
Cognitive burden
    decluttering to lessen, 108, 138, 141,
            142, 143, 145
    explicit axis titles to lessen, 199
Color
    accessibility and, 230
    axis lines and, 216, 218
    axis titles and, 176, 198, 216
    branding and, 214, 215, 216, 217, 218
    colorblindness and, 136, 154, 160,
            191, 218, 230, 291, 388
    data point highlighting using,
            114–115, 136, 158, 160
    decluttering by removing, 134, 202
    focusing attention using, 135–137,
            154, 155, 158, 159, 160,
            161, 162, 164, 169, 176,
            177, 188
    graphs and. *See* Heatmaps
    grey for background data and, 176
    hue as preattentive attribute and,
            147, 148, 149, 154
    hue changes to focus attention using,
            170
    importance of using sparingly, 155,
            164, 213
    intensity changes using, 161, 169
    iterations in applying, 135–137
    labels and, 127, 130–131
    line graphs with, 66–67
    logos and, 216
    negative and positive associations
            with, 218
    paying attention to detail exercise
            and, 209, 210, 211, 213

practice using with your tool, 188
relative value indicated by intensity
    changes in, 58
similarity principle and, 112, 115
in tables
    focusing attention to establish
        hierarchy of information, 57
    relative intensity of color to
        indicate relative value, 58
time to close deal graph for, 135–137
titles of graphs and, 132
transitioning from dashboard to story
    using, 271
two-sided layout and, 204
tying words to graphs using, 115, 119
visual hierarchy and, 202, 227
white space used in place of, for
    accessibility, 230
Colorblindness, 136, 154, 160, 191, 218,
    230, 291, 388
Compare and contrast, in refining Big idea,
    13
Comparison
    designing data in graphs for, 210–211
    horizontal bar chart for, 59–60
    single graph for, 55–58
    slopegraph for, 62–63
    two graphs for, 58–59
    vertical bar chart for, 61
Connection principle, 109, 111
    decluttering and, 118–119, 126, 139
    description and use of, 112
    tying words to graphs and, 118, 119
Consistency
    case (capitalization) and, 241
    detail in graphs and, 208, 229
    time intervals on graphs and, 88–89
Content
    organizing exercise for, 36–37
    planning process and, 1
    storyboarding for, 1
Context, understanding, 1–49, 388
    audience and
        getting to know exercises, 5–6,
            28–29, 41
        identifying action to take, 43
        narrowing exercises, 7–9, 42
    back-to-school shopping exercise for,
        7–9, 10–12, 13–14, 20–23

Big Idea for, 388
    completing worksheet exercises,
        10–12, 15–17, 31–35, 44
    creating as a team, 46
    critiquing your initial ideas, 18–19
    refining and reframing exercises,
        13–14, 30
    soliciting feedback, 45
CFO's update exercise, 31–32, 37–38
content, organizing exercise for,
    36–37
deciding on right amount of data
    and, 357
discussion questions at work and, 49
eliminating data to focus attention
    and, 171
exploratory vs. explanatory analysis
    and, 2
importance of, 2
overview of (main lessons from *SWD*
    book), 2–3
pet adoption pilot exercise for, 16–17,
    16–17, 24–27
planning process and, 1
practice exercises for, 4–49
    overview, 4
    practice at work, 41–49
    practice on your own, 28–40
    practice with Cole, 5–27
single "So what?" sentence on, 3, 309
storyboarding and, 388
    arranging potential components,
        36–37
    brainstorming step, 3, 20, 22, 24,
        26, 37–38, 46, 286
    CFO's update exercise, 37–38
    editing step, 3, 20, 24–25, 38, 286
    getting feedback step, 3, 21, 23,
        25, 27, 38, 48, 286
    organizing ideas, 47
    overview of process, 3
    revising, 39–40
    soliciting feedback exercise, 48
    sticky notes usage, 3, 20, 46
    three steps, 3
    university elections exercise, 38–40
storytelling and, 286
SWD working session on, 397

Continuity principle, 109, 111
     decluttering and, 139
     description and use of, 112
Contrast
     colorblindness and, 230
     decluttering nonstrategic use of, 109
     effectiveness of graphs using, 112
     how to use, 109
     market size over time graph and, 112
     preattentive attributes and, 164
Contrast and compare approach, in
          refining Big idea, 13
Critiques. *See also* Feedback
     Big Idea and, 18–19, 31
     storyboarding and, 38
Cross-functional teams, 376
Culture of organization
     feedback and, 385–387
     learning and, 377
Curvature, as preattentive attribute, 148

D
Dashboards
     regular data release using, 268
     reports generated from, 276
     transitioning to story from, 268–271
Dashed lines, for focusing attention, 168,
          188
Data
     bias in, 357
     critical role of words in communicating
          about, 195, 197, 199
     deciding on right amount of, 357
     deleting noncritical data, 227, 277
     designing to make sense in graphs,
          209–212
     direct labeling of, 130, 230
     as evidence for making your point, 2
     footnotes for, 226
     myths about, 357
     in storyboarding, 36
     visual hierarchy and, 227
     visualizing, 51. *See also* Effective
          visuals, choosing
Data labels
     adding for emphasis, 172–173
     audience focus and alignment of, 121

     bolding of, 160
     centering, 74
     color of, to match data, 130–131
     eliminating if not needed, 128–129,
          145
     eliminating, in decluttering, 128
     focusing attention using, 137, 158,
          160, 172–173
     line graph with, 71
     location on bars, 127–128
     proximity principle and, 112, 130
     streamlining redundant information
          in, 145
     weather forecast graph with, 82
Data markers, 78
     focusing attention and, 172, 173
Data overview for new HR head exercise,
          5–6
Data points
     changes over time and, 85
     color for highlighting, 114–115, 136,
          158, 160
     comparing across two graphs, 89
     connection principle and, 112
     critiquing graph for number of, 85
     labeling, 66, 78, 128, 145, 173, 187
     similarity principle and, 112, 117
     tying words to graphs and, 116, 117
Data stories. *See* Storytelling
Data visualization
     audiences and, 67
     benefits of decluttering, 123
     collections of examples of, 104
     common myths in, 356–357
     critical importance of words in, 241
     feedback on, 306
     goal of, 103, 357
     importance of design principles and
          accessibility in, 229
     learning from examples of, 98
     library of examples of, 103
     observing examples around us, 151,
          154, 220
     reviewing and critiquing in team
          meetings, 386, 387
     #SWDchallenge and, 98–99, 386
Data visualization specialist, 376

Dates
    axis labels with, 125, 126, 128, 209–210,
        211–212
    consistency in labels with, 208
    time intervals on graphs and, 88–89
Declutter exercises, 123–134, 141–143
Decluttering. *See* Clutter, identifying and
        eliminating
Demand and capacity by month graph,
        68–75
Designer, thinking like. *See* Thinking like a
        designer
Detail in graphs
    alignment and, 208
    audience assumptions based on, 208
    consistency and, 208
    footnotes for, 226
    making minor changes for major
impact exercise and, 221–222
    paying attention to detail exercises
            and, 206–213, 228–229
    practice at work exercise and, 228–229
    summarizing, to eliminate distractions,
            227
    thinking life a designer and, 389
Diabetes rates exercise, 330–341
Diagonal elements
    avoiding, 108, 126, 286
    decluttering and, 126
    how to use, when needed, 118
Discussion questions at work
    choosing effective visuals and, 105
    decluttering and, 146
    focusing attention and, 189
    storytelling, 283
    SWD process at work, 401
    thinking like a designer and, 233
    understanding context and, 49
Diversity hiring exercise, 359–360
Documents
    progression building of graph with
            fully annotated slide as, 257,
            267
    structuring for audience needs, 6
Dot plots
    attrition rate exercise for, 77
    demand and capacity by month
            exercise for, 74

practice with Cole on, 74, 77
    when to use, 83
Dotted lines
    continuity principle and, 112
    focusing attention with, 168, 188
    practice using with your tool, 188
    when to use, 112, 168
Drawing exercises, 388
    decluttering and, 144
    on paper, 68–70, 91, 144, 286
    practice at work using, 100, 144
    practice on your own using, 91–92
    practice with Cole using, 68–74
    using an online tool, 70–75, 92, 286
Duarte, Nancy, 3, 10

E
Editing step, in brainstorming, 3, 286
    back-to-school shopping exercise for, 20
    CFO's update exercise for, 38
    pet adoption pilot exercise for, 24–25
    questions to ask yourself during, 20, 25
Effective visuals, choosing, 51–105, 388
    attrition rate exercise for, 76–80
    average time to close a deal exercise
            for, 91–92
    bank index exercise for, 84–86
    choosing a graph exercise for, 94–95
    comparisons using, 55–63
    consistency in time intervals on graphs
            and, 88–89
    critiquing exercise for, 84–86
    data visualization library for, 103
    demand and capacity by month
            exercise for, 68–75
    discussion questions at work for, 105
    drawing exercises for, 388
        on paper, 68–70, 91, 100, 286
        using an online tool, 70–75, 92,
            286
    financial savings exercise for, 85–86
    improving graphs in, 87–90, 92–93
    iterations in, 51, 63, 97, 100
    learning from examples in, 98
    NPLs and loan loss reserves exercise
            for, 87–90
    overview of (main lessons from *SWD*
            book), 52–53

practice exercises for, 54–105
   overview, 54
   practice at work, 100–105
   practice on your own, 91–99
   practice with Cole, 55–90
practicing out loud with graphs and,
   102
resources, 104
response and completion rates
   exercise for, 96
simple text vs. graphs in, 52, 77
single "So what?" sentence on using,
   77
soliciting feedback and, 102–103
spotting what's wrong exercise, 96
starting point in using, 57
storytelling and, 286
#SWDchallenge and, 98–99
SWD working session on, 397
table improvement approaches, 55–67
   meals served over time exercise,
      64–67
   new client tier share exercise,
      55–63
table use vs. graphs in, 52
team goals and, 103
thinking critically about what we want
   to show on, 83
trying different representations using,
   63
types of visuals and, 52–53
visualizing and iterating exercises for,
   97, 100
weather forecast exercise for, 81–83
Enclosure
   as preattentive attribute, 148
   as signal on where to look, 154
Enclosure principle, 109, 111
   decluttering and, 116–117, 139
   description and use of, 112
   tying words to graphs and, 116–117
Encounters by type graph exercise, 369–370
Ending
   leading story with, 237, 256
   narrative arc with, 252, 253, 254, 255
Errors and reports graph, 366–367

Examples
   learning from
      choosing effective visuals, 98
      thinking like a designer, 220–221
   library of data visualization, 103
Excel
   conditional formatting in, 58, 65
   creating graphs in, 71, 74
   heatmap formatting using, 58, 65
Exercises for practice. *See* Practice at
   work; Practice on your own;
   Practice with Cole
Explanations
   action for audience to take in, 43
   conclusion in presentations and, 226
   differentiating between live and
      standalone stories exercise
      and, 257–267
   pithy, repeatable phrase exercise
      and, 278
   "So what?" question in, 279
   takeaway in, and titles, 241
   transitioning from dashboard to story
      exercise and, 268–271
   tying words to graphs in, 113, 157
Explanatory analysis, 2, 43, 188, 268
Exploratory analysis, 2, 188, 268
Eye movement
   focusing attention and, 287
      in graphs, 156–163
      in pictures, 151–155
      practice on your own, 178–181
      practice with Cole, 151–163
      where your eyes are drawn to,
         149, 151, 287, 388
   starting place and
      focusing attention, 149
      in tables, 57
   two-sided layout and, 204
   zigzagging "z" path in information
      processing on graphs and, 57,
      131, 198, 228, 247, 317

F

Falling action, in narrative arc, 252, 253,
   254, 255

Feedback
Big Idea
giving feedback, 18–19
questions to ask, 45
soliciting feedback, 35, 45
cultivating culture of, 385–387
drawing exercise and, 100
facial responses in, 103
giving and receiving exercise, 382–384
on graphs at work, 102–103
impromptu, 384
seeking after storytelling presentation,
400
storyboarding, 3, 23, 286
back-to-school shopping exercise
for, 21
CFO's update exercise for, 38
pet adoption pilot exercise for,
25, 27
practice at work, 48
questions to ask with your partner,
21, 25, 48
stakeholder and manager opinions,
48
team meetings and, 386, 387
Feedback culture, 385–387
Financial savings exercises, 85–86
Findings, in storyboarding, 36
Fonts
branding, 214, 215, 216, 217, 223, 228
size and readability of, 217
Footnotes
for acronyms, 307
for data, 226
for detailed information, 307
position of, 216
spacing with, 121
Form follows function, 192, 287
Framing Big Idea
back-to-school shopping exercise for,
13–14
benefits or risks defined during, 13,
14, 30
positive and negative framing, 13–14, 30
practice on your own for, 30, 35
practice with Cole on, 13–14

G
Gestalt Principles of Visual Perception
description and use of, 112
overview of, 109, 139
practice on your own using, 138–139
practice with Cole on, 111–112
tying words to graphs and, 113–119,
229
Goals
graphs stating, 132–133
Objectives and Key Results (OKRs) and,
380–381
pithy, repeatable phrase exercise and,
278
setting, exercise for, 380–381
Graphic Continuum, 104
Graphing applications
drawing exercises using, 70–75, 92
using default output exercise with,
200–205
Graphs. *See* specific charts and graphs
bank branch satisfaction exercise for,
84–86
choosing. *See* Effective visuals, choosing
comparisons using, 55–63
consistency in time intervals on, 88–89
critiquing exercise for, 84–86
data table embedded in, 93
deciding on right amount of data for,
357
demand and capacity by month
exercise for, 68–75
drawing exercises for
on paper, 68–70, 91, 100, 286
using an online tool, 70–75, 92, 286
financial savings exercise for, 85–86
goal stated in, 132–133
improving, 87–90, 92–93
iterations in, 51, 63, 97, 100, 133–134
learning from examples of, 98
monthly voluntary exercise rate graph
and, 113–119
myth about, 356
NPLs and loan loss reserves exercise
for, 87–90
overall "feel" of, 229

practice exercises for, 54–105
    overview, 54
    practice at work, 100–105
    practice on your own, 91–99
    practice with Cole, 55–90
practicing out loud with, 102
simple text vs., in presentations, 52, 77
soliciting feedback on, 102–103
spotting what's wrong exercise, 96
squint test for checking overall
    impression of, 227
starting point in reading, 57
summarizing in one sentence, 242–248
#SWDchallenge for, 98–99
table use vs., 52
thinking critically about what we want
    to show on, 83
titles of. *See* Titles
trying different representations using,
    63
tying words to graphs exercise for,
    113–119
types of, 52–53
zero baseline on, 356
Grey, for background data, 176
Gridlines, decluttering of, 123, 124–125,
    145, 202, 319

H

Heatmaps
    Excel formatting for, 58, 65
    meals served over time exercise for,
        64, 65
    new client tier share exercise for, 58
    practice with Cole on, 58, 64, 65
    relative intensity of color to indicate
        relative value in, 58
    when to use, 52
Highlighting
    color for, 313
    focusing attention using, 154, 156,
        259, 309
    techniques for, 227
    visual hierarchy and, 227, 233
Holden, Kritina, 227
Horizontal bar charts, 176, 204
    new client tier share exercise for, 58,
        59–60

practice with Cole on, 58, 59–60
space for x-axis labels on, 316–317
using two charts for comparison,
    59–60
when to use, 53
Horizontal elements
    alignment of, 108
    diagonal text vs., 126
How to use exercises, 355
Hue
    changing to focus attention, 170
    as preattentive attribute, 147, 148,
        149, 154

I

Information Is Beautiful Awards, 104
Intensity
    as preattentive attribute, 148, 164, 188
    practice using with your tool, 188
    relative value indicated by, 58
Interactive Chart Chooser, 104
Inversing elements, 227
Italics
    decluttering and, 131–132
    highlighting using, 227
    visual hierarchy and, 227

J

Justification
    of axis titles, 202
    of legends, 247
    of text in graphs, 121, 131
    of text in titles, 198, 202
    of titles, 131, 202, 214, 228, 247

K

Key results, and goals, 380–381

L

Labels. *See also* Axis labels and titles;
Data labels
    avoiding diagonal text in, 126
    axis charts with, 82, 127–128, 189
    case and typeface of, 227
    centering of, 74, 121
    consistency in, 208

color and, 127, 130–131, 158, 160
data points and, 66, 78, 128, 145, 173, 187
decluttering and, 125, 126, 127–128, 130
direct labeling of data, 130, 230
end labels on lines, 173
focusing attention and, 158, 160
line charts with, 71, 78, 86, 89, 189
lines on graphs and, 173, 202
paying attention to detail exercise for, 208–209
placement of, 247
practice using with your tool, 189
proximity principle and, 112, 130
reducing redundancy in, 209
removing data labels, 127–128
removing trailing zeros in, 125
Laundry detergent sales graph, 195–199
Learning culture, 377
Legends
for colors, 65
extra work moving back and forth to use, 88, 130, 209, 244, 247
heatmaps with, 65
labeling data directly vs., 130, 230
line graphs eliminating need for, 71
placement of, 71, 247, 319
Library, of data visualization examples, 103
Lidwell, William, 227
Linear (chronological) path
data event over time and, 296–297
moving to narrative arc from, exercise, 273–274
as narrative path of story, 237
storyboard example using, 332–333
Line graphs. *See also* Slopegraphs
annotations used on, 67
attrition rate exercise for, 78–79, 80
bar charts vs., 129
connection principle and, 112
demand and capacity by month exercise for, 71–72, 74
financial savings exercise for, 85–86
how to use, 356
labels on, 71, 78, 86, 89, 189
meals served over time exercise for, 64, 66–67

myth about, 356
plotting differences on, 74
practice with Cole on, 64, 66–67, 71–72, 74, 78, 80
shading used on, 74, 79
slopegraphs as, 52, 356
when to use, 52, 83, 356
Lines in graphs
decluttering by removing, 124
end markers and labels on, for focusing attention, 173
focusing attention on, 183, 188
labeling, 173, 202
length of, as preattentive attribute, 148
style of, for focusing attention, 168
width (thickness) of, 148, 167–168, 188, 217
Listening, in feedback sessions, 383
Logos, in branding, 214, 216, 217, 223, 224
Lowercase. *See also* Case titles and, 241

M
Main message. *See also* Big Idea
crafting and refining during planning, 1, 10, 48
Managers
audience insights from, 6
culture of learning and, 377
feedback and, 385
goals in Objectives and Key Results (OKRs) and, 380, 381
storyboard feedback from, 48
SWD working session and, 398
Market size over time graph, 111–112, 214–219
Marks, as preattentive attribute, 148
Meals served over time exercise, 64–67
Medical centers flu vaccination graph, 92–93, 184
Memory
repetition and, 237, 278
types of, 148
Message. *See* Big Idea; Main message
Model performance exercise, 306–313
Monthly voluntary exercise rate graph, 113–119

Motion
   graph example of, 171
   as preattentive attribute, 148

N

Narrative arc
   arranging stories along, 252–253,
      254–256, 279–280, 287
   building exercise for, 275
   components of, 281–282
   memorability of stories and, 235
   moving from linear path to, exercise,
      273–274
   stories with, 235, 236, 389
   storyboarding with, 282
   storytelling with, 235, 236, 287, 389
Narrative flow, 237
   storyboarding to determine, 20, 388
Narrative structure, 236, 279–280
Narrowing audience process
   back-to-school shopping exercise, 7–9
   having specific audience in mind, 7
   possible questions to ask, 7–8
   practice at work, 42
   practice on your own, 29
   practice with Cole, 7–9
   primary audiences, 7, 29, 42
   time factors in defining audience, 9
Negative framing of Big Idea, 13–14, 30, 35
Net Promoter Score (NPS) exercises,
      239–241, 342–353
New advertiser revenue exercise, 289–293
New client tier share exercise, 55–63
NPLs and loan loss reserves exercise, 87–90

O

Objectives and Key Results (OKRs), 380–381
100% stacked charts, 53, 245–246, 247
Oral presentations. *See also* Slides
   action for audience to take in, 237
   graphs vs. simple text in, 52
   learning from successes and failures
      of, 400
   live and standalone stories exercise
      for, 257–267
   moving from linear path to narrative
      arc exercise and, 273–274

pithy, repeatable phrase used in, 278
   practicing out loud with graphs in, 102
   progression building of graph on
      slide during, 259–267
   questions about graphs for, 101
   single-slide presentation, 203–204
   soliciting feedback on, 102–103
   time needed for talking about graphs
      in, 101
Organizing content, 36–37
Orientation, as preattentive attribute, 148
Overlapping bar charts, 72–73

P

Pet adoption pilot exercise, 16–17, 24–27,
      254–265
Physician prescription patterns graph,
      120–122
Pie charts
   choosing a graph exercise with, 94–95
   difficulties in using, 59
   myth about, 356
   new client tier share exercise for, 58–59
   practice with Cole on, 58–59
   when to use, 59, 356
Planning process
   audience identification during, 1
   Big Idea crafting and refining during,
      1, 10
   storyboarding
      back-to-school shopping exercise,
         20–23
      overview of process, 3
      pet adoption pilot program
         exercise, 24–27
      planning content, 1, 20
   three important aspects of, 1
   time spent on, 1, 41, 48
Plot, in narrative arc, 252, 253, 254, 255
Podcasts, on SWD website, 102, 381
Point of view, in Big Idea, 10, 18
Position
   graph example of, 159, 169
   practice using with your tool, 188
   as preattentive attribute, 147, 148,
      149, 164, 188
Positive framing of Big Idea, 13–14, 30, 35

Practice at work
 choosing effective visuals, 100–105
  data visualization library, 103
  discussion questions, 105
  drawing exercise, 100
  iterating with drawing tool, 100
  practicing out loud, 102
  questions about graphs, 101
  resources, 104
  soliciting feedback, 102–103
 focusing attention, 185–189
  discussion questions at work, 189
  figuring out where to focus, 188
  practicing strategies on your tool,
   186–187
  where your eyes are drawn to, 185
 identifying and eliminating clutter,
  144–146
  discussion questions at work, 146
  drawing exercise, 144
  questions to ask yourself, 145
 list of exercises, 379
 more practice exercises, 375–401
  assessment rubric, 389–391
  conducting SWD working session,
   396–398
  creating plan of attack, 379
  cultivating a feedback culture,
   385–387
  discussion questions, 401
  facilitating Big Idea practice
   session, 391–395
  giving and receiving effective
   feedback, 382–384
  how to use exercises, 375
  revisiting SWD process, 388–389
  setting good goals, 380–381
  tips for crafting successful data
   stories, 399–400
 storytelling, 278–283
  discussion questions at work 283
  employing narrative arc, 281–282
  finding exercise, 279–280
  pithy, repeatable phrase, 278
 thinking like a designer, 225–233
  accessibility design notes, 229–230
  creating visual hierarchy, 227–228
  data accessibility with words,
   225–226
  discussion questions at work 233
  garnering acceptance for designs,
   231–232
  paying attention to detail, 228–229
 understanding context, 41–49
  audience, 41–43
  Big Idea, 44–46
  storyboarding, 47–48
Practice on your own
 choosing effective visuals, 91–99
  choosing a graph, 94–95
  drawing exercises, 91–92
  improving a graph, 92–93
  learning from examples, 98
  spotting what's wrong, 96
  #SWDchallenge, 98–99
  visualizing and iterating, 97
 focusing attention, 178–184
  focusing on bars, 184
  focusing within tabular data,
   182–183
  multiple ways of directing
   attention, 183
  where your eyes are drawn to,
   178–181
 identifying and eliminating clutter,
  138–143
  alignment and white space, 140
  declutter exercises, 141–143
  Gestalt principles, 138–139
 more practice exercises, 355–373
  accounts over time, 365
  adverse effects, 362
  diversity hiring, 359–360
  encounters by type, 369–370
  errors and reports, 366–367
  how to use exercises, 355
  reasons for leaving, 363–364
  revenue forecast, 361
  sales by region, 360
  store traffic, 371–373
  taste test data, 368–369
 storytelling, 272–277
  building a narrative arc, 275
  evolving from report to story,
   276–277
  identifying tension, 272–273
  moving from linear path to
   narrative arch, 273–274

thinking like a designer, 220–224
    branding, 223–224
    learning from examples, 220–221
    making minor changes for major
        impact, 221–222
    ways of improving a graph,
        222–223
understanding context, 28–40
    audience, 28–29
    Big Idea, 30–35
    storyboarding, 36–40
website for downloading data and
    graphs for, 91
Practice with Cole
    choosing effective visuals, 55–90
        critiquing a graph, 84–86
        drawing exercise on paper, 68–70
        drawing exercise using an online
            tool, 70–75
        improving a graph, 87–90
        table improvement, 55–67
        ways of showing attrition rate
            data, 76–80
        weather bar charts, 81–83
    focusing attention, 151–177
        multiple ways of directing
            attention, 164–174
        visualizing all data, 175–177
        where your eyes are drawn to in
            graphs, 156–163
        where your eyes are drawn to in
            pictures, 151–155
    identifying and eliminating clutter,
        111–137
        alignment and white space,
            120–122
        declutter exercise, 123–134
        Gestalt principles, 111–112
        tying words to graphs, 113–119
    more practice exercises, 285–353
        back-to-school shopping, 314–329
        diabetes rates, 330–341
        how to use exercises, 285
        model performance, 306–313
        net promoter score, 342–353
        new advertiser revenue, 289–293
        sales channel update, 294–305
    storytelling, 239–271

arranging along narrative arc,
    254–256
differentiating between live and
standalone stories, 257–267
    identifying tension, 249–251
    putting graph into one sentence,
        242–248
    takeaway titles, 239–241
    transitioning from dashboard to
        story, 268–271
    using components of story,
        252–253
thinking like a designer, 195–219
    applying branding, 214–219
    paying attention to detail and
        design choices, 206–213
    using default output from tools,
        200–205
    using words wisely on graphs,
        195–199
understanding context, 5–27
    audience, 5–9
    Big Idea, 10–19
    storyboarding, 20–27
Preattentive attributes. *See also* specific
    attributes
    designing for accessibility and, 226
    focusing attention using, 147, 148,
        164, 173–174
Prescription patterns graph, 120–122
Presentations. *See* Oral presentations; Slides
Primary audiences, 7, 29, 41
Problem statement, in storyboarding, 36
Proximity principle, 109, 111
    decluttering and, 114–115, 130, 139
    description and use of, 112
    direct labeling of data and, 130
    tying words to graphs and, 114

Q

Questions, in feedback sessions, 383

R

Reasons for leaving graph, 363–364
Recommendations, in storyboarding, 36
Reddit: Data Is Beautiful, 104

Refining and reframing Big Idea
back-to-school shopping exercise for, 13–14
benefits or risks defined during, 13, 14, 30
compare and contrast in, 13
planning process and, 1, 10
positive and negative framing exercises for, 13–14, 30, 35
practice on your own for, 30
practice with Cole on, 13–14
Repetition
forming pithy, repeatable phrase exercise and, 278, 287
memory and, 237, 278
Reports, 237
evolving to story from, exercise, 276–277
learning from successes and failures of, 400
title consistency with, 199
Resonate (Duarte), 3, 10
Resources, for choosing effective graphs, 104
Response and completion rates exercise, 96
Revenue forecast exercise, 361
Revising, during storyboarding, 39–40
R Graph Gallery, 104
Ricks, Elizabeth Hardman, 330
Rising action, in narrative arc, 252, 253, 254, 255
Risks or benefits definition, in refining Big idea, 13, 14, 30

S

Saint-Exupery, Antoine de, 192
Sales by region exercise, 360
Sales channel update exercise, 294–305
Scatterplots
back-to-school shopping example of, 315
when to use, 52, 83
Shading
enclosure principle and, 112, 116
line graphs with, 74, 78
tables with, 57, 65
time intervals shown by, 89
tying words to graphs using, 116–117

Shape, as preattentive attribute, 148
Similarity principle, 109, 111
color in focusing attention and, 159
decluttering and, 115–116, 117, 119, 139
description and use of, 112
tying words to graphs and, 115–116, 117, 119
Size
as preattentive attribute, 147, 148, 149, 164
as signal on where to look, 154
visual hierarchy and, 227
Sketching. See Drawing exercises
Slideument, 257
Slides
alignment and white space on, 121
audience's path on, 204
practicing out loud with, 102
progression building of graph on, 259–267
single-slide presentation, 203–204, 213
takeaway titles for, 239–240, 241
title guidelines for, 199
tying words to graphs on, 113–119, 229
where your eyes are drawn to, 151, 178, 185
Slopegraphs, 356
choosing a graph exercise with, 94–95
comparison using, 62–63
as line graphs, 52, 356
practice with Cole on, 62–63
when to use, 52, 83
Solutions to exercises for practice. See Practice at work; Practice on your own; Practice with Cole
"So what?" sentence, 309
critiquing graphs using, 85
storytelling and, 279
understanding context and, 3
using effective visuals and, 77
Spatial position
graph example of, 159, 169
practice using with your tool, 188
as preattentive attribute, 147, 148, 149, 164, 188
Square area charts, 53

Squint test, 227
Stacked charts
    choosing a graph exercise with, 94–95
    demand and capacity by month
        exercise for, 69, 73, 74
    horizontal, 58, 60, 68, 69, 176, 204,
        316–317
    100% stacked, 53, 245–246, 247
    practice with Cole on, 69, 73, 74
    vertical, 53, 61, 316
    when to use, 53
    zero baseline on, 53
Starting place
    focusing attention and, 149
    key takeaway of graph in title and,
        226, 230
    legend placement and, 247
    tables and, 57
    testing where your eyes are drawn to
        and, 149
    titles of graphs and, 198, 202, 226,
        230, 239
    two-sided layout and, 204
    zigzagging "z" path in information
        processing on graphs and,
        57, 131, 198, 228, 247, 317
Sticky notes
    building narrative arc using, 275
    moving from linear path to narrative
arc exercise using, 274
    storyboarding using, 3, 20, 46
    storytelling using, 252, 253
Store traffic exercise, 371–373
Story. *See also* Storytelling
    answering "So what?" question to
        find, 279
    with capital "S," 279, 280
    components of, 235
    memorability of, 235
    narrative arc for structuring, 279–280
    with lowercase "s," 279, 280
Storyboarding, 20–27, 388
    arranging potential components of,
        36–37
    back-to-school shopping exercise for,
        20–23
    CFO's update exercise for, 37–38

    critiquing, 39
    definition of, 20
    discard pile in, 47
    narrative arc with, 282
    organizing ideas in, 47
    overview of process in, 3, 286
    pet adoption pilot program exercise
        for, 24–27
    practice at work for, 47–48
    practice on your own for, 36–40
    practice with Cole on, 20–27
    planning content using, 1, 3
    brainstorming step in, 3, 20, 22, 24,
        26, 37–38, 46, 286
    getting feedback step in, 3, 21, 23,
        25, 27, 38, 48, 286
    editing step in, 3, 20, 24–25, 38, 286
    revising, 39–40
    stakeholder and manager feedback
        on, 48
    sticky notes used in, 3, 20, 46
    storytelling and, 287
    three steps of, 3
    university elections exercise for, 38–40
Storytelling, 235–283, 389
    call breakdown over time graph and,
242–248
    evolving from report to story exercise,
276–277
    examples of approaches to, 285
    feedback after presenting, 400
    key elements of, 236, 252
    live and standalone stories exercise,
        257–267
    narrative arc in, 236, 287, 389
        arranging stories along arc,
            252–253, 254–256, 279–280
        building exercise, 275
        components, 281–282
        memorability of stories, 235
        moving from linear path to
narrative arc exercise, 273–274
    narrative flow in, 237
    narrative structure of, 236, 279–280
    Net Promoter Score (NPS) over time
        graph and, 239–241
    overview of (main lessons from *SWD*
        book), 236–237

pet adoption pilot program exercise
and, 254–265
potency of stories and, 235
practice exercises for, 238–283
overview, 238
practice at work, 278–283
practice on your own, 272–277
practice with Cole, 239–271
putting graph into one sentence
exercise and, 242–248
repetition in, 237
spoken vs. written narrative in, 237
steps in, 286–287
#SWDchallenge for, 98–99
SWD working session on, 397
takeaway titles exercise for, 239–241
tension and, 236, 279
action to be taken, 249, 251, 272
identifying exercises, 249–251,
272–273
memorability of stories, 235
story shape, 252, 253, 255
time to fill open roles graph and,
257–267
tips for crafting successful data stories
in, 399–400
transitioning from dashboard to story
exercise and, 268–271
using components of story exercise
and, 252–253
Storytelling with Data (SWD) book, review
of main lessons
context, 2–3
effective visuals, 52–53
focusing attention, 148–149
identifying and eliminating clutter,
108–109
storytelling, 236–237, 286–287
thinking like a designer, 192–193
Storytelling with Data website
(storytellingwithdata.com)
assessment rubric on, 391
Big Idea worksheet on, 44
blog on, 98, 229
downloading data and graphs for
exercises from, 91
podcasts available on, 102, 381
resources on, 405

#SWDchallenge on, 98–99, 386
SWD process son, 389
SWD blog, 98, 229
#SWDchallenge, 98–99, 386–387
SWD process
assessment rubric for, 389–391
conducting SWD working session in,
396–398
discussion questions on, 401
downloadable version of, 389
resources for, 405
summary of steps of, 388–389
using as final assessment of project, 391

T

Tableau Public Gallery, 104
Tables
appropriate level of detail in, 56
embedded bars used in, 58
embedding in graphs, 93
focusing attention to establish
hierarchy of information in, 57
focusing on contents in, 182–183
graphs vs., in live presentations, 52
heatmaps as, 52
shading vs. white space in, 57
starting point in using, 57
table improvement approaches
meals served over time exercise,
64–67
new client tier share exercise,
55–63
steps in analyzing a table, 55
trying different representations using,
63
when to use, 52
Takeaway titles
accessibility and, 230
color for, 158
primary point made in, 241
priming audience using, 170
storytelling and, 239–241
thinking like a designer and, 199,
226, 389
transitioning from dashboard to story
using, 271

Taste test data exercise, 368–369
Team, creating Big Idea working as, 46
Teams
cross-functional, 376
developing, 376
effective data visualization goal of, 193
embracing constraints by, 377
feedback time in meetings of, 385, 386
Objectives and Key Results (OKRs)
    and, 380–381
#SWDchallenge and, 386–387
Tension
action to be taken and, 249, 251, 272
identifying exercises and, 249–251,
    272–273
memorability of stories and, 235
narrative arc with, 279
story shape with, 252, 253, 255
Text boxes
alignment of, 121, 216
closure principle and, 112
position of, 216
white space around, 121
Text in graphs. *See also* Words in graphs
alignment of, 120, 121, 122
branding and size of, 217, 224
centering of, 57, 121, 131, 208, 216,
    217, 291
different audience perspectives
resulting in different interpretations of, 197
graphs vs. simple text, in
presentations, 52
justification of, 121, 131
simple text vs. visuals, 52, 77
two-sided layout using, 204
white space with, 120, 121–122
Thinking like a designer, 191–233, 388–389
acceptance by audience of designs
    and, 191, 193, 220, 231–232
accessibility and, 191, 193, 220,
    229–230
aesthetics and, 191, 193, 220
affordances and, 191, 192, 220
axis titles and, 198, 202
branding exercises for, 214–219,
    223–224
car sales over time graph and,
    200–205

critical role of words in communicating
    data and, 195, 197, 199
data accessibility with words exercise
    and, 225–226
designing data to make sense in,
    209–212
different audience perspectives
    resulting in different
    interpretations of text and,
    197
discussion questions at work and, 233
form follows function in, 192, 287
laundry detergent sales graph and,
    195–199
learning from examples in, 220–221
making minor changes for major
    impact exercise and, 221–222
market size over time graph and,
    214–219
overall design critique in, 201, 202,
    205, 229
overall "feel" of, 229
overview of (main lessons from *SWD*
    book), 192–193
paying attention to detail and,
    206–213, 228–229, 389
practice exercises for, 194–233
    overview, 194
    practice at work, 225–233
    practice on your own, 220–224
    practice with Cole, 195–219
storytelling and, 287
SWD working session on, 397
takeaway titles and, 199, 226, 388
touchpoints per customer over time
    graph and, 206–213
two-sided layout in, 204
using default output from tools
    exercise, 200–205
using words wisely on graphs
    exercise, 195–199
visual hierarchy and, 201, 202,
    227–228, 389
ways of improving a graph exercise
    and, 222–223
word choice and, 200, 202
3-minute story, 3

Time
        planning and need for, 1, 41, 48
        time intervals on graphs, 88–89
Time factors
        defining audience using, 9
        feedback session scheduling and, 382
        footnotes on, 226
        talking about graphs and, 101
Time to close deal graph, 123–137
        decluttering exercise with, 123–134
        focusing attention and, 135–137
Time to fill open roles graph, 257–267
Titles. *See also* Takeaway titles
        of axis. *See* Axis labels and titles
        of graphs
                branding, 217, 218, 224
                centering, 202
                color, 132
                decluttering, 131, 132
                guidelines for, 199, 225
                orientation, 131
                placement of, 131, 202, 214,
                        228, 247
                starting place in graphs, 198,
                        202, 226, 230, 239
                takeaway titles, 226, 230,
                        239–241, 388
                two-sided layout and, 204
        of slides and oral presentations
                pithy, repeatable phrase, 278
                word choice, 239, 241
Title text in graphs
        alignment of, 198, 202
        case (capitalization) of, 227, 241
        color of, 160
        focusing attention using, 158, 160,
                170, 202
        key takeaway of graph placed in, 226,
                230, 239–241, 388
        typeface of, 227
        wording changes for clarity of, 197–198
Tools
        default output exercise with, 200–205
        drawing exercises using, 70–75, 92
Touchpoints per customer over time graph,
        206–213
Two-sided graph layout
        detail and design choices exercise for,
                206–213

        revising content to create, 204
        transitioning from dashboard to story
                using, 271
Typeface
        as signal on where to look, 154
        visual hierarchy and, 227

U
Underlining, for highlighting, 227
United Airlines, 216–217
Universal Principles of Design (Lidwell,
Holden, and Butler), 227
University elections exercise, 33–35, 38–40
Uppercase. *See* All caps; Capitalization; Case

V
Vaccine rate exercise, 17–18
Vertical bar charts
        comparison using, 61
        horizontal bar chart vs., 316
        practice with Cole on, 61
        when to use, 53
Vertical elements, alignment of, 108
Visual hierarchy
        focusing attention to establish, 57
        practice at work exercise and, 227–228
        thinking like a designer and, 201,
                202, 227–228, 389
        tips on, 227–228
Visualizing data, 51. *See also* Effective
visuals, choosing
Visuals
        choosing. *See* Effective visuals,
                choosing
        simple text vs., 52, 77
        types of, 52–53

W
Waffle charts, 53
Waterfall charts, 53
Weather forecast exercise, 81–83
Web Content Accessibility Guidelines, 230
"Where are your eyes drawn?" test, 388
        combining preattentive attributes
                and, 173–174
        graphs and, 156–163

how to perform the test, 149, 151
pictures and, 151–155
practice at work and, 185
practice on your own and, 178–181
practice with Cole and, 151–163
tables and, 57
White space
accessibility and, 230
bar graphs with, 71
effectiveness of graphs and, 112
decluttering and, 120–122, 140, 286
market size over time graph and, 112
paying attention to detail with, 228
physician prescription patterns graph
for, 120–122
practice on your own and, 140
practice with Cole and, 120–122
two-sided layout using, 204
visual order using, 108
when to use, 230
Words in graphs. *See also* Text in graphs
axis label clarity and, 197, 198, 320
branding and, 217
critical role of, 195, 197, 199, 241
data accessibility with words exercise,
225–226
different audience perspectives
resulting in different
interpretations of, 197
key takeaway and, 226
laundry detergent sales graph and,
195–199
memorability of stories and, 235
monthly voluntary exercise rate
graph and, 113–119
paying attention to detail exercise
and, 213
slide titles and, 239, 241
takeaway titles exercise and
choosing, 239–241
transitioning from dashboard to story
using strategic choice of, 271, 277
tying words to graphs and, 113–119,
229
using words wisely exercise and,
195–199

X
x-axis
connection principle and, 112
eliminating diagonal text on, 126
labels for. *See* Axis labels and titles
practicing out loud with graphs and,
102
time intervals on, 88–89
Xenographics, 104

Y
y-axis
connection principle and, 112
dual y-axes, 88
labels for. *See* Axis labels and titles
practicing out loud with graphs and,
102
secondary, 308
starting at zero, 82

Z
zigzagging "z" path in information
processing on graphs, 57,
131, 198, 228, 247, 317